MCAT®
VERBAL REASONING
REVIEW

Related Titles

Kaplan MCAT Biology Review*

Kaplan MCAT General Chemistry Review*

Kaplan MCAT Organic Chemistry Review*

Kaplan MCAT Physics Review*

Kaplan MCAT Verbal Reasoning*

Kaplan MCAT Premier

Kaplan MCAT 45

MCAT Flashcards

Get into Medical School*

Med School Rx*

Applications for iPhone

MCAT Comprehensive Flashcards

MCAT Review Notes

*Also available in eBook format

MCAT®
VERBAL REASONING
REVIEW

The Staff of Kaplan

KAPLAN) PUBLISHING

New York

© 2012 by Kaplan, Inc.

Published by Kaplan Publishing, a division of Kaplan, Inc.
395 Hudson Street
New York, NY 10014

Printed in the United States of America

10 9 8 7 6 5 4 3 2

ISBN: 978-1-60978-604-5

Kaplan Publishing books are available at special quantity discounts to use for sales promotions, employee premiums, or educational purposes. For more information or to purchase books, please call the Simon & Schuster special sales department at 866-506-1949.

Contents

KAPLAN'S EXPERT MCAT TEAM

Kaplan has been preparing premeds for the MCAT for more than 40 years. In the past 15 years alone, we've helped more than 400,000 students prepare for this important exam and improve their chances for medical school admission.

Marilyn Engle

MCAT Master Teacher; Teacher Trainer; Kaplan National Teacher of the Year, 2006; Westwood Teacher of the Year, 2007; Westwood Trainer of the Year, 2007; Encino Trainer of the Year, 2005

John Michael Linick

MCAT Teacher; Boulder Teacher of the Year, 2007; Summer Intensive Program Faculty Member and Academic Director

Dr. Glen Pearlstein

MCAT Master Teacher; Teacher Trainer; Westwood Teacher of the Year, 2006

Matthew B. Wilkinson

MCAT Teacher; Teacher Trainer; Lone Star Trainer of the Year, 2007

Thanks to Jason Baserman, Jessica Brookman, Da Chang, John Cummins, David Elson, Jeff Koetje, Alex Macnow, Andrew Molloy, David Nagle, Deeangelee Pooran-Kublall, Josh Rohrig, and Amjed Saffarini.

How to Use this Book

Kaplan MCAT Verbal Reasoning Review, along with the other four books in our MCAT Review series, brings the Kaplan classroom experience to you—right in your home, at your convenience. This book offers the same Kaplan content review, strategies, and practice that make Kaplan the #1 choice for MCAT prep. All that's missing is the teacher.

Unlike the other books in this MCAT series, there is no content to review for the Verbal Reasoning. The questions are written in such a way as not to presume necessary funds of knowledge. In other words, all the support that is needed to answer the questions correctly is found in the corresponding passages.

To guide you through this complex content, we've consulted our best MCAT instructors to call out **Key Concepts** and **Key Equations** synopses of important and complex information; to offer **MCAT Expertise**—which illuminate conceptual patterns used by the test maker; and to encourage you with **You Can Do This!**—strategies to eliminate bad answer choices on tough questions. When you see these sidebars, you will know you're getting the same insight and knowledge that classroom students receive in person. Look for these expert margin notes throughout the book.

Please continue to **Introduction to the MCAT**, which contains important information about the entire MCAT, as well as specific information on the verbal reasoning section.

The bulk of this book is devoted to 6 full-length Verbal Reasoning section practice tests. Once you have read the introductory chapters on critical reading, mapping, key words, and the Verbal Reasoning question types, you should begin to work through the section tests. Although each of these section tests has a suggested time limit of 60 minutes (the time of the real MCAT Verbal Reasoning section), you may find it helpful, in the early stages of your preparation, to break some of these section tests into smaller configurations of passages (e.g. pairs of passages) to help you build your passage and question management skills without feeling overwhelmed. As you become more confident in your mastery of the Kaplan verbal passage and question strategies, you can begin to address issues of section management, timing, and pacing by taking the remainder of these section practice tests under timed (Test Day) conditions.

We're confident that this guide and our award-winning instructors can help you achieve your goals of MCAT success and admission to med school. Good luck!

Introduction to the MCAT

The Medical College Admission Test (MCAT) is different from any other test you've encountered in your academic career. The knowledge-based exams you took in high school and college placed an emphasis on memorizing and regurgitating information. However, medical schools can assess your academic prowess by looking at your transcript. The MCAT isn't like other standardized tests you may have taken, where the focus was on assessing your general skills.

Medical schools use MCAT scores to assess whether you possess the foundation upon which to build a successful medical career. Though you certainly need to master the content to do well, the stress is on the thought process, because the MCAT is, above all else, a critical thinking test. That's why it emphasizes reasoning, analytical thinking, reading comprehension, data analysis, and problem-solving skills.

The MCAT places more weight on your thought process, but you must have a strong grasp of the required core material. The MCAT is not a perfect gauge of your abilities, but it is a relatively objective way to compare you with students from different backgrounds and undergraduate institutions.

The MCAT's power comes from its use as an indicator of your abilities. Strong scores can open doors. Your advantage comes from sound preparation and a focused mindset, as the key to MCAT success is knowing what you're up against. That's where this section of this book comes in. We'll explain the philosophy behind the test, review the sections one by one, show you sample questions, share some of Kaplan's proven methods, and clue you in to what the test makers are really after. You'll get a handle on the process, find a confident new perspective, and achieve your highest possible scores by MCAT Test Day. Let's get started.

ABOUT THE MCAT

Information about the MCAT CBT (Computer-Based Test) is included below. For the latest information about the MCAT, visit **www.kaptest.com/mcat**

MCAT CBT

Format	U.S.—All administrations on computer
	International—Most on computer with limited paper and pencil in a few isolated areas
Breaks	Optional break between each section
Length of MCAT Day	Approximately 5.5 hours
Test Dates	Multiple dates in January, April, May, June, July, August, and September
	About 24 administrations each year.
Delivery of Results	Within 30 days. If scores are delayed notification will be posted online at www.aamc.org/mcat
	Electronic and paper
Security	Government-issued ID
	Electronic thumbprint
	Electronic signature verification
Testing Centers	Small computer testing sites

PLANNING FOR THE TEST

As you look toward your preparation for the MCAT, consider the following advice:

Complete your core course requirements as soon as possible. Take a strategic eye to your schedule, consult with your pre-health advisor, and get core requirements out of the way earlier rather than later.

Take the MCAT once. The MCAT is a notoriously grueling standardized exam that requires extensive preparation. It is longer than the graduate admissions exams for business school (GMAT), law school (LSAT), and graduate school (GRE), which are all about 3.5 hours long. You want to do well the first time–so that it's your last MCAT administration. Plan and prepare accordingly.

THE ROLE OF THE MCAT IN ADMISSIONS

More people are applying to medical school, so that means more people are taking the MCAT. It's important for you to recognize that while a high MCAT score is a critical component of gaining admission to a top-ranked medical school, it's not the only factor. Medical school admission officers weigh your grades, interviews, MCAT scores, level of involvement in extracurricular activities, as well as personal essays.

In a Kaplan survey of 130 pre-med advisors, 84 percent called the interview a "very important" part of the admissions process, followed closely by college grades (83%) and MCAT scores (76%). Kaplan's college admissions consulting practice works with students on all of these issues so that they can position themselves as strongly as possible. In addition, the AAMC has made it clear that scores will continue to be valid for a three year time period.

REGISTRATION

The only way to register for the MCAT is online. The registration site is: www.aamc.org/mcat.

You should access the site approximately six months before your test date. Payment must be made by MasterCard or Visa.

Go to www.aamc.org/mcat/registration.htm and download *MCAT Essentials* for information about registration, fees, test administration, and preparation. For other questions, contact:

MCAT Care Team

Association of American Medical Colleges

Section for Applicant Assessment Services

2450 N. St., NW

Washington, DC 20037

www.aamc.org/mcat

Email: mcat@aamc.org

Keep in mind that you will need to take the MCAT the year prior to your planned medical school start date. For example, if you are on a four-year plan at your institution, you would take your MCAT during your junior year, in preparation for applications and interviews during your senior year. Don't drag your feet gathering information. You'll need time not only to prepare and practice for the test, but also to get all of your registration work completed.

The MCAT should be viewed just like any other part of your application: This is an opportunity to show the medical schools who you are and what you can do. Take control of your MCAT experience.

ANATOMY OF THE MCAT

Before mastering strategies, you need to know exactly what you're dealing with on the MCAT. Let's start with the basics: The MCAT is, among other things, an endurance test.

Approach it with confidence and stamina, so that you don't lose your composure. To succeed, you need to be in control of the test.

The MCAT consists of four separately timed sections, three of which include Physical Sciences, Verbal Reasoning, and Biological Sciences. Starting in January 2013 and continuing through 2014, the Writing Sample will no longer be a part of the MCAT administration. If you do take the test in 2012, your Writing Sample score will be valid for the next 3 years. In its place, a voluntary, unscored trial section will be added. What does this mean for you? This experimental section won't affect your overall score, but it's something to be prepared for before Test Day. Topics including psychology, sociology, and biochemistry will be trial-tested, and starting in 2015, they will count as a score-qualifying section. All of the testing times will remain the same in 2013 and 2014. Later in this section we'll take an in-depth look at each MCAT section, including sample question types and specific test-smart hints, but here's a general overview, reflecting the order of the test sections and number of questions in each.

Physical Sciences

Time	70 minutes
Format	• 52 multiple-choice questions: approximately 7–9 passages with 4–8 questions each • approximately 10 stand-alone questions (not passage-based)
What it tests	basic general chemistry concepts, basic physics concepts, analytical reasoning, data interpretation

Verbal Reasoning

Time	60 minutes
Format	• 40 multiple-choice questions: approximately 7 passages with 5–7 questions each
What it tests	critical reading

Biological Sciences

Time	70 minutes
Format	• 52 multiple-choice questions: approximately 7–9 passages with 4–8 questions each • approximately 10 stand-alone questions (not passage-based)

What it tests	basic biology concepts, basic organic chemistry concepts, analytical reasoning, data interpretation

Experimental Section

Time	60 minutes
Format	• Trial multiple choice questions (UNSCORED) • What it tests psychology, sociology, and biochemistry

The sections of the test always appear in the same order:

Physical Sciences
[optional 10-minute break]
Verbal Reasoning
[optional 10-minute break]
Biological Sciences
[optional 10-minute break]
Experimental Section

SCORING

Each MCAT section receives its own score. Physical Sciences, Verbal Reasoning, and Biological Sciences are each scored on a scale ranging from 1–15, with 15 as the highest. In 2013 or 2014, the Writing Sample will be replaced by an experimental, unscored section. Starting in 2015, topics such as psychology, sociology, and biochemistry will be tested in a new scored section, once again on a scale of 1-15.

The number of multiple-choice questions that you answer correctly per section is your "raw score." Your raw score will then be converted to yield the "scaled score"—one that will fall in the 1–15 range. These scaled scores are reported to medical schools as your official MCAT scores. All multiple-choice questions are worth the same amount—one raw point—and ***there's no penalty for guessing***. That means that *you should always select an answer for every question, whether you get to that question or not!* This is an important piece of advice that you shouldn't forget. Never let time run out on any section without selecting an answer for every question.

The raw score of each administration is converted to a scaled score. The conversion varies with administrations. Hence, the same raw score will not always give you the same scaled score.

Your score report will tell you and your potential medical schools not only your scaled scores, but also the national mean score for each section, standard deviation, national scoring profile for each section, and your percentile ranking.

WHAT'S A GOOD SCORE?

There's no such thing as a cut-and-dry "good score." Much depends on the strength of the rest of your application (if your college GPA is near a 4.0, the pressure to score high on the MCAT is less intense) and on where you want to go to school (different schools have different score expectations). Here are a few interesting statistics:

For each MCAT administration, the average scaled scores are approximately 8s for Physical Sciences, Verbal Reasoning, and Biological Sciences. You need scores of at least 10–11s to be considered competitive by most medical schools, and if you're aiming for a top-tier medical school (Harvard, Yale, Johns Hopkins, etc.), you need to perform at a higher level, with scores of 12s and above in each of the sections. However, you will also need strong recommendation letters, volunteer/research experience, and a good GPA as well.

Here's the bottom line: you don't have to be perfect to do well. For instance, on the AAMC's Practice Test 5R, you can get as many as 10 questions wrong in Verbal Reasoning, 17 in Physical Sciences, and 16 in Biological Sciences and still score in the 80th percentile. To score in the 90th percentile, you can get as many as 7 wrong in Verbal Reasoning, 12 in Physical Sciences, and 12 in Biological Sciences. Even students who receive "perfect" (raw score: 45) scaled scores get a handful of questions wrong.

With that being said, it's important to maximize your performance on every question. Just a few questions one way or the other can make a big difference in your scaled score. Here's a look at recent score profiles so you can get an idea of the shape of a typical score distribution.

Physical Sciences		
Scaled Score	Percent Achieving Score	Percentile Rank Range
15	0.1	99.9–99.9
14	1.2	98.7–99.8
13	2.5	96.2–98.6
12	5.1	91.1–96.1
11	7.2	83.9–91.0
10	12.1	71.8–83.8
9	12.9	58.9–71.1
8	16.5	42.4–58.5
7	16.7	25.7–42.3
6	13.0	12.7–25.6
5	7.9	04.8–12.6
4	3.3	01.5–04.7
3	1.3	00.2–01.4
2	0.1	00.1–00.1
1	0.0	00.0–00.0
Scaled Score Mean = 8.1 Standard Deviation = 2.32		

Verbal Reasoning		
Scaled Score	Percent Achieving Score	Percentile Rank Range
15	0.1	99.9–99.9
14	0.2	99.7–99.8
13	1.8	97.9–99.6
12	3.6	94.3–97.8
11	10.5	83.8–94.2
10	15.6	68.2–83.7
9	17.2	51.0–68.1
8	15.4	35.6–50.9
7	10.3	25.3–35.5
6	10.9	14.4–25.2
5	6.9	07.5–14.3
4	3.9	03.6–07.4
3	2.0	01.6–03.5
2	0.5	00.1–01.5
1	0.0	00.0–00.0
Scaled Score Mean = 8.0 Standard Deviation = 2.43		

Biological Sciences		
Scaled Score	Percent Achieving Score	Percentile Rank Range
15	0.1	99.9–99.9
14	1.2	98.7–99.8
13	2.5	96.2–98.6
12	5.1	91.1–96.1
11	7.2	83.9–91.0
10	12.1	71.8–83.8
9	12.9	58.9–71.1
8	16.5	42.4–58.5
7	16.7	25.7–42.3
6	13.0	12.7–25.6
5	7.9	04.8–12.6
4	3.3	01.5–04.7
3	1.3	00.2–01.4
2	0.1	00.1–00.1
1	0.0	00.0–00.0
Scaled Score Mean = 8.2 Standard Deviation = 2.39		

WHAT THE MCAT REALLY TESTS

It's important to grasp not only the nuts and bolts of the MCAT, so you'll know *what* to do on Test Day, but also the underlying principles of the test so you'll know *why* you're doing what you're doing on Test Day. We'll cover the straightforward MCAT facts later. Now it's time to examine the heart and soul of the MCAT, to see what it's really about.

THE MYTH

Most people preparing for the MCAT fall prey to the myth that the MCAT is a straightforward science test. They think something like this:

> *"It covers the four years of science I had to take in school: biology, chemistry, physics, and organic chemistry. It even has equations. OK, so it has Verbal Reasoning, but that is just to see if we're literate, right? The important stuff is the science. After all, we're going to be doctors."*

Well, here's the little secret no one seems to want you to know: The MCAT is not just a science test; it's more importantly a critical thinking test. This means that the test is designed to let you demonstrate your thought process in addition to your thought content.

KAPLAN

The implications are vast. Once you shift your test-taking paradigm to match the MCAT modus operandi, you'll find a new level of confidence and control over the test. You'll begin to work symbiotically with the MCAT rather than against it. You'll be more efficient and insightful as you prepare for the test, and as a result, you'll be more relaxed on Test Day. In fact, you'll be able to see the MCAT for what it is rather than for what it's dressed up to be. We want your Test Day to feel like a visit with a familiar friend instead of an awkward blind date.

THE ZEN OF MCAT

Medical schools do not need to rely on the MCAT to see what you already know. Admission committees can measure your subject-area proficiency using your undergraduate coursework and grades. Schools are most interested in the potential of your mind.

In recent years, many medical schools have shifted pedagogic focus away from an information-heavy curriculum to a concept-based curriculum. There is currently more emphasis placed on problem solving, holistic thinking, and cross-disciplinary study. Be careful not to dismiss this important point, figuring you'll wait to worry about academic trends until you're actually in medical school. This trend affects you right now, because it's reflected in the MCAT. Every good tool matches its task. In this case the tool is the test, used to measure you and other candidates, and the task is to quantify how likely it is that you'll succeed in medical school.

Your intellectual potential—how skillfully you annex new territory into your mental boundaries, how quickly you build "thought highways" between ideas, how confidently and creatively you solve problems—is far more important to admission committees than your ability to recite Young's modulus for every material known to humankind. The schools assume they can expand your knowledge base. They choose applicants carefully because expansive knowledge is not enough to succeed in medical school or in the profession. There's something more. It's this "something more" that the MCAT is trying to measure.

Every section on the MCAT essentially tests the same higher-order thinking skills: analytical reasoning, abstract thinking, and problem solving. Most test takers get trapped into thinking they are being tested strictly on biology, chemistry, and so on. Thus, they approach each section with a new outlook on what's expected. This constant mental gear-shifting can be exhausting, not to mention counterproductive. Instead of perceiving the test as parsed into radically different sections, you need to maintain your focus on the underlying nature of the test: It's designed to test your thinking skills, rather than your information-recall skills. Each test section presents a variation on the same theme.

WHAT ABOUT THE SCIENCE?

With this perspective, you may be left asking these questions: "What about the science? What about the content? Don't I need to know the basics?" The answer is a resounding "Yes!" You must be fluent in the different languages of the test. You cannot do well on the MCAT if you don't know the basics of physics, general chemistry, biology, and organic chemistry. We recommend that you take at least one year each of biology, general chemistry, organic chemistry, and physics before taking the MCAT, and that you review the content in this book thoroughly. Also, starting in 2015, the MCAT will test the basic principles of biochemistry, so we also recommend at least one semester of biochemistry or its equivalent. Knowing these basics is just the beginning of doing well on the MCAT. That's a shock to most test takers. Often, students presume that once they recall or relearn their undergraduate science, they are ready to do battle against the MCAT, but that is wrong! They merely have directions to the battlefield. They lack what they need to beat the test: a copy of the test maker's battle plan!

You won't be drilled on facts and formulas on the MCAT. You'll need to demonstrate ability to reason based on ideas and concepts. The science questions are painted with a broad brush, testing your general understanding.

TAKE CONTROL: THE MCAT MINDSET

In addition to being a thinking test, as we've stressed, the MCAT is a standardized test. As such, it has its own consistent patterns and idiosyncrasies that can actually work in your favor. This is the key to why test preparation works. You have the opportunity to familiarize yourself with those consistent peculiarities, to adopt the proper test-taking mindset.

The following are some overriding principles of the MCAT mindset that will be covered in depth in the chapters to come:

- Read actively and critically.
- Translate prose into your own words.
- Save the toughest questions for last.
- Know the test and its components inside and out.
- Do MCAT-style problems in each topic area after you've reviewed it.
- Allow your confidence to build on itself.
- Take full-length practice tests a week or two before the test to break down the mystique of the real experience.
- Review and learn from your mistakes—get the most out of your practice tests.
- Look at the MCAT as a challenge, the first step in your medical career, rather than as an arbitrary obstacle.

That's what the MCAT mindset boils down to: taking control. Being proactive. Being on top of the testing experience so that you can get as many points as you can as quickly and as easily as possible. Keep this in mind as you read and work through the material in this book and, of course, as you face the challenge on Test Day.

Now that you have a better idea of what the MCAT is all about, let's take a tour of the individual test sections. Although the underlying skills being tested are similar, each MCAT section requires that you call into play a different domain of knowledge. So, although we encourage you to think of the MCAT as a holistic and unified test, we also recognize that the test is segmented by discipline and that there are characteristics unique to each section. In the overviews, we'll review sample questions and answers and discuss section-specific strategies. For each of the sections—Verbal Reasoning, Physical/ Biological Sciences—we'll present you with the following:

- **The Big Picture**
  You'll get a clear view of the section and familiarize yourself with what it's really evaluating.
- **A Closer Look**
  You'll explore the types of questions that will appear and master the strategies you'll need to deal with them successfully.
- **Highlights**
  The key approaches to each section are outlined, for reinforcement and quick review.

TEST EXPERTISE

The first year of medical school is a frenzied experience for most students. In order to meet the requirements of a rigorous work schedule, students either learn to prioritize and budget their time or else fall hopelessly behind. It's no surprise, then, that the MCAT, the test specifically designed to predict success in the first year of medical school, is a high-speed, time-intensive test. It demands excellent time-management skills as well as that sine qua non of the successful physician—grace under pressure.

It's one thing to answer a Verbal Reasoning question correctly; it's quite another to answer several correctly in a limited time frame. The same goes for Physical and Biological Sciences—it's a whole new ballgame once you move from doing an individual passage at your leisure to handling a full section under actual timed conditions. When it comes to the multiple-choice sections, time pressure is a factor that affects virtually every test taker.

So when you're comfortable with the content of the test, your next challenge will be to take it to the next level—test expertise—which will enable you to manage the all-important time element of the test.

THE FIVE BASIC PRINCIPLES OF TEST EXPERTISE

On some tests, if a question seems particularly difficult you'll spend significantly more time on it, as you'll probably be given more points for correctly answering a hard question. This isn't true for the MCAT. Remember, every MCAT question, no matter how easy or hard, is worth a single point. There's no partial credit or "A" for effort, and because there are many questions to do in a timed-section, it would be foolish to spend 10 minutes on one question and miss an opportunity for easy points later on.

Given this combination—limited time, all questions equal in weight—you must develop a game plan to attack each of the test sections to make sure you get as many points as quickly and easily as you can. Here are the principles that will help you do that

1. FEEL FREE TO SKIP AROUND

One of the most valuable strategies to help you finish the sections in time is to learn to recognize and deal first with the questions that are easier and more familiar to you. That means you must temporarily skip those that promise to be more challenging and time-consuming, if you feel comfortable doing so. You can always come back to these at the end, and if you run out of time, you're much better off not getting to questions you may have had difficulty with, rather than missing out on quick points on Test Day. Of course, because there's no guessing penalty, always click on an answer to every question on the test, whether you get to it or not.

This strategy is difficult for most test takers; we're conditioned to do things in order. Nevertheless, give it a try when you practice. If you take the test in the exact order given, you're letting the test makers control you. YOU control how you take this test. On the other hand, if skipping around goes against your moral fiber and makes you a nervous wreck—don't do it. Just be mindful of the clock, and don't get bogged down with the tough questions.

2. LEARN TO RECOGNIZE AND SEEK OUT QUESTIONS YOU CAN DO

Another thing to remember about managing the test sections is that MCAT questions and passages are not presented in order of difficulty, unlike items on the SAT and other standardized tests. There's no rule that says you have to work through the sections in any particular order; in fact, the test makers scatter the easy and difficult questions throughout the section, in effect rewarding those who actually get to the end. Don't lose sight of what you're being tested on along with your reading and thinking skills: efficiency and cleverness.

Don't waste time on questions you can't complete with the time constraints. We know that skipping a tough question is easier said than done; we all have the natural instinct to plow through test sections in their given order, but this strategy doesn't pay off on the MCAT. The computer won't be impressed if you get the toughest question right. If you dig in your heels on a tough question, refusing to move on until you've cracked it, well, you're letting your ego get in the way of your test score. A test section (not to mention life itself) is too short to waste on lost causes.

3. USE A PROCESS OF ANSWER ELIMINATION

Using a process of elimination is another way to answer questions both quickly and effectively. There are two ways to get all the answers right on the MCAT. You either know all the right answers, or you know all the wrong answers. Because there are three times as many wrong answers, you should be able to eliminate some if not all of them. By doing so you either get to the correct response or increase your chances of guessing the correct response. You start out with a 25 percent chance of picking the right answer, and with each eliminated answer, your odds go up. Eliminate one, and you'll have a $33\frac{1}{3}$ percent chance of picking the right one; eliminate two, and you'll have a 50 percent chance; and, of course, eliminate three, and you'll have a 100 percent chance. Increase your efficiency by crossing out the wrong choices on the screen with the strike-through feature, using the right-click button on the mouse. Look for wrong-answer traps when you're eliminating. Some answers are designed to seduce you by distorting the correct answer.

4. REMAIN CALM

It's imperative that you remain calm and composed while working through a section. You can't allow yourself to become so rattled by one challenging passage that it throws off your performance on the rest of the section. Expect to find at least one passage like this in every section, but bear in mind that you won't be the only one to have trouble with it. The test is curved, taking this tough material into account. A difficult question isn't going to ruin your score—but getting upset about it and letting it throw you off track will. When you understand that part of the test maker's goal is to reward those who keep their composure, you'll recognize the importance of not panicking when you run into challenging material.

5. KEEP TRACK OF TIME

Of course, the last thing you want to happen is to have time called on a particular section before you've gotten to half the questions. Therefore, it's essential that you pace yourself, keeping in mind the general guidelines for how long to spend on any individual question or passage. Have a sense of how long you have to do each question, so you know when you're exceeding the limit and should start to move faster.

Always keep track of time. We'll talk more about strategies for this in your MCAT course. You don't want to fall into the trap of spending a disproportionate amount of time on any one question or group of questions. Also, give yourself about a minute or so at the end of each section to fill in answers for any questions you haven't gotten to.

SECTION-SPECIFIC PACING

Now, let's look at the section-specific timing requirements and some tips for meeting them. Keep in mind that the times per question or passage are only averages; there will be questions that take less time, and others that take more. Try to stay balanced. Since every question is weighed equally, don't spend more than a minute on any one.

VERBAL REASONING

Allow yourself approximately eight to ten minutes per passage and corresponding questions. It may sound like a lot of time, but it goes by quickly. Also, keep in mind that some passages are longer than others. On average, give yourself about three or four minutes to read and then four to six minutes for the questions.

PHYSICAL AND BIOLOGICAL SCIENCES

Averaging over each section, you'll have about one minute and 20 seconds per question. Some questions, of course, will take more time, and some less. A science passage plus accompanying questions should take about eight to nine minutes, depending on how many questions there are. Stand-alone questions can take anywhere from a few seconds to a minute. Again, the rule is to do your best work first. Also, don't feel that you have to understand everything word-for-word in a passage before you move on to the questions. You may not need a deep understanding to answer the questions because some information in the passage can be extraneous. Overcome your perfectionism and use your time wisely.

COMPUTER-BASED TESTING STRATEGIES

ARRIVE AT THE TESTING CENTER EARLY

Get to the testing center early to jump-start your brain. However, if they allow you to begin your test early, decline.

USE THE MOUSE TO YOUR ADVANTAGE

If you are right-handed, practice using the mouse with your left hand for Test Day. This way, you'll increase speed by keeping the pencil in your right hand to write on your scratch paper. If you are left-handed, use your right hand for the mouse.

KNOW THE TUTORIAL BEFORE TEST DAY

You will save time on Test Day by knowing exactly how the test will work. Click through any tutorial pages on practice tests and familiarize yourself with them, and on Test Day you will save time.

PRACTICE WITH SCRATCH PAPER

Going forward, always practice using scratch paper when solving questions because this is how you will do it on Test Day. Never write directly on a written test.

REMEMBER YOU CAN ALWAYS GO BACK

Just because you finish a passage or move on, remember you can come back to questions about which you are uncertain. You have the "marking" option to your advantage. However, as a general rule try not to mark up more than one question per passage.

MARK INCOMPLETE WORK

If you need to go back to a question, clearly mark the work you've done on the scratch paper with the question number. This way, you will be able to find your work easily when you come back to tackle the question.

LOOK AWAY AT TIMES

Taking the test on computer leads to faster eye-muscle fatigue. Use the Kaplan strategy of looking at a distant object at regular intervals. This will keep your mind alert throughout the test.

PRACTICE ON THE COMPUTER

This is the *most critical* aspect of adapting to computer-based testing. Like anything else, in order to perform well on computer-based tests, you must practice. Spend time reading passages and answering questions on the computer. You often will have to scroll when reading passages.

KAPLAN

About Verbal Reasoning

Remember the last time you were given a required reading list? You probably sighed and tried to figure out how long it would take you to read all those books. Well, there's required reading on the MCAT too, but the good news is that you know exactly how long it will take you—60 minutes—and you don't have to write a research paper or book report at the end. You just have to answer some questions (correctly—we're not interested in incorrect answers!), and you have an excellent, time-tested strategy for doing it: the Kaplan way. Fundamentally, the Verbal section of the MCAT requires you to do three things: read, think, and analyze. These are skills you already have in abundance or you wouldn't be studying for MCAT right now. Of course, you have to tweak them for MCAT, but that's why you have this review book.

There are four things you really need to know about MCAT reading:

First, you're not reading to learn anything. This is not information you need to carry with you for weeks, months, or years. You just need to use it in the next few minutes, and you will refer back to the source (the passage) when you need it.

Second, you're not reading to remember anything. If you try to remember what you read, you'll rely on memory—which is notoriously faulty—and your mind will be taken up with what you're trying to remember. That's not helpful. Your mind needs to be open and focused on the really important parts of the MCAT: the questions. Anything you think is important enough to remember will go on your map, which we'll discuss in the next chapter.

Third, you don't need any outside knowledge to read the passage well. All of the correct answers are supported in the passage, and if you use what you already know, you'll be tempted to answer questions based on your own knowledge, not on the passage. That's a classic way to choose wrong answers.

And fourth, you're not reading to understand everything. After all, if there's no question on the part you didn't understand, it doesn't matter anyway. So you're not going to read and reread; you're just going to keep moving ahead and let the questions determine what you need to reread.

The MCAT Verbal section tends to be the scariest for students—after all, for the most part, you're a science expert—but remember that Verbal is the section that is probably the most responsive to strategy, and strategy is exactly what you'll learn through practice with this book. So let's take an overall look at Kaplan strategy. And remember: You *can* improve your critical reading between now and Test Day; we'll show you how!

Content of the Passage

Let's say you've looked at that required reading list and noticed that the topics are all over the place. And let's say that you don't enjoy reading philosophy or literary studies. Okay, but what about anthropology and history? The nice thing about MCAT Verbal Reasoning passages is that they cover a great variety of subjects. Past MCATs have had passages on everything from Native American life in Alaska to Sartre's philosophy, so you're bound to come across some passages that interest you and are easier to read and understand than others. It's usually a matter of familiarity with the subject matter, but as we've already said, you don't need any outside knowledge—the passage itself provides you with all of the information that you need to answer the questions. And here's a tip: You probably started on that required reading list by reading the books you thought you'd like. Do the same on the MCAT. Start with the passages on which you think you can do best. You don't have to read the passages in the order the test maker presents them. Once you've chosen a passage, all you have to do is concentrate on reading and thinking critically. And even better, regardless of whether you're dealing with a humanities, social science, or science text, every passage can be handled easily if you follow some general principles that you learned in class and that we'll review in the next chapter, Reading the Kaplan Way. But first, we'll look at how everyday reading differs from the active reading you'll do on MCAT Verbal Reasoning.

Reading on the MCAT versus Everyday Reading

Ordinarily, we read for one or both of two simple reasons: to learn something or to pass the time pleasantly. Needless to say, neither of these reasons has anything to do with the MCAT. Furthermore, on a daily basis, we tend to read for content. "What's the deeper meaning here?" we ask ourselves, or "What's this book *about*?" But anyone who tries to read for content during the MCAT is missing the point. There's just no time under strict test conditions to understand everything that's written—and, as we'll see, there's no payoff in it, either.

So what do you really need to get from reading an MCAT passage that's different from everyday reading? Broadly stated, there are two primary goals in reading an MCAT passage:

Reading for author **PURPOSE**—the "why" of the text—what does the author really want me to get from this paragraph and passage?

Reading for passage **STRUCTURE**—the "how" of the text—how does the author present her ideas?

MCAT Expertise

Familiarity with a wide variety of content will help you feel comfortable with many MCAT passages, so start reading outside your comfort zone. Read anything that puts you at ease with the terminology and content of subjects other than science. You don't need to learn anything; you just need to relax and be confident with any passage.

KAPLAN

Almost every MCAT Verbal Reasoning question fundamentally hinges on your ability to step back from the text and analyze *why* the author is writing in the first place and *how* she puts her text together.

Why does the MCAT test these particular skills?

You can think of this in two ways: short-term and long-term. Let's start with the long term. From this point of view, MCAT critical reading is very reflective of what you need to do as a practicing physician. Think about yourself in those terms. Let's skip over the MCAT, med school, internship, and so on and picture you as a fully qualified doctor. When a patient comes into your office for the first time and starts talking to you about his problems, what do you really need to understand? You need to know why this patient is here. What is the really important, basic point this patient is making? And how do all those symptoms, experiences, personal feelings, and physical complaints fit into that big picture? Essentially, with each patient, you're looking for the "why" and the "what"—just as you are on the MCAT.

As for the short term, here's the deal: Demanding that we figure out the author's purpose and the passage structure is the best way to test how each of us thinks about the prose we read. And thinking is always being tested, one way or another, on every MCAT question.

Look at it this way. You have probably written a term paper that begins something like this:

> The purpose of this paper is to examine the Christian imagery employed by John Milton in *Paradise Lost* and then to compare it to the pagan imagery in *Paradise Regained*. I will show that Milton's views of divinity and predestination, in particular, underwent a metamorphosis as he . . .

Most of us would say, *Sure, I was taught to begin papers with that kind of statement of intent. And yes, I was also told to describe how I planned to achieve that purpose.* In other words, most of us were trained to announce our "why" and "how" right at the beginning of the paper.

Now there are good reasons, of course, to urge students to write in this fashion. If you (as a student writer) lay out the "why" and "how" of your paper up front, you're more likely to write with unity and clarity as you go along.

However, more sophisticated writing—like the prose you'll see on the MCAT—doesn't always reveal its secrets quite so quickly and clearly. Authors always have a purpose, of course, and always have a structural plan for carrying out that purpose. But MCAT writers may not announce their purposes, which puts an extra burden

MCAT Expertise

Did you know that many medical schools consider your MCAT Verbal score the most important of the section scores? That's because the Verbal section reflects what you will do as a doctor. And what is that? You'll think critically!

on the reader to analyze what's stated, read between the lines, and draw inferences. Consider this first sentence of a typical passage:

> The great migration of European intellectuals to the United States in the second quarter of the twentieth century prompted a transmutation in the character of Western social thought.

See? We can figure out why the author is writing: His purpose, we might say, is to discuss a change in Western social thought that was brought about by the arrival of European eggheads in the mid-20th century (your phrasing might be a bit different, but the gist is probably the same). So there is a definite purpose here. And we can anticipate the structure: paragraphs that explain what the change is and how it happened. The author didn't state this, but we *can* figure it out; we just have to work a little harder than we usually do.

So remember that the MCAT Verbal section really tests critical reading and thinking—knowing the "why" and the "how." As you move on to the next chapter, Reading the Kaplan Way, you'll learn (1) to use a strategy that focuses on exactly those two ideas and (2) how that strategy will turn into points on MCAT Test Day.

Key Points to Remember

You Can Do This!

Reading the Kaplan way is reading with a strategic approach. It's this approach to the passage, rather than how much you really understand, that gets you points on MCAT.

- MCAT reading is not the same as most reading; you need a strategic approach.
- Read for purpose and structure, not for detail or solid understanding.
- Keep asking yourself "Why?" instead of "What?"
- You don't need any outside knowledge; in fact, using outside knowledge could be detrimental to your score.
- Read outside of science to become comfortable with—not knowledgeable about—many different content areas.

Reading
the Kaplan Way

Principles That Will Reward You

Do any of these problems sound familiar? You sometimes "glaze over" while you're reading a paragraph so when you reach the end, you realize you weren't really paying attention. Or you read for detail instead of purpose, so you get bogged down when faced with a patch of dense text or a cluster of thorny details. Or you think you have to understand everything fully before you can move on to the questions. Be honest with yourself, but don't worry; with practice, you'll learn to manage these problems by being an active reader and identifying the important parts of a passage. When you do, you'll find yourself getting "glazed and bogged" less and less.

When it comes to MCAT Verbal Reasoning, let's make sure we understand one extremely important point: For 99 percent of MCAT passages, it's all about the author. Again: It's *all* about the author. You'll get questions about the author's ideas, his purpose (obviously, to get his ideas across), what can be inferred from his passage, and how he puts it together. If you understand little more than the author's intent, you'll still have enough to go to the questions. So your focus as you read must always be on the author. Detail questions—those that ask about the "what"—are very rare on the MCAT. By contrast, questions that ask about the "why" and the "how"— i.e., global, deduction, evaluation, application, and incorporation questions—are the mainstay of the Verbal Reasoning section. That's where your critical thinking skills come into play.

Have you ever been followed around by a little kid who keeps asking "Why? Why? Why?" It's annoying, to be sure, but that kid has a point. "Why?" is a great question. It makes you look below the surface of the obvious words and gets you to the real point: why the author wrote those words.

On the MCAT, the passage exists only because the author has a specific purpose in mind. So as you read, keep asking yourself "Why?": *Why are you telling me this, author? Why are you discussing this theory? Why are you citing this opinion? Why are you including this particular detail at this particular place in the text?* Even when the text is more objective—a descriptive "storytelling or information download" text—you have to keep asking *why* and *how*, not *what*.

Details are the "what," and they never exist in a vacuum; they're always in a passage to support an idea. The function of a detail isn't unique to MCAT. Think about why you make a shopping list of grocery items. You make it to remind yourself of your purpose: to buy these things. Since details (bread, butter, milk) are secondary to main ideas on MCAT passages (if I don't buy these items, I won't eat tonight), don't get caught up in details. Ask yourself why those details are there. In other words, what is the idea the details are supporting? Read over details quickly; then reread them more closely only when questions demand it.

Of course, there's no payoff in just "getting through the passage" without comprehension; on the other hand, reading all of the content carefully is a waste of time. Instead, know what's important in a passage and what isn't. The author's ideas and purpose are the important points; the details can always be researched if there are questions on them (mostly in science passages). Remember that the MCAT is a timed test; use your time wisely and focus on the author.

You already know that paragraphs are the fundamental building blocks of the passage. Paragraphs introduce ideas, or add support, or take you in a different direction. There's always a reason why the author writes each and every paragraph, just as there is when you write an essay. MCAT passages aren't so different from your own writing, though they tend to be denser and more vague than what we usually write. But the basics are the same. So as you read, look for the purpose of every paragraph rather than the details. For example, ask yourself: Is the paragraph the author's main idea or a small supporting example? Is the author using an analogy in a paragraph to strengthen her point or to refute someone else's contrary idea? It all goes back to the "why." Why is this paragraph here, and why is it at this particular place in the passage?

The Skills Behind the Principles

MAPPING

By now you might be saying to yourself, "Okay, I get the idea, but how in the world do I make it work on the passages?" Relax—it's not that hard. Take a deep breath and don't panic. You're going to learn the Kaplan strategy step-by-step, practice it slowly and deliberately, internalize it so it's second nature, then watch it boost your MCAT score. Ready? Here's the first step.

Pause Frequently to Summarize. Don't Glaze!

Yes, we've already mentioned this, but now let's get specific. You know what we mean by "glazing," right? It's when you've finished reading a passage and realize you have no idea what you just read. Your first instinct is to read it again, but you don't have time to do that on MCAT. How can you avoid glazing? Stop briefly after each paragraph and write a short summary that captures the main idea of the paragraph. This will be your **passage map**, paragraph by paragraph, and it's going to come in very handy. Just like a road map, it will tell you where you started, where you ended up, and how you got there. Using the map will be your first step in researching the questions, since it will remind you where to look in the passage.

MCAT Expertise

Always read the entire paragraph and passage. Just know what parts are important so you can gain time by reading quickly over the less important parts.

Take a look at the following text and think about how you could put it in your own words.

> Most of the developed countries are now agreed on the need to take international measures to reduce carbon emissions into the atmosphere. Despite this consensus, a wide disagreement among economists as to how much emission reduction will actually cost continues to impede policy making. Economists who believe that the energy market is efficient predict that countries that reduce carbon emission by as little as twenty percent will experience significant losses to their gross national product. Those who hold that the market is inefficient, however, estimate that costs will be much lower . . .

A good **paraphrase** of this text would be something like this: *An international policy to reduce carbon emissions has been held up by arguments about how much it would cost.* That's the basic idea here; the rest is just detail. You probably came up with different words, but as long as you have the gist of the paragraph, you'll be fine.

There's another reason why mapping is important. MCAT answer choices are frequently just paraphrases of what was stated in the passage. When you paraphrase and map, you'll be focused on correct answer choices.

The key to reading and mapping MCAT passages successfully is to read actively. Don't just let the words glide by while your mind wanders to other subjects (like your anxieties about getting into med school, for instance). Pause after each paragraph to summarize and paraphrase quickly what you've just read. A good reader checks her understanding frequently without getting bogged down on any one section. And you check your understanding by putting the ideas down in your own words.

Three Concepts You Need to Know

Your map will have two parts: (1) the purpose of each paragraph, which you jot down immediately after you read the paragraph, and (2) the overall Topic, Scope, and Purpose of the passage. Let's look at these ideas and make sure we're clear on the three concepts:

The **Topic** is the author's basic subject matter—World War I; or volcanoes; or Charles Dickens's *Bleak House*; or, in the case of this book, MCAT.

The **Scope** is the specific aspect of the topic on which the author focuses—the causes of World War I, or competing theories about predicting volcanic eruptions, or Dickens's critique of the English legal system, or the Verbal Reasoning section of the MCAT.

MCAT Expertise

Paraphrase and map after each paragraph. Don't map before reading the entire paragraph, and don't wait until the end of the passage. Mapping takes practice. Initially you'll go slowly, but don't give up; this is an important strategy that must be mastered and applied.

Key Concept

There's no such thing as a perfect map. We'll all come up with different words for the same paragraph. Since paraphrasing means putting ideas into your own words, whatever words you use will work.

The **Purpose** is the reason why the author wrote the passage—to dispute a common belief about the causes of World War I, or to describe competing theories about predicting volcanic eruptions, or to support Dickens's critique of the English legal system, or to describe the Kaplan method.

Find the Purpose of Each Paragraph

Here's the second step of the Kaplan method. Remember when we said that it's all about the author? The author's Purpose, paragraph by paragraph and in the passage as a whole, always shows up in MCAT questions. So you need to pay attention to the ideas in each paragraph and map them in your own words. For most passages, the Topic and Scope remain the same throughout the passage, but that's not necessarily true of each paragraph. You need to get to the gist of each one to have a good handle on the author's intent and build your map.

Each paragraph always serves a Purpose in the larger context of the passage: An author never writes just to pass the time but rather to make a point. (And no, the point is *not* to confuse you.) In other words, the Purpose of a paragraph is the major point that the author wants you to take away from the paragraph—e.g., "World War I was caused by European competition for overseas colonies, not by alliance arrangements in Europe," or "so-and-so's theory of volcanic eruptions is the most credible because of such-and-such," or "Dickens's critique of the English legal system was flawed by his inability to understand legal arguments."

As an MCAT test taker, your goal is to identify this Purpose in order to ace the questions. Of course, the author has to support or explain his purpose with evidence, which will come in the form of details. Don't get stuck on those details; go for the idea they support. Let's give it a try.

DRILL #1: DISTINGUISHING THE PURPOSE OF A PARAGRAPH FROM SUPPORTING DETAILS

Instructions: Read each of the following paragraphs and, in your own words, jot down the Purpose and supporting details of each paragraph. Then check your answers against those provided.

1. In the early 20th century, impoverished Southern black farmers migrated in large numbers to Northern cities in search of steady employment. With a rapidly expanding industrial base, Chicago was the destination for much of this wave of migration. Many of these farmers were eventually able to find jobs in Chicago's factories, but life was not easy for them. They received very low wages for long hours of physically demanding work. Moreover, they were

Key Concept

Here's an important tip for finding the purpose of each paragraph. Look for contrast keywords such as *while*, *but*, and *however*. They clue you in to the author's purpose and focus you on what he really wants you to know. (More about keywords in the next chapter.)

often torn from their families, with wives and children left behind out of economic necessity. And though discrimination was less intense in the North than in the South, black migrants were still subject to unfair treatment in matters of pay, promotion, and job security.

Purpose:

_____

Supporting details:

_____

2. Theropods, or three-toed dinosaurs, were traditionally thought of as unsociable, land-bound creatures who preferred to scavenge rather than hunt. But recently uncovered fossil evidence has led to a thorough reassessment of this view. The discovery of numerous sets of three-toed tracks at many fossil sites, for instance, has convinced paleontologists that theropods moved in packs, at least when feeding. Furthermore, some fossil sites were underwater when dinosaurs roamed the earth, indicating that theropods could swim. In fact, paleontologists now think that they were excellent swimmers who experienced little trouble capturing prey in the water. Their ability to swim has also undermined the belief that they were scavengers rather than hunters, because scavengers look for carrion on land, not in the water.

Purpose:

_____

Supporting details:

_____

3. The poetry of the earliest Greeks was completely impersonal. It was folk poetry, whose purpose was to express the thoughts and feelings of the entire community. During the later age of heroes, however, the focus of Greek poetry switched from the community to the individual. This poetry celebrates the lives of important personages such as kings and warriors. In so doing, it reflects the changing nature of ancient Greek life: A society that had initially been free of stark class differences eventually developed a hierarchical structure, with a small ruling elite in control of the masses.

Purpose:

_____

Supporting details:

_____

ANSWERS TO DRILL #1

1. **Purpose:** Poor black farmers who migrated to Chicago in search of jobs often found employment, but life remained difficult for them.

   Supporting details: low wages for hard work; family separation; job discrimination

2. **Purpose:** Contrary to traditional thinking, recent findings have shown that theropods were sociable hunters capable of swimming, rather than solitary, land-bound scavengers.

   Supporting details: numerous sets of theropod tracks at fossil sites, including some underwater at the time theropods roamed earth

3. **Purpose:** The change in Greek poetry from an emphasis on the community to an emphasis on the individual reflected larger changes in Greek society.

   Supporting details: folk poetry the norm in early Greek society when no classes existed; heroic poetry the norm later when society ruled by small elite of warriors and kings.

Find the Topic, Scope, and Purpose of the Passage

Finally, step 3: Review and characterize. By the time you finish reading the entire passage and mapping it paragraph by paragraph, you'll be able to step back, look at everything you read, and characterize the entire passage's Topic, Scope, and Purpose. These three final components of a map—Topic, Scope, and Purpose—help you check your overall understanding of what the author wrote and why. Remember, we're looking for overall Topic, Scope, and Purpose. Just to refresh your memory:

The **Topic** is the author's basic subject matter.

The **Scope** is the specific aspect of the topic on which the author focuses.

The **Purpose** is the reason why the author wrote the passage.

Always write the Purpose starting with a verb. For one thing, a verb shows *action*, and the Purpose is the reason why the author *acted* to write the passage. Not only that, but on the rare occasion when the test maker gives you a Purpose question, she may start each answer with a verb. If you know the author is neutral and your Purpose verb reflects that, all you have to do is get rid of any answer that doesn't start with a neutral verb.

Identifying these parameters of a passage makes it easier to attack. Because all correct answers are supported by or inferred from the passage, reminding yourself what is and is not in the passage keeps you focused on the author.

Let's assume that the following blocks of text constitute the entire passage (MCAT passages, however, are never this short) and see if we can pull out the Topic, Scope, and Purpose out of each one.

DRILL #2: FINDING TOPIC, SCOPE, AND PURPOSE

Instructions: Practice being an active reader. As you go through each paragraph, think about the Topic, Scope, and Purpose. Then, using your understanding of each paragraph, match the numbered statements that follow with the appropriate paragraph. There may be more than one correct statement for each paragraph, and not every statement necessarily matches up with one of the paragraphs.

A. At the Battle of Gettysburg in July 1863, 75,000 Confederate troops faced 90,000 Union soldiers in one of the largest battles of the American Civil War. For two days, both armies suffered heavy casualties in constant fighting, without either gaining a clear advantage. On the third and final day of the battle, Confederate forces mounted one last effort to penetrate Union lines. But the attempt ended in complete failure, forcing Confederate troops to withdraw far to the south . . .

B. In January 1863, seven months before the decisive Battle of Gettysburg, President Lincoln issued the Emancipation Proclamation, in which he declared an end to slavery in the United States. Some historians cite Lincoln's edict as proof that he wanted to do away with slavery because he considered it morally repugnant. While Lincoln certainly opposed the institution on ethical grounds, the timing of the proclamation suggests that he was out to weaken the Confederacy rather than to undertake a moral crusade . . .

C. Gettysburg was a turning point in the Civil War. Before the battle, Confederate forces under General Robert E. Lee had defeated their Union counterparts in a string of major engagements. After the battle, however, Union forces took the initiative, finally defeating the Confederacy less than two years later. By invading

MCAT Expertise

To find Scope, ask yourself: What about the topic? If the topic is MCAT Verbal Reasoning, what about it? You're reading about the definitions of Topic, Scope, and Purpose. That's the Scope. It's important to note this because many wrong answers go out of scope—outside the parameters of the passage. Writing Scope reminds you of what is and isn't in the passage.

MCAT Expertise

To find Purpose, first ask yourself if the author is neutral or has a point of view. If he's neutral, start Purpose with a neutral verb such as *explain*, *describe*, *show*, or *compare*. If he has a point of view, what is it? "To advocate?" "To criticize?" "To compare two theories and support one?"

Union territory, the Confederate leadership had sought to shatter the Union's will to continue the war and to convince European nations to recognize the Confederacy as an independent nation. Instead, the Union's willingness to fight was strengthened, and the Confederacy squandered its last chance for foreign support . . .

D. The Confederacy had hoped that France and Great Britain would intervene militarily on its side in order to restore the European-American cotton trade. But once President Lincoln issued the Emancipation Proclamation—which changed the focus of the Civil War from a conflict over states' rights to one over slavery—both the French and British concluded that their status in the international community would be jeopardized were they, in effect, to support slavery . . .

Remember to watch for those Purpose verbs; they reflect the author and help you focus on the right answer.

1. Argues that the outcome of the Battle of Gettysburg undermined the Confederacy's military and political goals in the Civil War.
2. Discusses the course of one of the most important battles of the Civil War.
3. Points out that Lincoln's primary motive for delivering the Emancipation Proclamation was to strengthen the Union in its struggle with the Confederacy.
4. Describes the effect of the Emancipation Proclamation on the Confederacy's foreign relations.
5. Conveys a sense of the close relations that existed between the Confederacy and European nations before the Battle of Gettysburg.
6. Settles an ongoing debate among historians about the importance of the Emancipation Proclamation to the Confederacy's defeat at the Battle of Gettysburg.
7. Proposes that the Battle of Gettysburg played a crucial part in changing the course of the Civil War.
8. Refutes the view that the Emancipation Proclamation stemmed from Lincoln's desire to destroy slavery.
9. Explains the cotton trade's role in turning the international community against the Confederacy.
10. Shows that the Union won the Battle of Gettysburg because it had more troops than the Confederacy.

ANSWERS TO DRILL #2

Statements 1 and 7 match up with paragraph C: Topic is the Battle of Gettysburg; Scope is the battle's role in determining the outcome of the Civil War; and Purpose is to assert that Gettysburg was a turning point in the eventual defeat of the South and victory of the North.

Statement 2 matches up with paragraph A: Topic is the Battle of Gettysburg; Scope is the battle itself; Purpose is to describe what happened during the battle.

Statements 3 and 8 match up with paragraph B: Topic is Emancipation Proclamation; Scope is Lincoln's motive for issuing the proclamation; Purpose is to argue that Lincoln did so in order to weaken the Confederacy.

Statement 4 matches up with paragraph D: Topic is Confederate foreign relations; Scope is the connection between the Emancipation Proclamation and Confederate foreign relations; Purpose is to describe the effect of the proclamation on Confederate foreign relations.

Statement 5 doesn't match up with any paragraph: paragraphs C and D do mention Confederate-European relations, but neither speaks of close relations before Gettysburg.

Statement 6 doesn't match up with any paragraph: None of the paragraphs refer to a debate among historians on this point.

Statement 9 doesn't match up with any paragraph: Paragraph D does refer to the cotton trade, but it doesn't draw any connection between the cotton trade and the international community's rejection of the Confederacy.

Statement 10 doesn't match up with any paragraph: Paragraph A mentions the number of troops deployed by each side at Gettysburg, but its purpose isn't to argue that the Union won at Gettysburg because it had more troops.

What If I Don't Know What to Map?

Even with the excellent Kaplan strategy, MCAT passages can be really tough—especially the abstract humanities readings that are about philosophy, literary criticism, or the nature of mankind. Sometimes you just don't understand the paragraph and have no idea what to map. Here's what you do: Map what you do understand and write down interesting, unique words from the paragraphs that baffle you. Previously, we said that you don't need to understand everything in order to go to the questions; this is what we mean.

Be confident that there will always be *something* you understand. Even the most obfuscatory of authors occasionally uses simple words. Map what you can from them. Also, know that MCAT authors tend to be redundant. They frequently say the same thing over and over using different words and examples (there's a redundant sentence for you). That's great, because if you didn't catch the author's ideas the first time, keep going—she'll probably repeat them.

For example, how much of this paragraph (taken from a passage you may see later in this book) do you really understand?

> For historico-deductivists, the problem of *a posteriori* overdetermination is a case in point. In the natural sciences, replicability and verifiability afford the finds of laboratory experimentation potentially nonmothetic status. In international relations, however, such lawlike generalizations about cause and effect are rarely if ever possible, not only because events are unique, but also because of the multiplicity of potential causes. Whether World War I resulted from a disequilibrium in the international distribution of power, the ascendancy of government factions committed to aggression, or the accuracy of an assassin's bullet is, ultimately, unknown. For opponents of positivism, it is better to recognize darkness than to pretend to see light.

It's a dense paragraph, but some things are probably clear. First, there is such a thing as historico-deductivists (whoever they are). Did you see the contrast word *however*? That tells us that what comes next is important, and it's something about the causes of events in international relations being difficult to pinpoint. That's as much as you need for a map of the paragraph. If you couldn't get even this, just leave it at mapping words: historico-deductivists, overdetermination, details re: WWI causes. That doesn't say much, but it could well be enough for you to know where to reread if a question asks about it.

Here's the moral of MCAT critical reading: Never give up—you can do this!

Key Points to Remember

- Read for the author's purpose; the "why," not the "what."
- Don't get bogged down in details.
- Map every paragraph with the primary idea of the paragraph.
- When you're finished reading, map for overall topic, scope, and purpose.
- If you don't know what to map, pick out words that seem important or unusual or that reflect the author's ideas.

3

Keywords

Keywords and phrases are just that: keys to open the locks that tell you the passage structure and author's intent. The rest is detail—which may or may not be important, depending on whether the questions relate to the details. So let's take a little quiz on keywords. Read the paragraph below as you would normally, then answer the question that follows.

> Although keywords pop up all the time, we seldom pay attention to them. In fact, sometimes we skip right over them. Consequently, they don't seem important. But they are very important. Why? Because they help you to become an active, critical reader who scores well on the Verbal Reasoning section of the MCAT.

Here's the quiz question: How many keywords did you see in this passage, and more importantly, were you able to use them quickly to get the structure and author intent? Let's look at the paragraph again, sentence by sentence, and read critically, the Kaplan way.

> Although keywords pop up all the time, we seldom pay attention to them.

The sentence starts with a **contrast keyword**, *although*. This tells you that there's opposition here: We see the keywords, but we don't read them critically. Here's the author's Topic: keywords. Contrast keywords are the most important in any MCAT passage. They indicate the author's purpose, point of view, and voice. Remember what we said previously: It's all about the author!

> In fact, sometimes we skip right over them.

In fact is a **continuation keyword**; we're getting more of the same. But once you know what the issue is—in this case, keywords—you don't need much more of the same. This is not a particularly important sentence, and you don't need to spend a lot of time on it. So when you see a continuation keyword, you can speed up your reading.

> Consequently, they don't seem important.

Consequently tells us someone's **conclusion**, though not necessarily the author's. Here the conclusion seems to be that people don't read keywords carefully. Stay alert—there's another keyword coming that *will* be the author's conclusion.

> But they are very important.

MCAT Expertise

Using appropriate keywords is also important for your MCAT essay!

Ah, another contrast keyword: *But*. This one indicates Scope—the author's intent in writing about the topic. Now we know the author's voice—his point of view: Keywords are important. By the way, the ideas that the keywords signal are what you'd map for this paragraph.

Why?

Rhetorical questions are lovely. Since they exist only as literary devices to allow the author to continue with his real purpose, they act as another clue to the author's point of view.

Because they help you to become an active, critical reader who scores well on the Verbal Reasoning section of the MCAT.

Because is an **evidence keyword** and introduces the author answering his own rhetorical question; that is, giving his conclusion. But you knew that would come next, didn't you? When you read actively, you're marching right up there with the author, not trying to play catch-up. Active reading allows you to read faster and with more understanding.

So what does the critical reader quickly take from this paragraph? Keywords are important in gaining points on MCAT Verbal Reasoning. That's it. The rest is background and detail. *But don't think you can just skip from keyword to keyword*. Always read the entire paragraph and passage. Just know what parts are important so you can gain time by reading quickly over the less important parts.

We've seen different types of keywords in this little exercise so you know that each type has a specific function. The most important and common categories of keywords on MCAT are evidence, conclusion, contrast, and (to a lesser extent) emphasis—because these are the words that will lead you to either the structure or the purpose of each paragraph.

CONTRAST KEYWORDS

Contrast keywords, as you've already seen, are among the most significant in Verbal Reasoning because so many passages are based on contrast or opposition. Almost certainly, something important is happening when a contrast keyword shows up. The author is shifting direction in order to take the reader to her real purpose for writing the passage. There are lots of common contrast words:

but	however	although	not	nevertheless
despite	alternatively	unless	though	by contrast
yet	still	otherwise	while	notwithstanding

> **Key Concept**
>
> It's not a question of saying: "Aha—here's a keyword!" It's more an issue of what that keyword tells you about the paragraph.

The really alert MCAT reader also pays attention to the more subtle contrast words, such as *traditionally, initially*, and *originally*. These words always indicate "something's going to change" and that change is going to be the author's focus.

EMPHASIS KEYWORDS

Emphasis keywords are almost as welcome as contrast keywords. After all, if we're supposed to read for the author's point of view—and we are—what better way than to stumble across words and phrases whose sole purpose is to announce "I, the author, find this important"? Note these:

above all	most of all	primarily	in large measure
essentially	especially	particularly	indeed

As useful as these words are, we don't see a lot of them in MCAT passages. They're too personal for the tone most authors take.

CONCLUSION KEYWORDS

Conclusion keywords signal that the author is about to sum up someone's thesis. But a passage could contain several ideas, so conclusions could sum up a thesis other than the author's. We saw that in the previous exercise, right? Still, it's nice when the author uses a conclusion keyword for his own thesis. The most common conclusion word is *therefore*, to which we can add these:

thus	believes	consequently	we can conclude that
in conclusion	so	it can be seen that	[Toynbee] claims that

Pay attention to conclusion keywords when you see them, but don't expect them always to sum up the passage because passages are lifted from longer works, so the end of a passage is not necessarily the end of the book, chapter, or other source. Rest assured, though, that everything you need to answer the questions correctly is in the passage.

EVIDENCE KEYWORDS

Evidence keywords tell you that the author is about to provide support for a point; that is, give you evidence for what the author has already said. Thus, evidence keywords tend to indicate details. And what do you do with details? Not much other than to note where they are so you can refer to them if a question requires it. Here are the "big four" evidence keywords:

because	for	since	the reason is that

CONTINUATION KEYWORDS

Continuation keywords announce that more of the same is about to appear. The word *and* is probably the most common continuation keyword in the English language. Others include the following:

also	furthermore	in addition	as well as
moreover	plus	at the same time	equally

Also (there's a signal for you!), the colon sometimes does the same job: It usually tells you that what follows expands upon, or continues, what came before. Continuation keywords serve essentially the same purpose as evidence words. Don't spend a lot of time worrying over what's being continued.

ILLUSTRATION KEYWORDS

Illustration keywords signal that an example is about to arrive. *One example* and *for instance* are the most obvious. But think about these:

As [Maya Angelou] says,	For historians,	In the words of [Hannah Arendt],
According to these experts,	To [Proust],	

In each case, what's about to come is an example of that person's thinking.

SEQUENCE KEYWORDS

Sequence keywords are the author telling you, "Hey, there's some sort of order at work here." These are helpful words, when used (which is seldom). They allow you to map a passage as, for example, "¶1 Step 1, ¶2 Step 2, ¶3 Step 3." Nice and easy, right? Here are some sequence keyword examples:

Secondly, (and thirdly, fourthly, etc.)	Next,	Finally,
Recently,		

A Keywords Exercise

The best MCAT test takers are attentive to purpose and structure at every moment, and when keywords come along, these readers automatically tend to anticipate where the author will probably take the passage next. As a result, the reader stays ahead of the author (rather than behind) and is less likely to be confused by dense detail or to lose sight of the structure as a whole.

Instructions: Each of the following pieces of text—any of which might be found in a Verbal Reasoning passage—ends with a familiar keyword. After you read it, try to formulate an idea of what ought to follow the keyword; then look at the three possibilities listed. Choose the one that would be the most logical completion of the sentence: Which one (if any) comes the closest to your expectation?

> **Key Concept**
>
> Pay attention to keywords and what they tell you about the author and the structure of the passage. Your MCAT Verbal score will thank you for it.

1. The latest research seems to suggest that people who consume alcohol in moderation may be healthier, on average, than either teetotalers or heavy drinkers. Hence,

    A. people who enjoy a single glass of wine with dinner need not fear that they are endangering their health.
    B. at least one clinical study rates both nondrinkers and heavy drinkers as less psychologically stable compared with moderate drinkers.
    C. without more data, it would be premature to change one's lifestyle on the basis of these findings.

2. The photograph being copied must be in good condition; otherwise,

    A. it should be examined with a magnifying glass under strong white light.
    B. its dimensions must be identical to those of the desired duplicate.
    C. the duplicate will exhibit the same scratches or smears as the original.

3. The fresco was completed after Giotto's death by an apprentice whose skills were not quite up to the task, and

    A. he clearly attempted to imitate the master's strokes.
    B. neither the perspective nor the colors are convincing.
    C. he had studied with the master for only a short time.

4. The evidence suggesting that the two species of felines may have existed simultaneously on the African veldt is purely circumstantial. For example,

    A. with no direct proof to the contrary, many experts still believe that the giant cats died out long before their smaller relatives appeared.
    B. fossil traces of both species have been found in separate areas in sediments that are thought to have been laid down by the same floodwaters.
    C. since all of the giant fossils found so far have been male, some scientists suspect that the smaller ones represent the females and young of the same sexually dimorphic species.

5. Only one day care facility in this city bases its fees on a sliding scale according to family income, and there are over three hundred children on its waiting list. Consequently,

    A. it is nearly impossible for most poor mothers to work outside the home while providing care for their children.

    B. the blame for the lack of affordable child care alternatives must be placed on state legislators, who have stymied every attempt to redress the situation.

    C. the number of high- and middle-income families who place their pre-school children in day care primarily to give them an educational advantage continues to rise.

6. The purpose of the proposed advertising campaign is, first, to increase public awareness of the company's new logo. For instance,

    A. it is hoped that the new commercials will reinforce brand loyalty among consumers.

    B. a major portion of the budget has been allocated to create a striking and memorable design.

    C. television viewers should be able to identify the design correctly after seeing the commercial only once.

7. Tobacco companies often advertise cigarettes with filter tips or with lower levels of tar and nicotine as "lighter," implying that they are less damaging to health than regular cigarettes. But

    A. several studies have shown that people who smoke such cigarettes tend to inhale more deeply, thereby delivering at least as much tar and nicotine to their lungs as if they were smoking regular cigarettes.

    B. in manufacturing and marketing these products, the tobacco companies are responding to the widespread awareness and fear, even among habitual smokers, of the harmful effects of smoking.

    C. the impression created by these advertisements is that people—particularly young women—who care about their health may smoke these cigarettes without having to worry about developing cancer or emphysema.

8. Many methods of contraception work by preventing sperm from fertilizing the ovum. Alternatively,

    A. latex condoms and diaphragms present physical barriers to sperm; the contraceptive efficacy of these methods can be increased chemically via spermicides.

    B. these methods, however varied their mechanisms, are all prophylactic in nature, in that no embryo is ever created.

    C. pregnancy can be averted after fertilization by causing the fertilized egg to be expelled from the body rather than implanting in the uterine wall.

9. That Nabokov's novels found a mass audience in the United States, a country in which relatively few people study foreign languages, is mystifying, especially given

    A. his appeal to academics and literary critics.

    B. his penchant for multilingual puns.

    C. the ribald adult content of his books.

DISCUSSION

1. A

Hence is a conclusion keyword, and (A) is the only one of the choices that can reasonably be concluded from the previous sentence. (B) provides additional evidence along the same lines and would more logically follow a continuation keyword such as *moreover*. (C), which takes a different view, would probably start off with a contrast keyword such as *however*.

2. C

The contrast keyword *otherwise* warns of some undesired consequence to follow if the photo is in bad shape; (C) fits the bill. (A) is a precondition to ensure that the original photo is okay; it should take a conclusion keyword such as *therefore*. (B) describes a second requirement that is distinct from the photo's condition; it needs a continuation keyword such as *also* to set it up.

3. B

And expresses continuation, another piece of evidence that points in the same direction. Replacing *and* with a wordier evidence keyword—such as *as evidenced by the fact that*—would make (B) even more clearly correct. The contrast keyword *although* would more appropriately introduce (A), which expresses a subtle contrast (the apprentice didn't succeed, although he tried). (C) attempts to explain why the apprentice wasn't up to snuff; an evidence keyword such as *since* should set up this choice.

> **You Can Do This!**
>
> Every time you see practice drills or questions for passages, you'll always also see full explanations of right and wrong answers. Study these, even if you got the answer right. You want to make sure you know why the answer is right and why others are wrong.

4. B

For example, one of the most common illustration keywords, sets the stage for (B), a specific piece of the circumstantial evidence mentioned in the first part of the sentence. (A) suggests an opposing conclusion—that the two species did not coexist—and would probably be introduced by a conclusion keyword such as *thus*. (C) brings in additional evidence pointing to an alternative conclusion and would be more effectively set up by the continuation phrase *in addition*.

5. A

The conclusion keyword *consequently* leads nicely to (A), a natural result of the first sentence. Placing blame, (B), is not a result but a completely different idea (the legislators have stymied every attempt to redress the situation). (C) discusses a simultaneous but different trend. *At the same time*, which is a continuation phrase with subtle overtones of contrast, would set it up better.

6. C

The illustration keyword *for instance* should lead to an example of how the campaign would increase public awareness; (C) would be a reasonable result to hope for. A sequence keyword such as *secondly* would more effectively indicate that (A) raises a new issue, brand loyalty, that is an additional purpose of the campaign, unrelated to public awareness. (B) requires a conclusion keyword such as *hence* to show that the previously stated objective requires a hefty design budget for the new logo.

7. A

But, one of the bluntest contrast keywords in the English language, leads to (A), an outcome diametrically opposed to the claims in the cigarette ads. (B) is an attempt to infer why the tobacco companies would make such claims; a conclusion phrase such as *it can be concluded that* would clarify the logical connection. (C) seems to be a result of the ads, so a conclusion keyword, not a contrast one, would work here.

8. C

The contrast keyword *alternatively* has to introduce contraceptive methods that don't rely on preventing fertilization; (C), preventing implantation after the fact, is a good alternative. (A), which describes specific contraceptive methods that prevent fertilization, would be better introduced by an illustration keyword such as *for example*. An emphasis keyword such as *essentially* would help (B) point out what all these methods have in common.

9. B

Especially is an emphasis keyword. (B) is the only choice that would make Nabokov's mass appeal in a linguistically provincial country even more mystifying. His appeal to academic and literary critics might explain his mass readership, or at least render it less mystifying; (A) should thus be introduced by a contrast keyword such as *despite*. (C), the adult content of the books, has nothing to do with the language in which Nabokov wrote and so wouldn't make his books any more or less mystifying.

How did you do? Don't worry if this was tough—it's just the beginning of your Kaplan strategy practice. Mastery will come from thorough, focused practice and result in a higher MCAT Verbal score.

Key Points to Remember

- Keywords and phrases give you lots of important information—use them well.

- The most important keywords are contrast words because they introduce the author's point of view.

- Keywords also help you identify what's really important in the passage and what you can read less carefully, saving you time.

- Make sure you review the complete explanations for all practice items.

- Mastery comes from practice; practice wisely and well.

Key Concept

Rule of thumb: It should take you twice as long to review the explanations as it took to answer the questions.

4

Dissecting Arguments

The Structure of Arguments

Critical reading takes you a long way toward scoring points on Verbal Reasoning, but most of the questions you'll face will require more than finding, paraphrasing, or categorizing the appropriate text; they'll require that you understand arguments.

An argument, in the logic sense of the word, has nothing to do with angry exchanges between people. In Verbal Reasoning, an argument simply means a conclusion (what someone wants or believes) plus its supporting evidence (the reasons why). Don't be misled by the word conclusion—it can appear in the beginning, middle, or end of a passage or paragraph.

Remember, since outside information is not relevant in the Verbal Reasoning section, evaluating an argument will never require that you decide whether the evidence is true—just that you evaluate the structure of the argument itself.

Breakdown of an Argument

Part	Function
Opinion	Stated Conclusion
Fact	Stated Evidence
Inference	Implied Conclusion
Assumption	Implied Evidence

Every argument needs a *conclusion* and *evidence*, which might consist entirely of the stated *opinion* and *facts*. An argument might allow one to make an unstated *inference*, which is part of the argument but not necessary for the argument to be complete. An argument might rely upon an unstated *assumption*, which is necessary for the argument to be complete. As used here, *facts* and *opinions* mean the parts of the argument that you find in the text, rather than the unstated *inferences* or *assumptions*.

The strongest arguments are those with conclusions that must be true if the evidence is true. For example:

Evidence: All Central High School volleyball players are over six feet tall, and Sally plays volleyball for Central High.

Conclusion: Therefore, Sally is over six feet tall.

Don't allow your own biases to mislead you when answering Verbal Reasoning questions. An argument can be strong even if you reject its conclusion or weak even if you believe its conclusion is true.

Stated Parts of an Argument

Try your hand at identifying the stated parts of arguments. Identify the *conclusion* or *opinion* first and then the *evidence* or *facts* supporting the conclusion.

1. The school board's decision to seize the high school newspaper was not censorship. The board was merely trying to protect the students from dangerous ideas. The paper contained an editorial in favor of communism. Protecting students from dangerous ideas is not censorship.

   Conclusion _____

   Evidence _____

2. An ordinance should be passed banning midtown street vendors from selling food within a certain proximity to restaurants. With their high rents and operating costs, restaurants cannot be expected to compete with the vendors. Even though the vendors often sell food that is completely different from the restaurants' bills of fare, their lower prices are enough to attract customers who otherwise would have eaten in the restaurants.

   Conclusion _____

   Evidence _____

3. An investigation must be launched into the operations of the private group that is training recruits to fight against Country Z. The Neutrality Act plainly forbids citizens from engaging in military campaigns against any nation with which we are not at war. Since no war has been declared between Country Z and us, we should bring charges against these fanatics who are in open defiance of the law.

   Conclusion _____

   Evidence _____

DISCUSSION

1. **Conclusion:** The school board's decision to seize the high school newspaper was not censorship.

   (Again, conclusions are not about individual sentences; they're about ideas.)

   Evidence: The board was merely trying to protect the students from dangerous ideas.

2. **Conclusion:** Street vendors need to be restricted from selling food around restaurants.

   Evidence: Restaurants cannot compete with the vendors' lower prices.

3. **Conclusion:** An investigation must be launched into the operations of the private group that is training recruits to fight against Country Z.

   Evidence: The Neutrality Act forbids citizens from engaging in military campaigns against any nation with which we are not at war. This group of citizens is training recruits to fight against Country Z, with which we are not at war.

SORTING THE OPINION (STATED CONCLUSION) FROM THE FACTS (STATED EVIDENCE)

The *opinion* should answer the question "what is the author's point?" The *facts* should answer the question "why should we believe the *opinion* is true?"

When you know what *facts* support which *opinion*, restate the argument in your own, simplified words:

> The author believes the *conclusion* because of the *evidence*.

This will give you a consistent form to work with, whatever the questions ask. With practice, this step will be automatic and instantaneous by Test Day—saving, not using, time.

Restate the argument made in the following paragraph:

> The "Robber Baron" industrialists of the late 19th and early 20th centuries are often portrayed as having no interest in the well-being of society as a whole in their ruthless pursuit of power and personal fortunes. Quite apart from the incidental benefits they provided to society through industrial development, this view ignores the philanthropic endeavors with which most of the Robber Barons were associated. Admittedly a good deal of their philanthropy took the form of bequests; still, these industrialists are responsible for many of our best museums and symphony halls, and the foundations they established continue to rank among the most important sources of charity to this day.

Argument _____

DISCUSSION

You probably used different words, but the basic idea is: These industrialists were better than most people think because they developed industry and because they were very philanthropic.

Note that this argument is never affirmatively stated in the passage: It's expressed as a rebuttal of a common opinion, with the author's opinion apparent in the words this view ignores. The statement "quite apart from" indicates that the first part of the sentence—about the industrial benefits the Robber Barons provided—is in contrast to the more significant evidence that their philanthropy is sufficient to redeem their reputations. "Admittedly" is another evidence Keyword; you admit facts that weaken or refute your conclusion. Although we discuss many of the Keywords present in our passages, remember that you shouldn't worry about catching every Keyword—they reinforce each other, and you only need to note enough to grasp the flow of the argument.

Now try identifying the *conclusion* and *evidence* (stated parts of the argument) in this paragraph.

> While this may be the most commonly held belief, more enlightened scholars argue that these figures are actually Shinto religious images. They point out that Shinto artists often borrowed Buddhist iconography, so an image that resembles a lion cannot unequivocally be interpreted as a Buddhist piece. Furthermore, Shinto art characteristically displays a peculiar appreciation for the wood (reflecting the belief that a deity may reside in any natural object) and the artist who sculpted these statues carefully followed the natural direction of the wood grain in sculpting curls of the mane and the curves of the forelegs.

1st Sentence _____

2nd Sentence _____

3rd Sentence _____

DISCUSSION

The first sentence is the conclusion. It's what the author wants you to believe. If the sentence said simply "other scholars argue" this could be evidence, citing one branch of scholarship on the topic. But the author describes these scholars as "more enlightened"—and that's the author's opinion. The Keyword "While" prepares you for the second half of the sentence contrasting with the opening clause. Keywords "argue" and "actually" further identify the opinion. You can see that it isn't necessary to recognize every keyword, since they often reinforce each other throughout passages.

The second sentence is evidence identified by the keywords "they point out that"—this is some of the supporting detail provided by the experts. Notice the opinion of this group of scholars, introduced by "so," is supported by the fact that Shinto artists borrowed from Buddhist iconography.

The third sentence is more evidence—as the word "Furthermore" indicates.

The Unstated Parts of Arguments

The process of deciphering what the author implies is deduction, and deduction questions are the most common type on the MCAT Verbal Reasoning Section. There are two types of deduction questions that you will have to answer: *assumption* and *inference.*

ASSUMPTIONS

Assumptions are the evidence that the author does not state but, based on the evidence she does state, must be true. For this reason, assumptions don't veer far away from the conclusion and evidence; an assumption will be a logical idea connecting the two. On the MCAT, the answers to assumption questions are not usually found explicitly stated in the text.

Read the following argument, and write the *assumption* on the line below.

> Sally plays volleyball for Central High School; therefore, Sally must be more than six feet tall (assuming that…)

Assumption _____

DISCUSSION

The keyword "therefore" tells us that "Sally is more than six feet tall" is the conclusion, so "Sally plays volleyball…" is supporting evidence. But what's missing?

> All those who play volleyball for Central High are more than six feet tall.

This assumption directly links the evidence to the conclusion, and it must be true if the conclusion follows from the stated evidence. Note that either fact could have been left unstated in this argument. If you are told: "All volleyball players for Central High are more than six feet tall, therefore Sally must be more than six feet tall" then the author must be assuming that Sally plays volleyball for Central High.

INFERENCES

A Verbal Reasoning *inference* is an implied part of an argument that must be true if the evidence or facts are true.

Consider the following:

> Sally plays volleyball for Central High School. All of Central High's volleyball players are more than six feet tall (therefore, we can infer...)

We can infer that Sally is over six feet tall. We are given facts that necessarily add up to this conclusion.

Note the difference between an *inference* and an *assumption*: The former is a conclusion supported by the given facts; the latter is an unstated fact necessary to support the stated opinion. They aren't interchangeable parts. Suppose you were told:

> Sally plays volleyball for Central High School and Sally is more than six feet tall.

Because "and" is used instead of "therefore," you wouldn't be able to assume that "all volleyball players for Central High School are over six feet tall" as you did in the exercise on assumptions; it's only a possibility. The information given doesn't support that statement as a conclusion.

Now try another familiar type of example. What is the *inference* in this argument?

> Either you or I must clean this room, and I won't do it!

Conclusion _____

Evidence _____

DISCUSSION

Conclusion: You have to clean the room.

Evidence: Either you or I have to clean the room, and I won't.

This is another implicit conclusion—an *inference* of a type that occurs commonly in conversation. Only evidence is stated in the argument. Note that, when there is no stated conclusion, there are not likely to be keywords indicating the different roles played by the parts.

THE DENIAL TEST

If you are uncertain about an *assumption* or *inference* answer choice, it may be easier to see what happens if that choice is not true. This is Kaplan's Denial Test. It's more time-consuming than predicting the correct answer, but it can be very powerful. Use it while you're practicing to confirm your predictions; use it on the test when you can't predict.

Let's see how this would work with a simple argument:

> Sally plays volleyball for Central High School; therefore, Sally is more than six feet tall.

Assumption: All Central High volleyball players are over six feet tall.

Denial: Not all Central High volleyball players are over six feet tall.

If we deny the assumption, we are no longer able to conclude for certain that Sally is more than six feet tall; therefore, the assumption must be valid for the argument to be true. Restate arguments with implied parts in the same simplified form you use for arguments with only stated parts:

> The author believes the *conclusion* because of the *evidence* plus the *assumption*.

> The *inference* must be true because of the *evidence* and *conclusion*.

Practice by restating the argument in the following passage excerpt.

> It is a historical fact that only in conditions of profound societal instability are great works of literature produced. During the first century B.C., Rome experienced almost constant civil war accompanied by social upheaval. It wasn't until the ascension of Nerva to the throne in 96 A.D. that the situation stabilized. Throughout the second century A.D., Rome experienced a century of uninterrupted peace and stability.

Argument _____

DISCUSSION

The author left the conclusion unstated, but the facts left no room for doubt about it. A reasonable restatement might be:

> Great Roman literature could have been created during the first centuries B.C. and A.D., but not during the second century A.D., because great literature requires social unrest, which Rome experienced in the first centuries B.C. and A.D. but not the second century A.D.

Understanding Passages

Recognizing the Author's Voice

On the MCAT, recognizing the author's voice is the most important part of any Verbal Reasoning passage, because so many questions ask about it in one way or another.

The author's voice reflects the author's opinion or purpose. When you break down the author's argument into its conclusion and evidence, the author's voice will provide the conclusion. And when you map the author's purpose on Test Day, you will essentially be making note of the author's voice.

The author's voice may be straightforward, subtle, or neutral; nevertheless, you'll always want to note it when it appears. If there are several opinions expressed in a passage, you'll want to be clear about which opinion belongs to the author of the passage and which opinions reflect ideas of others mentioned in the passage.

In the following paragraphs, underline the author's voice and restate it in your own words. If there are two opinions, focus on and rephrase that of the author.

1. A scientific trial found that the administration of AZT (zidovudine) to HIV-positive women during pregnancy and delivery, and to their babies after birth, reduced the transmission of HIV to the infants by two-thirds, compared to a placebo. The validity of the study's result, however, is debatable. The design did not account for important variables: in particular, whether the amount of HIV in the subjects' bodies might have contributed to the difference in transmission rates.

   Restate the author's opinion

   _____

   _____

   _____

2. The position of the parfleche—an envelope-shaped rawhide container used by the Plains people for storing clothes, food, and personal items—held symbolic position in the lodge. It was stored beneath the bed of older women, not only because they were careful guardians but also because they were closer to Grandmother Earth, from whose union with the lightning spirit the animals and plants of the middle worlds came to provide food and shelter. The

symbolism of the parfleche, therefore, reflects the Cheyenne belief in a complementary worldview: the blending of the masculine spirit and the feminine physical matter.

Restate the author's opinion

_____

_____

_____

3. Early biologists tried to explain why, contrary to expectations, family size decreased after the Industrial Revolution, which ushered in a new prosperity. By drawing comparisons with the animal world, biologists suggested that animals that have many young tend to live in hostile, unpredictable environments. Since the odds against any offspring's survival are high, having many offspring increases the chance that at least one or two of them will survive. However, in more stable, affluent times, animals will have fewer children since more of them are apt to survive. Critics of this theory argue instead that changes in social attitudes are adequate to explain this phenomenon.

Restate the author's opinion

_____

_____

_____

4. Containing invasive fish and animal species has become a focal point for environmentalists. However, scientific evidence is lacking about which containment measures work, and about how serious the threat posed by various invasive species actually is. Simply identifying an environmental threat does not mean we should automatically give it priority over other important issues. Instead, scientific data should be treated as just that—data that allow us to make informed and balanced policy decisions.

Restate the author's opinion

_____

_____

_____

5. In the fast new choreography of American compassion, explanation is twirled into excuse, and the spotlight's shine gives feeling a prominence that facts could only hope for. How we perceive something has become more important than its reality. We prefer to understand viewpoints rather than discern truths.

Restate the author's opinion

_____

_____

_____

DISCUSSION

1. "The validity of the study's result, however, is debatable." The author's voice disagrees with the study's conclusions. The key here is the word "however." Contrast words may sometimes introduce the author's point of view. The rest of the passage will probably explain his objection and may also provide an alternative suggestion to the study.

2. "The symbolism of the parfleche, therefore, reflects the Cheyenne belief in a complementary worldview: the blending of the masculine spirit and the feminine physical matter." The parfleche is important to the Cheyenne as a symbol of their beliefs. As noted by the word "therefore," the author is stating her conclusion about the parfleche. She is summing up, essentially saying that everything she wrote previously comes down to this one idea.

3. "Early biologists tried to explain why, contrary to expectations, family size decreased after the Industrial Revolution, which ushered in a new prosperity." The author simply states that people tried to explain why families got smaller even though they had more resources and money. We have a neutral author here, since there is no particular point of view expressed—just a paradox. Note that when passages start with paradoxes or questions, the rest of the passage will give at least one explanation. You should actively read for the general idea behind the explanation, rather than the details.

4. "However, scientific evidence is lacking about what containment measures work, and about how serious the threat posed by various invasive species actually is." Again we have the contrast word "however," indicating the author's point of view. This statement indicates that the author doesn't agree with previous ideas about how to control invasive species and how serious the problem is. The rest of the paragraph—the details, or evidence—will probably support his opinion.

5. "How we perceive something has become more important than its reality. We prefer to understand viewpoints rather than discern truths." The author makes her opinion clear right up front. Specifically, she concludes that we are more interested in how we feel about things than in the facts about them. The rest of the passage will support this idea in the form of examples and details. Even though the details will be alluded to in questions, the author's point of view will be most important in getting the questions right.

Attacking Tough Passages

How many "tough" passages will you encounter on Test Day?

At least two and at most three.

Which passages are usually the "tough" ones?

Passages from subject areas that lend themselves to abstract language (e.g., social science and humanities) and passages from the world of philosophy or higher abstract thought.

What makes these passages "tough"?

They present difficult ideas in a difficult framework. They tend to be abstract, dense, and rather dull. In fact, they tend to have few or no proper nouns, which makes establishing relationships very difficult.

Take this example:

In deciding the characteristics of a legitimate state, what conception of humanity should we use? Hobbes was quite explicit on this point, making his case with what he considered to be the worst image of people. To find Nozick's opinion on the question, we again look to his discussion of Locke; and for Nozick, the position from which we justify the state is Locke's state of nature. In Locke's state of nature, people have rights, and people generally respect one another's rights. Nozick accepts this, and proceeds to make his case without assuming any further responsibilities towards others. The resulting picture of humanity resembles a population of disinterested choosers, who need not have any concern for their fellows beyond respecting their basic rights.

Topic _____

Scope _____

Purpose _____

DISCUSSION

Topic: the legitimate state

Scope: the conception of humanity that pertains to it

Purpose: to describe 3 different views: Hobbes—people are low, Locke—people are respectful, Nozick—people are self-centered and distant, indirectly respectful.

So you can see that by breaking down tough passages into discrete bits of information, you gain a better understanding of the author's purpose.

HINTS FOR ATTACKING TOUGH PASSAGES

HINT #1: Make mental pictures.

Tough passages are often confusing since students are erroneously focusing on the prose, and not the ideas behind the prose. One excellent way to animate those ideas is to picture what is happening mentally. Let's take an example:

> Researchers have never directly observed the formation or existence of these super-heavy elements. The emission of hydrogen nuclei, presumably from the element's decay, is the only evidence that the experiments have succeeded.

DISCUSSION

For the "emission of hydrogen nuclei," picture sparks flying from a sort of core. That may keep you tuned into the fact that "these super-heavy elements"—whatever they are—actually exist, even though no one has seen them. You will now be ready to add or alter to this mental picture as more details pile on.

HINT #2: Pay the greatest attention to sentences in which the author clearly voices an opinion.

It's no surprise that the author's opinion is paramount on Test Day. This hint is just a reminder that when a passage is baffling or off-putting, you can get a handle on it simply by skipping past all the objective facts and highlighting the opinions instead. Look at the sample paragraph below:

> Marsupials are not known to exhibit protective behavior. Indeed, scientists have reported that frightened female kangaroos will drop their pouch-young as they flee, drawing a predator's attention to the less able offspring while the adult escapes. This behavior, whether purposeful or accidental, instantaneously relieves the female marsupial of the mechanical difficulties of pregnancy with which her placental counterpart would be burdened, while marsupials can replace any lost young quickly. Thus, in the absence of any need for close

maternal supervision, sacrificing their offspring in this manner may well have been favored in selection. Pointing to the absence of the "virtue" of maternal protectiveness in marsupials is an instance of how mistaken those theorists are who see similarities with humans as marks of evolutionary sophistication.

Summary _____

_____

DISCUSSION

Summary: Some people use human standards to gauge just how evolved other animals are or have become. But, according to the author, they are wrong to do so, and this extended example is evidence of why. The keywords indicating this lies in the last sentence, "how mistaken those theorists are…"

HINT #3: Really "dumb it down."

Students (especially perfectionist pre-med students) mistakenly think that they are supposed to read like an expert in the given field of a passage, but that is not at all the case! When one is not an expert in that field, it's rational to expect to pick up only the bare bones of what is being said. This is especially true when you add the strict time limits on Test Day (only 8-9 minutes per passage)! Practice getting just the gist with the following example:

> Social analysts of the 1950s sought to demonstrate how the increasing industrialization, urbanization, and bureaucratization of American society had, beginning in the early nineteenth century, altered the American psyche. Writers of the day like David Riesman and William H. Whyte argued that the achievement motive and the Protestant ethic of hard work had virtually died as Americans began to turn to communal togetherness. Riesman posited a transformation of the American character structure from inner direction (responding to a fixed internal code of morality) to other direction (responding to the demands of others in complex situations). Whyte believed that values themselves had changed, suggesting that the old value system of the Protestant ethic, defined as the drive for individual redemption, had been replaced by the social ethic whose basic tenet stressed the importance of the group, the many.

Bare bones gist _____

_____

DISCUSSION

Bare bones gist: In the 1950s, some scholars thought that increasing industrialization, urbanization, and bureaucratization had changed American values; that Americans had turned from caring about themselves to caring about others.

You should worry about the other details, like Riesman and Whyte, when they appear in a question, not before.

HINT #4: Relate it to your world.

This is similar to the hint "make a mental picture," except that this requires you to conjure up a specific real-life example of the phenomenon described. If you can relate the ideas to "real life"—yours or somebody else's—you will be less intimidated by them and more able to answer questions about them. Be careful NOT to substitute your own ideas for the author's, though!

Try your hand at this hint in the passage excerpts below:

> The justification of political institutions is perhaps the fundamental question of political philosophy. For centuries, one of the leading theories in state justification has been contract theory. The general approach is as follows: Citizens of a state enter into a contract with that state. The terms of that contract determine what is permissible. The state is justified insofar as it fulfills its responsibilities as defined in the contract. The state is also entitled to restrict the freedom of its citizens according to the terms of the contract. The key is consent; the contract is justified because we agreed to it.

Real life example _____

_____

> To apply extensionism, one starts with a set of individuals who are assumed to have moral value. Then these individuals are examined to determine what it is about them that entitles them to moral consideration. Having found that set of qualities X, any other thing that also has X also deserves moral consideration. That is, by virtue of having X, a thing may have moral consideration extended to it.

Real life example _____

_____

DISCUSSION

Political Philosophy Example: "citizens of a state enter into a contract with that state"—Income tax, or the rule of law as administered by police and judges.

Extensionism Example: "individuals who are assumed to have moral value"—The clergy, social crusaders, writers who point the moral truths of life for us in words and images.

HINT #5: Concentrate on the first and last sentence of each paragraph.

Over the years, Kaplan has found MCAT passages from the test maker (especially the denser and more abstract ones), the tougher prose is generally framed with more straightforward sentences at the beginning and at the end of the paragraph. The following paragraph illustrates this point really well:

> *Animal behavior was formerly thought to consist of simple responses, some of them innate and some of them learned, to incoming stimuli.* Complex behavior, if it was considered at all, was assumed to be the result of complex stimuli. However, a particular group of ethologists has established a new view of animal behavior. They have shown that the animal brain possesses certain specific competencies, that animals have an innate capacity for performing complex acts in response to simple stimuli. *The discovery that complex behavior patterns were inherited was a vitally important contribution to the study of evolution.*

DISCUSSION

The middle of the paragraph is essentially just filler, so reading just the first and last sentences can be a good way to save time if time is running low on Test Day.

HINT #6: There'll always be a few points there for the taking.

When students hit a tough passage, they tend to get discouraged and assume that because the passage is baffling them, the questions will as well. But remember that the passage is NOT an all-or-nothing scenario. All passages come equipped with a set of questions of varying difficulty levels, from easy questions that most students can handle to tough ones that few can.

So even when you think a passage is tough, you can still be confident that you will be able to answer a few of the questions correctly.

HINT #7: Use the answer choices to fill in content gaps.

If, even after all of the hints above, the main purpose of the passage is still elusive, you have one lifeline available to you: the answer choices! You can always work backward from them to help you reason out what must be true for that part of the passage.

HINT #8: Be confident!

A positive attitude can only help you on Test Day. Thanks to your preparations and your wise investment in Kaplan, you will be able to overcome any obstacles on the road to Verbal Reasoning success!

Question Types

Here's a riddle for you. On MCAT Verbal Reasoning, when does doing more result in getting less? Before you read the answer, take a guess. Ready? The answer is that when you do more reading—slowly, carefully, even more than once—you have less time to work on the questions, and that results in less opportunity to raise your score. Remember, there are no points gained from the passages; all MCAT points come from answering questions correctly. So use your time wisely; read and map quickly (no more than four to four-and-a-half minutes except for the very worst passages) and spend most of your time on the questions. How closely does that answer match your guess? At Kaplan, we don't call that a guess but a prediction. A guess is sort of a blind shot in the dark, while a prediction is a considered, intelligent idea about the general direction of the right answer, if not exactly what it is.

Predicting is a really important part of the Kaplan question strategy: **Stop, Think, Predict, Match.** You already know to predict, and the "match" part of that is simply to look over the answers and choose the one that matches the prediction. You always want to make a prediction based on what you've gone back and researched in the passage. Without a prediction, all four answers might look good, and you'll spend a lot of time considering each one carefully. Since there's always only one right answer, studying each answer carefully means you're studying three wrong answers carefully—a total waste of time. You can avoid that by predicting and matching. But what about "stop" and "think"? They're really two parts of the same step. Stop and consider what the question is really asking, and think about the best way to answer it. The best way depends on the kind of question it is and the most efficient and effective way to get the right answer. And don't let a difficult question drag you down. Almost everyone's going to get something wrong; just shrug it off and move on. Every question is another opportunity to get another point.

> **You Can Do This!**
>
> Attack the question! Don't creep up on it with fear and loathing. Barge right in with confidence (after all, you're using the time-tested Kaplan strategy). You can do this!

So let's take a look at some typical MCAT questions, how to identify them, and the fastest way to answer them correctly. And commit yourself to practicing using the Stop, Think, Predict, Match strategy and developing a really good understanding of the question types. You'll love the bump in your MCAT score.

Global

- Global questions ask for the "central thesis," "primary purpose," or "main idea."
- The correct answer will reflect the overall Scope and Purpose.

To answer global questions, just refer to your Topic, Scope, and Purpose—but backward. Start with Purpose. After all, the author's Purpose is to tell you his main idea. With practice, answering these questions will be fast and easy. Unfortunately, you won't see many global questions on the MCAT. These are more SAT-level questions.

COMMON QUESTION STEMS

1. The author's central thesis is that...
2. The author's primary purpose is...
3. Which of the following titles most accurately describes the passage?

STRATEGY

Finding the topic, scope, and purpose of the passages is crucial to answering global questions correctly since, together, these three things represent the author's main point.

PRACTICE

Read the following Humanities passage using the Kaplan method, and then try the Global questions below:

> Sibilla Aleramo's autobiographical novel, *Una Donna (A Woman),* has been described as both a "personal catharsis" and a "cultural revolution." Written in 1906 in Italy, *Una Donna* explores one woman's quest for self-fulfillment in the face of a stifling familial and societal structure. The account, written several years after the incidents upon which it is based, represents a conscious move away from highly contextualized personal narrative to a more generalized account that would appeal to a broader audience and thus bolster the burgeoning feminist movement of the day.
>
> The bulk of 19th and early 20th century feminist literature consisted of novels of "awakening" to the limitations placed on women within patriarchal society. Charlotte Perkins-Gilman's *The Yellow Wallpaper* and Kate Chopin's *The Awakening* are two examples of this genre, in which women seek release from their subjugation through madness or suicide. Both novels are representative of what Carolyn Heilbrun describes as the traditional genre of women's autobiography in her book, *Writing a Woman's Life*. Heilbrun notes that the writer of such books "tends to find beauty even in pain and to transform rage into spiritual acceptance."
>
> In *Una Donna,* the protagonist neither accepts her preordained role, nor does she find beauty in it—with the exception of her love for her son. By dissenting from the traditional female path, by divorcing her husband and beginning a life alone, she places herself in a unique personal position, and hence Aleramo the author places herself in a distinct literary one as well.

Topic _____

Scope _____

Purpose _____

MCAT Expertise

Every question is relevant to the passage. There are no questions that don't rely on passage information or inference.

1. The author's main purpose is to:

    A. criticize Aleramo's dissent from her literary feminist contemporaries.

    B. support autobiographical feminist literature as a form of "personal catharsis."

    C. contrast Aleramo's literary approach with that of other feminist writers of her day.

    D. describe how autobiography can connect individuals to more general issues of the human condition.

2. Which of the following statements best summarizes the main idea of the passage?

    A. Concurrent literary and political movements demonstrate little connection other than that of time.

    B. Autobiographical fiction dictates that the author distance herself from the prose.

    C. Traditional feminist literature depicts the struggle for spiritual acceptance.

    D. Literary trends can provide insight into the transformation of social movements over time.

DISCUSSION

Topic: The book *Una Donna*

Scope: Its content and context—what's in it, and its relationship to previous literature

Purpose: To argue that *Una Donna* represents a revolutionary new feminist approach

1. C

Remember what we noted as the purpose of the passage: that *Una Donna* represents a new feminist approach, in contrast to the literature that preceded it. What do you do when your pre-phrasing doesn't seem to be there? You attack the choices, remembering that one of them has been set up as right and three of them have been set up as flawed. (C) has the topic and scope right, and conveys the author's intent. **Correct choice (C).**

(A) The author is hardly critical of Aleramo. Quite the contrary. This is what we will call a "180."

(B) The last choice was wrong in claiming this passage was "attacking" Aleramo. But while the author admires her book, "support" seems off as a descriptive verb as well. This passage isn't about for-and-against. (B) also fails to mention the topic, *Una Donna*, and blows up the detail about "personal catharsis."

(D) This is way too broad, utterly missing the topic and scope.

2. D

This question is another way of asking the same thing. But note: none of the choices mentions the topic of *Una Donna*. So a pre-phrasing here will come up short! The test maker wants to approach this from a broader perspective. Go through the choices in order.

(A)'s focus is on literary and political movements. The latter seems to be far removed from the literary works under discussion. And if anything the author would argue that these movements *overlap* rather than "demonstrate little connection."

(B) Neither *Una Donna* nor the traditional works seem to be examples of an author distancing herself. This seems to distort one detail or another.

(C) would be fine but it ignores the contrast between "traditional" literature and the approach Aleramo chooses in *Una Donna*. (C) blows up a detail into the main idea.

Don't get nervous and worry that maybe (D) won't be any good either. Since we've found concrete reasons why the other three are bad—unless we're way off—(D) must be right! And it is, a paraphrase of the way in which a book like *Una Donna* can "bolster the burgeoning feminist movement of [its] day." **Correct choice (D).**

Detail

- Detail questions ask what was stated in the passage.
- The correct answer will be in the passage.

Look for expressions such as *according to* or *as stated in the passage* to identify detail questions. Refer to your map to home in on the paragraph that contains the answer, reread the relevant information, predict, and then match your prediction with an answer choice. As you might expect, science passages will have the greatest number of detail questions. On other passage types, you won't see more than one or two detail questions at most.

COMMON QUESTION STEMS

1. According to the passage...
2. As stated in the passage...
3. Based on information given in the passage...

STRATEGY

The answers to these passages will be stated explicitly in the passage. Look for keywords and phrases and use your passage map to help you investigate.

PRACTICE

Refamiliarize yourself with the details of the passage (reprinted below) then attempt the detail questions below:

Sibilla Aleramo's autobiographical novel, *Una Donna (A Woman),* has been described as both a "personal catharsis" and a "cultural revolution." Written in 1906 in Italy, *Una Donna* explores one woman's quest for self-fulfillment in the face of a stifling familial and societal structure. The account, written several years after the incidents upon which it is based, represents a conscious move away from highly contextualized personal narrative to a more generalized account that would appeal to a broader audience and thus bolster the burgeoning feminist movement of the day.

The bulk of 19th and early 20th century feminist literature consisted of novels of "awakening" to the limitations placed on women within patriarchal society. Charlotte Perkins-Gilman's *The Yellow Wallpaper* and Kate Chopin's *The Awakening* are two examples of this genre, in which women seek release from their subjugation through madness or suicide. Both novels are representative of what Carolyn Heilbrun describes as the traditional genre of women's autobiography in her book, *Writing a Woman's Life.* Heilbrun notes that the writer of such books "tends to find beauty even in pain and to transform rage into spiritual acceptance."

In *Una Donna,* the protagonist neither accepts her preordained role, nor does she find beauty in it—with the exception of her love for her son. By dissenting from the traditional female path, by divorcing her husband and beginning a life alone, she places herself in a unique personal position, and hence Aleramo the author places herself in a distinct literary one as well.

3. According to the passage, which of the following statements about *Una Donna* describes a way in which it differs from traditional novels of "awakening"?

A. The author generalizes a personal account so that it will appeal to a broad audience.

B. The protagonist finds beauty in her distress and transforms her rage into spiritual acceptance.

C. The protagonist chooses to dissent from her predetermined social role.

D. The novel was constructed as a means of bolstering the feminist movement in Italy.

4. The author of the passage implies that prior to 1900, a novel by a feminist would most probably feature:

A. specific details of a protagonist's life.

B. elements designed to enhance the reader's political awareness.

C. symbolic characters representing societal forces.

D. patriarchal oppression impossible to transcend.

DISCUSSION

3. C

Question 3 asks for a specific and explicit distinction between *Una Donna* and other "awakening" novels. This evokes paragraph 3—or rather the connection between paragraphs 2 and 3. *Una Donna's* "donna" does not "[accept] her preordained role..." and in paragraph 2 we see that protagonists like those in the Perkins-Gilman and Chopin books do exactly that. Aleramo's protagonist "dissent[s] from the traditional female path." **Correct choice (C).**

(A) is what we'll be calling "FUD": faulty use of detail. Aleramo's use of generalizing (paragraph 1) is not contrasted with paragraph 2's novels of awakening.

(B) is a 180: the exact opposite of what the question asks for.

(D) is false because we're not told what the purpose of the earlier novels was (nor whether they were aimed at the Italian market), while (C) gives us a distinction we know to be true.

4. A

What would be found in a pre-1900 feminist novel—a "novel of awakening," in other words? This one is tougher than question 3 because we cannot be sure which of the several mentioned traits of pre-1900 novels the test maker has chosen for the right answer. Sometimes you just have to move to the four choices and remember: One of them has been written to be explicitly supported by the passage text, and three of them have been set up to be off somehow. (A) *Una Donna*, according to paragraph 1, was "a conscious move away from highly contextualized personal narrative." Paragraph 2 makes it clear that the last phrase refers to the pre-1900 novel of awakening. The "context" of a personal narrative (as opposed to "a more generalized account") would have to involve specific details. **Correct choice (A).**

But: Once you think you have found the right answer, you *have* to check the other three to try and find explicit reasons against them or ways in which they go wrong. Such a practice insures against too-quick acceptance of a faulty choice.

(B) Political awareness is expected from the post-1900 *Una Donna*

(C) Social forces and symbolism are traits we'd expect from the post-1900 *Una Donna*.

(D) While a pre-1900 novel would likely feature the oppressiveness of a patriarch, it's a distortion of the text to allege that such a state would be "impossible to transcend."

SCATTERED DETAIL

- Scattered detail questions ask you to determine the "odd man out." They often use the words *except*, *everything except*, or *everything but*.
- These have to be researched methodically, starting with your map to determine where the answer might be in the passage. They are not inherently difficult questions, but they can be time consuming.

Global and detail questions are relatively rare today. The most common MCAT Verbal Reasoning questions are the critical-thinking questions, particularly the ones you'll see next.

Evaluation

- Evaluation questions ask how the author put together the argument.
- Correct answers stick to the scope of the argument and identify how the author moves between evidence and conclusion.

Most evaluation questions end in the words *in order to*. They're really just "why" questions—why does the author refer to this, that, or the other? So research the quoted phrase and ask yourself what function it has in the passage. In other words, why is it there?

Some evaluation questions ask you how the author organized her argument. They'll have answer choices that say something like "Paragraph 1 introduces a conundrum, paragraph 2 outlines three explanations . . ." and so on.

COMMON QUESTION STEMS

1. The author mentions "third-order discontinuities" primarily in order to...
2. The author organizes his argument by...
3. In context, the phrase [...] most nearly means...

Which type of MCAT passage is LEAST likely to include an evaluation question, and why? Science passages, because they are largely fact-based and don't often traffic in author opinion. This isn't to say that science passages *never* yield evaluation questions—one draws conclusions in science, too. But in general, the MCAT editors tend to base their evaluation questions on the arguments made in Humanities and Social Science passages.

STRATEGY

Evaluation questions on the MCAT are a type of logic question; they ask you how the author built his argument. So, remember that an argument consists of the author's explanation of what he believes (the conclusion), and why he believes it to be so (the evidence).

PRACTICE

For each of the following arguments:

1. Identify the conclusion.

2. Identify its evidence.

3. Sum up the gist of the argument in your own words, according to the following form: "The author believes X (conclusion) because Y (evidence)."

   a. High school administrators should not be concerned about the problem of teenage alcoholism, because, when surveyed, fewer than ten percent of nearly 10,000 high school students agree that alcoholism is a problem among those of their age group.

   b. Many underdeveloped areas suffer from air pollution even though there are no factories or combustion engines in use. Evidently, the connection between industrialization and air pollution has yet to be proved.

   c. Tests show a strong correlation between cardiovascular fitness and exercise. It is essential that everyone run or swim for at least 30 minutes three times each week.

   d. Government support for the arts cannot help but interfere with the free flow of the creative process. Money will accumulate around established artists when a certain philosophy prevails, or just as swiftly revert to more experimental artists when the political pendulum swings. Individual creators will attempt to keep pace, pursuing funding at the expense of their own sure and inner-directed development.

DISCUSSION

a. "Because" signals evidence. The conclusion is the recommendation in the first clause that administrators rest easy about teen alcoholism, and everything after "because" explains *why* that is so. In other words, the author believes high school admins shouldn't worry about teenage alcoholism because only a small percentage of high school students surveyed think their peers have such a problem.

b. "Evidently" could be replaced by "therefore" or "thus." It's a conclusion keyword. Why has the connection between those two things not yet been proved? Sentence one—the evidence—tells us why. Therefore, the author believes that the connection between industrialization and air pollution has to yet to be proved since many underdeveloped areas suffer from air pollution even though there are no factories or combustion engines in use.

c. We're given two sentences, one argument, and no keywords to signal the structure. Now we must "hear" the keywords implied even when they're not actually present. Where does the insertion of "because" make most sense? Which of these sentences provides support for the other? The *reason* for sentence 2's recommendation is provided by sentence 1. So sentence 1 is the evidence and sentence 2 is the conclusion. Everyone should run or swim half an hour three times a week *because* there is a strong correlation.

d. Read the first sentence aloud. Does it sound like a conclusion? *YES.* Does it sound like it needs supporting evidence? *YES.* Does the rest of the paragraph provide such evidence? *YES.* That's how you decide that sentence 1 is the conclusion and all the rest acts as evidence. The last few sentences spell out why, to the author, government artistic support stifles or retards creativity.

Sometimes, an MCAT Verbal Reasoning point can come merely from identifying pieces of the structure. This can be seen in question 1 below the following short passage:

The best-tasting premium ice cream requires milk from organically raised cows. When milk supplies are obtained from non-organic sources, ice cream manufacturers are unable to ensure that their products are free of pesticide residues, and taste tests have shown that only those products that are free of pesticide residues meet the highest quality standards for taste.

1. The purpose of the claim that ice cream products can meet the highest quality taste standards only if they are free of pesticide residues is to act as:

A. support for the argument's conclusion.
B. a logical consequence of the argument.
C. an assumption upon which the argument depends.
D. the argument's conclusion.

DISCUSSION

The stem asks about the *purpose of the claim*. The claim referenced shows up in the last 16 words of the passage. The opening sentence is the author's expressed opinion that great tasting premium ice cream requires milk from organically-raised cows, and the rest of it explains why: *You have to get rid of pesticide waste for best taste, and you can't ensure that milk from other, non-organic, cows lacks pesticide waste.* So the claim in question is part of the evidence. **Correct choice (A).**

(B) and (D) Sentence 1 is the conclusion. Both choices imply that the claim in question is a conclusion rather than a premise.

(C) is wrong because: assumptions on the MCAT are usually unstated, and the claim in the question is stated flatly.

Deduction Questions

This is the single MOST common question type on the MCAT. In addition, the principles behind this question type apply to the *Incorporation* and *Application* question types as well.

To understand what is being asked of you in a deduction question, you need to remember the definition of an argument.

ARGUMENT = CONCLUSION + EVIDENCE

In a passage, that translates to the conclusion being *mapped* as the main purpose and the evidence being treated as supporting details.

There are two types of deduction questions: Inferences and Assumptions. Deduction questions require you to use your broader understanding of the passage to identify logical conclusions (inferences) or crucial pieces of evidence (assumptions) that are unstated in the passage information. Note that creative interpretation isn't rewarded here. The correct answer will definitely be true based on the passage.

INFERENCE QUESTIONS

An inference is a statement that must be true based on the passage text and is implicit in the argument in the passage.

$$\text{ARGUMENT} = \text{CONCLUSION} + \text{EVIDENCE}$$

unstated $\downarrow$

INFERENCE

COMMON QUESTION STEMS

1. The author of the passage would most likely agree that…
2. It can be inferred from the passage that…
3. It can be justifiably concluded that…

STRATEGY

When answering inference questions, stick close to the text, since you are looking for something that the author does not state but strongly implies using the evidence in the passage. Always remind yourself of the author's ideas and the overall scope of the passage since they will guide you in the right direction.

PRACTICE

Read the passage below, map it, and answer the inference questions provided.

A pioneering figure in modern sociology, French social theorist Emile Durkheim examined the role of societal cohesion on emotional well-being. Believing that scientific methods should be applied to the study of society, Durkheim studied the level of integration of various social formations and the impact that such cohesion has on individuals within the group. He postulated that social groups with high levels of integration serve to buffer their members from frustrations and tragedies that could otherwise lead to desperation and self-destruction. Integration, in Durkheim's view, generally arises through shared activities and values.

Paragraph 1 _____

Durkheim distinguished between mechanical solidarity and organic solidarity in classifying integrated groups. Mechanical solidarity dominates in groups in which individual differences are minimized and group devotion to a common aim is high. Durkheim identified mechanical solidarity among groups with little division of labor and high rates of cultural similarity, such as among more traditional and geographically isolated groups. Organic solidarity, in contrast, prevails in groups with high levels of individual differences, such as those with a highly specialized division of labor. In such groups, individual differences are a powerful source of connection, rather than of division. Because people engage in highly differentiated ways of life, they are by necessity interdependent. In such societies, there is greater freedom from some external controls, but such freedom occurs in concert with the interdependence of individuals, not in conflict with it.

Paragraph 2 _____

Durkheim realized that societies may take many forms and consequently, that group allegiance can manifest itself in a variety of ways. In both types of societies outlined above, however, Durkheim stressed that adherence to a common set of assumptions about the world was a necessary prerequisite for maintaining group integrity and avoiding social decay.

Paragraph 3 _____

Topic _____

Scope _____

Purpose _____

DISCUSSION

¶**1:** Highly integrated societies buffer folks against heartache, and integration comes when people share the same values and things to do.

¶**2:** Two ways in which societies can maintain social integration

¶**3:** A broader context for interpreting the evidence in ¶2

Topic: Durkheim

Scope: how people's emotional state is affected by how "connected" society is

Purpose: to discuss Durkheim's view

1. The passage contrasts mechanical solidarity and organic solidarity along which of the following parameters?

    A. The degree to which each relies on objective measures of group coherence.

    B. The manner in which members are linked to the central group.

    C. The length of time that each has been used to describe the structure of societies.

    D. The effectiveness of each in serving the interests of its members.

2. It can be inferred from the passage that:

    A. as societies develop, they progress from organic solidarity to mechanical solidarity.

    B. group integration enables societies to mask internal differences to the external world.

    C. individuals from societies with high degrees of organic solidarity would be unable to communicate effectively with individuals from societies that rest on mechanical solidarity.

    D. the presence of some type of group integration is more important for group perpetuation than the specific form in which it is manifest.

DISCUSSION

1. B

This is an inference question because nowhere does the author explicitly say "here's how I (or Durkheim) compare the two." After evaluating all of the choices and our paragraph map, we find that (B) reflects the author's ideas (even though not in the same explicit terms). (B) paraphrases the gist of paragraph 2: "Manner" of linkage to the core group. **Correct choice (B)**

(A) "Objective measurements" of anything, let alone group coherence, are never alluded to. Each type of solidarity describes a way in which societies can flourish naturally.

(C) As far as we can tell, the two types were simultaneously conceived by Durkheim. Rather than a traditional vs. more recent view, we are shown two different ways in which societies that share a worldview can function.

(D) brings into question the effectiveness of each, but the last paragraph makes it clear that either one can serve its members' needs equally well.

2. D

In this question, there are no real clues, so you have to jump right to the answer choices.

(A) Neither the transformation of societies over time, nor the relationship of each type to each other, is mentioned.

(B) The passage never gets into the relationship of individual societies to the world at large.

(C) makes a comparison between the two types of social solidarity and their ability to communicate; the sentiment is utterly lacking in passage support.

(D) must be right since it is the only choice remaining. Since paragraph 3 indicates that many kinds of social solidarity are possible, clearly the specific form is less important than the presence of some kind of force unifying a society. The author doesn't say so verbatim, but she must believe it, or paragraph 3 is false. **Correct choice (D)**

ASSUMPTION QUESTIONS

Assumptions are evidence that the author does not state but which, based on the evidence he does state, he must believe to be true. For this reason, don't veer far away from the conclusion and evidence; an assumption will be a logical idea inherent between the two.

ARGUMENT = CONCLUSION + EVIDENCE

Unstated (but still a crucial link)

ASSUMPTION + EVIDENCE = CONCLUSION

COMMON QUESTION STEMS

1. It can be reasonably concluded that the author assumes…

STRATEGY

Look for an answer which stays within the parameters of the evidence and conclusion—the scope of the argument—and watch out for out of scope answer choices.

PRACTICE

1. Through their selective funding of research projects, pharmaceutical companies exert too much influence on medical research in universities. Only research proposals promising lucrative results are given serious consideration, and funding is usually awarded to scientists at large institutions who already have vast research experience. As a result, only larger universities will be able to continue developing adequate research facilities, and graduate students will learn that their future research must conform to the expectations of the corporation. Research will continue to be conducted at the expense of human welfare.

Conclusion _____

Evidence _____

Assumption _____

The argument above depends upon which of the following assumptions?

A. As universities become primarily research institutions, teaching will be neglected.
B. Graduate students are not motivated by humane interests.
C. Smaller universities would be better suited to serve as product development laboratories for pharmaceutical companies.
D. The interests of pharmaceutical companies and human welfare are usually incompatible in research.

2. It has been against the law for federal agencies and federal contractors to discriminate against a qualified job applicant because of a disability. Now that Congress has approved legislation to expand these existing provisions to cover private industry as well, the number of disabled people who are involuntarily unemployed will drop substantially.

Conclusion _____

Evidence _____

Assumption _____

The author of the argument above must be assuming which of the following?
A. Many congressmen were reluctant to pass the new legislation to prevent discrimination against the disabled.
B. In the past, some private employers deliberately chose not to hire qualified but disabled job applicants.
C. The federal government currently employs more disabled people than does private industry.
D. The approved legislation would stop discrimination against the disabled in the public and private sectors.

3. Doubling the cost of public transportation to compensate for money lost by declining ridership would be disastrous. The greater expense would only further discourage commuters who are already dissatisfied with the poor condition of buses and trains. If the fares are increased, many commuters will choose to drive cars instead, increasing pollution and traffic congestion while decreasing city revenues.

Conclusion _____

Evidence _____

Assumption _____

Which of the following is an assumption made in advancing the argument above?

A. Commuters who decide to drive rather than use public transportation will not share rides with one another.

B. Commuters will not park their cars in garages and thereby spend more money than they would by using buses or trains.

C. The condition of public transportation will not improve as a result of the fare increase.

D. A significant number of people who now use public transportation have cars or can easily obtain them.

4. I know that Tucson is a great place to live: I read it in *Newsweek*.

What assumption is the author making in connecting her evidence to her conclusion?

_____

5. When my high school principal was told that the students wanted the freedom to design their own curricula, he replied that that was "a ridiculous notion, and I'll tell you why: students don't have enough maturity or experience to equal the ability of those currently doing the job."

Conclusion _____

Evidence _____

Assumption _____

6. Researchers, perplexed by the development of measles immunity in children who were not given the measles vaccination, believe that they now understand this phenomenon. The children in question were all raised from birth on a baby formula produced by the manufacturer Dihydro. The Dihydro formula contains a synthetic chemical known as dihydron-X, which has been shown in lab tests to rapidly destroy cells infected with measles. Researchers have concluded that those children who ingest the Dihydro formula maintain dihydron-X in their bloodstreams indefinitely. When measles-infected cells proliferate in the child's body, the dihydron-X responds to the invasion by quickly killing off all infected cells, thus arresting the progress of the disease so rapidly that the child is perceived to have a measles immunity.

An assumption made by the researchers in their reasoning is that:

A. some children who receive measles vaccinations develop immunity to measles.
B. some children who develop immunity to measles do not receive vaccinations against other childhood diseases.
C. dihydron-X can only be found in the formula produced by Dihydro.
D. it is not possible that children who do not receive measles vaccinations develop immunity to measles.

7. The influence of McTell's work on Waters' formulation of psychosocial theory has long been recognized in the academic community. McTell was Waters' mentor and main confidant during the 1950s, the time just before Waters published his revolutionary findings. There is ample evidence of communication during this time between the two regarding the core issues that would eventually coalesce in Waters' theory. However, a recently discovered letter dated 1947—years before Waters met McTell—indicates that Waters had already formulated the basic conceptions of his psychosocial theory. Therefore, while McTell may certainly have helped Waters develop his theories, McTell cannot have influenced the formulation of Waters' scholarship in the manner originally believed.

The author of the argument about McTell's influence on Waters assumes that Waters

A. did not know of or read McTell's work before he met McTell.
B. did not model his theory on the work of some scholar other than McTell.
C. did not allow McTell to influence any aspect of his psychosocial theory.
D. did not benefit in any way from his association with McTell in the 1950s.

8. Recently, the research and development departments at major pharmaceutical companies have been experimenting with new injections that provide the boost in iron that anemic children need to reverse their condition. These companies have expressed confidence that children who are suffering from anemia will be cured relatively simply through the use of such biochemical supplements.

In concluding that the biochemical remedy being developed will have its desired effect, the pharmaceutical companies assume that:

A. the use of biochemical supplements is the safest way to cure anemia in children.

B. a low iron level in the body is the major factor influencing the incidence of anemia in children.

C. a diet rich in iron cannot improve the conditions of children suffering from anemia to the point that biochemical supplements would become unnecessary.

D. children afflicted with anemia will find out about and submit to injections that can reverse the condition.

9. The proliferation of colloquialisms is degrading the English language. A phrase such as "she was like, 'no way,' you know?"—a meaningless collection of English words just a few decades ago—is commonly understood by most today to mean "she was doubtful." No language can admit imprecise word usage on a large scale without a corresponding decrease in quality.

The argument about colloquialism and the English language relies on which one of the following assumptions?

A. Colloquialisms always evolve out of a meaningless collection of words.

B. The colloquialisms appearing in the English language introduce imprecision into the language on what would be considered a large scale.

C. The English language would not be degraded if there did not exist an alternative informal way to express the sentiment "she was doubtful."

D. The widespread use of colloquialisms represents the most serious form of language degradation.

DISCUSSION

1. D

Conclusion: Research will be conducted at the expense of human welfare.

Evidence: Pharmaceutical companies exert too much influence on university medical research through selective funding. The first sentence states this point.

Assumption: This is a classic case of a new term being introduced in the conclusion. Nowhere in the evidence is human welfare discussed. So, the correct answer will have to tie human welfare back to research funded by pharmaceutical companies. **Choice (D) does that best.**

(A) Out of Scope. The focus of choice (A) is teaching, and the focus of the stimulus is research.

(B) Out of Scope. This choice introduces the irrelevant issue of what motivates graduate students.

(C) Distortion. This choice confuses the contrast between smaller and larger universities.

2. B

Conclusion: The number of involuntarily unemployed disabled people will drop.

Evidence: Congress has passed legislation making it illegal for private industry employers to discriminate against qualified job applicants because of disabilities.

Assumption: The conclusion speaks to the number of disabled people who have been discriminated against, which the evidence does not cover. In order to conclude that the new legislation will have the intended effect, the author must assume that the targeted discrimination does in fact happen. That makes **Choice (B) the correct answer.**

(A) Out of Scope. This issue is the effect of the new legislation, not how the legislation was passed.

(C) Distortion. This choice has an irrelevant contrast between federal and private employers.

(D) Extreme. The legislation will help substantially lower the amount of discrimination. To say that it will "stop discrimination" takes the argument too far.

3. D

Conclusion: Increasing public transportation fares would lead to increased pollution and traffic congestion while decreasing city revenues.

Evidence: Commuters, already dissatisfied with public transportation, would choose to drive cars instead of using public transportation if fares are increased.

Assumption: When a conclusion predicts an outcome, the author assumes that the predicted outcome is possible. In this specific case, the author assumes that commuters can indeed start driving themselves to work. But because the argument doesn't state that the commuters actually have cars, it's a fact that must be assumed in order for the argument to work. If the commuters don't have cars, then the prediction cannot come to pass. **Choice (D) is the correct answer**.

(A) This one looks close, but be careful. It isn't necessary to assume that commuters won't share rides. Whether they carpool or drive themselves is basically irrelevant to the final prediction, which is that there will be more cars on the road. The extent of the increase isn't central to the argument.

(B) Out of Scope. Where commuters park their cars is irrelevant to the increase in pollution and congestion.

(C) Out of Scope. Two factors are at play here: increased fares and poor conditions. The author's point is that the increased expense combined with poor conditions will lead to an increased number of cars on the road. Whether the conditions will improve after the fare increase is irrelevant; the commuters will have already traded in their bus and train passes for their cars.

4.

The assumption that the author is making to connect the evidence and conclusion is that "*Newsweek* is a reliable evaluator of places to live." That has to be true for the argument to hold up.

5.

Conclusion: It'd be ridiculous to let the kids design their own curricula.

Evidence: They're not mature or experienced enough.

Assumption: One needs maturity and experience to design curricula.

6. A

The author's conclusion is that the formula causes immunity. The assumption in this case is that being vaccinated with the measles vaccine can lead to immunity to the disease. Answer (A) is better than the other three answers, and if the measles vaccination didn't provide immunity, the author would never have mentioned it in the first sentence to begin with. Therefore, the **correct choice is (A)**.

(B) This answer is out of scope since the lack of other vaccinations has no effect on the solution to the mystery.

(C) This is a distortion of the idea that the ingredient in the formula led to the measles immunity; after all, that doesn't imply that dihydron-X is unavailable anywhere else.

(D) This is an opposite answer choice because, far from assuming that measles immunity is "impossible" for unvaccinated children, the researchers are noting that very phenomenon and investigating it.

7. A

The gist of the argument in this example is that McTell couldn't have influenced Waters' theories as was long believed, because Waters' ideas (on the evidence of the letter) were formed, or begun, before they met. Given this argument, it is clear that the author ignores any possibility that Waters could have been influenced by McTell in any way before actually knowing him. Therefore, **choice (A) is the correct** assumption.

(B) This answer is out of scope since the issue isn't whether Waters was influenced by just anyone, but by McTell specifically.

(C) The author readily admits that McTell may have helped Waters "develop his theories"—he just didn't help in the formulation of it.

(D) This is an opposite answer because it is contrary to the assertion that McTell was Waters' mentor and main confidant during the 50s.

8. D

In this case, the value of the question stem becomes evident since it gives us the conclusion of the argument, "The remedy will cure kids' anemia." A summary of the evidence tells us that injections will boost iron to levels necessary for cure. So what must the pharmaceutical company assume? For the injections to work as the researchers hope, anemic kids have to know about the injections and submit to them. If the kids rebel, then the injections cannot possibly work. Therefore the **correct choice is (D).**

(A) Distortion. Drug companies aren't committed to the belief that there is no better way or safer way than the injections, just that the injections will work.

(B) Out of Scope. This focuses on anemia's "incidence" rather than cure. Furthermore, we don't know enough about the way anemia works to decide whether the problem is simply low iron levels, or if the iron-boosting injections address only one part of a more complex set of causes.

(C) The possibility of another potential treatment (diets richer in iron) does not affect whether the injections will or won't work.

9. B

For this problem, the conclusion lies in the first sentence: slang is killing English. The evidence can be summarized as follows: if language is imprecise, its quality suffers. What is the crucial link between these two? The idea that English slang is imprecise. Therefore, slang must be introducing imprecision into the language—**correct choice (B)**.

(A) Out of Scope since the evolution of slang is not discussed.

(C) Faulty Use of Detail because it blows up the importance of the one cited example; even if there were another way to express "she was doubtful," there still might be a vast array of imprecise slang degrading English.

(D) Extreme/Distortion of the sentiment that slang is degrading the English language: It can be doing so without being the "most serious" degradation.

Incorporation Questions

Incorporation questions ask you to identify what strengthens or weakens arguments. It is actually quite logical to progress from assumptions to this concept because an argument is most vulnerable when the author makes an assumption. Therefore, one of the most effective ways to strengthen an argument is to shore up its assumptions, while you can tear apart an argument by discrediting an unstated assumption.

So what do we mean by strengthen or weaken an argument?

Well, strengthen does NOT mean prove. To strengthen means to forge a tighter connection between the evidence and conclusion.

And weaken does NOT mean disprove. To weaken means to lessen the connection between the evidence and conclusion.

Note that you are more likely to see weaken questions than strengthen ones, since it is easier for the test maker to create scenarios that weaken an argument than ones that indubitably strengthen it.

COMMON QUESTION STEMS

1. Which of the following would most likely strengthen (or weaken) the author's argument?
2. Which of the following scenarios would support (or deny) the author's main purpose?

Either the question stem or the answer choices will be about a paragraph long.

STRATEGY

The first step is to identify the conclusion and evidence (use keywords like *therefore* and *because* respectively) and then predict the answer choice that makes the conclusion more (strengthen) or less (weaken) likely a result of the evidence.

PRACTICE

1. Assume that each of the following statements is true. What is the effect of each of the following statements—does it strengthen the argument, weaken the argument, or have no effect on the argument?

   In his apartment, Jim has a bronze statue with the words "Johor Baharu" inscribed on the base. Jim must have gone to Malaysia at some point in his life.

   A. Jim rents a furnished apartment.
   B. "Johor Baharu" is a city in Malaysia.
   C. Jim's fiancée Shimi lived in Malaysia for many years before Shimi and Jim met.
   D. In Malaysia, copper is much cheaper than bronze.
   E. The statue can be separated from its base.
   F. Jim owns several authentic Malaysian art objects that he has ordered through the Internet.

2. The proliferation of colloquialisms is degrading the English language. A phrase such as "she was like, 'no way,' you know?" a meaningless collection of English words just a few decades ago, is commonly understood by most today to mean "she was doubtful." No language can admit imprecise word usage on a large scale without a corresponding decrease in quality.

   Which one of the following, if true, most weakens the argument about colloquialisms and the English language?

   A. The use of imprecise language on a small scale generally does not impair understanding.
   B. Many colloquialisms that appeared in earlier forms of the English language have disappeared over time.
   C. Dissemination of a new word or phrase by the mass media determines whether it will become a colloquialism.
   D. Languages of the highest quality often evolve over time out of a collection of colloquial usages woven into a given people's formal dialect.

3. The harbor town of Osceola has determined that the channeling of recycled wastewater into the harbor is endangering residents' health. A sharp increase in cases of the intestinal illness giardiasis has been directly attributed to parasites which began to appear in drinking water supplies immediately following the implementation of the wastewater recycling program. The town has proposed adding the synthetic enzyme tripticase to the water during recycling. The addition of this enzyme would solve the health problem by eliminating the parasite that causes giardiasis.

Which one of the following statements, if true, most weakens Osceola's solution to its health problem?

A. The tripticase enzyme also acts to break down parasites causing intestinal conditions other than giardiasis.
B. No other illnesses aside from giardiasis have increased significantly in Osceola since the wastewater recycling program began.
C. Giardiasis may be caused by the ingestion of contaminated food as well as contaminated drinking water.
D. The tripticase enzyme also breaks down chlorine that is essential to maintaining a safe drinking water supply.

4. Cross-species studies of animal groups indicate that offspring who are separated from their mothers during the first months of life frequently develop long-lasting aggression disorders. During group feedings, for example, separated offspring exert excessive force in the struggle over food, continuing to strike at other offspring long after the others have submitted. The best explanation for this observed behavior is the hypothesis that aggression disorders are caused by lack of proper parent-led socialization during the first stage of an offspring's development.

Which one of the following, if true, provides the most support for the hypothesis that a lack of parent-led socialization causes aggression disorders in animals?

A. Wildebeests not separated from their mothers during infancy display excessive aggression as they seek a place in the dominance hierarchy.
B. Human babies adopted in the first three months of life often display aggressive behavior disorders during early childhood.
C. Chimpanzees raised in captivity in environments simulating traditional parent-led socialization display far less aggression in mating-related conflicts than do chimps raised without such social interaction.
D. Elephants separated from their mothers during the first months of life do not display excessive aggression in food or social dominance struggles.

DISCUSSION

1.

A. **Weakens** the argument since it makes it less likely that Jim must have gone to Malaysia because of the statue in his possession. If the apartment is furnished it is at least as likely that the statue came with the place as it is that Jim got it in Malaysia.

B. **Strengthens** the argument because if it is true, then we have succeeded in connecting the seemingly unrelated terms in the argument, namely the words "Johor Baharu" and the country Malaysia.

C. **Weakens** the argument since it is a plausible alternative explanation of how the statue came to be in Jim's possession. It is no less possible that Shimi obtained the statue all by herself than if Jim went there to get it.

D. **No effect** on the argument because the fact that copper is cheaper doesn't affect the likelihood that Jim obtained the statue in Malaysia. We know nothing of his purchasing power, etc.

E. **No effect** on the argument since all the statement does is change the nature of the object, not the evidence. We don't know whether the separate base & statue came from the same place. Nevertheless, the conclusion is still based on an object that Jim possesses (the base) that says "Johor Baharu," so the argument is undamaged.

F. **Weakens** the argument because it's no more likely that Jim went to Malaysia to get the piece than that it was one more email order. This is another plausible alternative explanation of the phenomenon of Jim's having the statue.

2.   D

Given the argument that slang is killing English because its imprecision is eating away at the language's quality, one assumption is that English slang is imprecise on a large scale. Another assumption, however, is that the process of introducing slang cannot, over time, have a beneficial effect. If one can show that English slang is not imprecise or that slang can have a positive effect, the argument would be weakened. **The correct choice is (D).**

(A) This answer is out of scope since the issue of impaired understanding and a "small scale" are not discussed.

(B) This is out of scope since "disappearing slang" doesn't mean that it didn't degrade the quality of the language when it was around.

(C) This answer is also out of scope since the concern with the way changes in language are transmitted is irrelevant.

3.   D

The gist of the passage is that tripticase needs to be added to the town's water during recycling because it would kill the parasites that is getting into the water supply during recycling. This assumes that adding tripticase wouldn't cause additional problems for the health of those drinking the water. Therefore, **choice (D) is the answer** because if the cure has deleterious effects, it would weaken the argument.

(A) Besides the fact that other diseases are out of scope, this answer might actually strengthen the notion that adding tripticase would solve the problem of the town's health.

(B) Again other illnesses are out of scope since the argument only deals with giardiasis.

(C) The goal is not to eliminate giardiasis, it's to solve the specific health problem at hand.

4.   C

The hypothesis states that when animals are separated from their mothers early in life, they can become violent because of the lack of proper parent-led socialization early in life. The question asks for support of this theory and the **correct choice is (C)** since it cements aggressive behavior to the phenomenon of absent-parent socialization, and also presents a kind of control group in which the presence of such socialization causes less aggressiveness. The observed chimp behavior makes the hypothesis more persuasive.

(A) This choice actually weakens the explanation by suggesting that the source of aggression must lie other than in parental absence. The word NOT is important here.

(B) Adoption takes us into a gray area: Because such a human child is both absent from the birth mother and in the presence of the adopting mother, the source of the aggressive behavior cannot be pinpointed to the degree the question is asking for.

(D) This answer choice is the exact opposite of what we are looking for.

Application Questions

Application questions are unique to the MCAT Verbal Reasoning section. They test students' understanding of the relationship between the author's ideas and outside areas, altered passage information, or hypothetical situations.

Some application questions simply provide more information—as, for instance, a quotation by the subject of the passage, or a new fact—which you have to combine with the ideas in the passage in some way.

Some of them ask you to consider a possible alteration of a detail in the passage.

However, the majority of application questions involve hypothetical information brought to bear on the situation in the passage; our job is to infer how the author would react or what would happen to the author's ideas as a result.

COMMON QUESTION STEM

1. "Suppose it was discovered that instead of…, the author of the passage would probably argue that…"

Note that either the question stem or answer choices will be about a paragraph long in application questions.

STRATEGY

Accept the new information provided as fact. Look to the passage for support of the new information. In other words, you are drawing an analogy between the passage information and the new information.

PRACTICE

1. An economic or political crisis in a poor country can lead to a lack of faith in the country's leaders, often followed by violent behavior, dissent, and even revolt among specific segments of the population. In many cases, propaganda that is immediately issued from media outlets quells such reactions by downplaying the extent of the recent crisis and thereby helping to restore belief in the efficacy of the government. However, the habitual violence exhibited by certain groups of disaffected youths in such countries almost never has to do with a lack of faith in their leaders, but rather is the consequence of an endemic boredom and lack of any vision of a positive future for themselves.

Assume that propaganda from media outlets is effective in decreasing youth violence in a poor country. Based upon the information in the passage, it can be inferred that the effect of the propaganda was:

A. not based on its impact on the psyches of individual disaffected youths.
B. probably not the result of restoring the youths' faith in their country's leadership.
C. not the only external factor contributing to the reduction of youth violence.
D. primarily related to its ability to alter people's fundamental belief systems.

2. The financial burden imposed by job-related costs is greatest for individuals who earn a salary of $30,000 to $40,000 per year, and less for those who earn much lower or much higher salaries. That is because individuals in low-paying entry-level positions earning far less than $30,000 per year generally find fewer costs associated with maintaining their jobs, such as wardrobe costs, dry cleaning, and medical bills due to work-related stress. The burden of these costs increases as one is promoted to higher-ranking positions, but lessens as the salary levels commensurate with further promotions become more than adequate to offset such costs.

Suppose that Jenny, who currently earns $40,000 per year as an administrative director, will be promoted with greater compensation over the next five years. On the evidence of the passage, it is most probable that:

A. She will be less financially burdened by job-related costs over the next five years.
B. Over the next several years, Jenny's employer will provide benefits that will help reduce stress-related medical costs.
C. The subordinates she supervises over the next five years will struggle with job-related costs more than Jenny will.
D. The costs related to Jenny's previous job were not as high as the costs related to her current position.

DISCUSSION

1. B

The gist of the paragraph is that youth rebellion is different than ordinary unrest in a poor country because the youths' problem is boredom and lack of personal vision, not a lack of faith in leaders. How does the new hypothetical situation relate to the text? Essentially, the success of media propaganda in cooling down youth violence may or may not have had to do with relieving youth boredom and/or providing a positive vision, but it did NOT have to do with restoring faith in government leaders. That is not an issue that interests youths. Since youth violence "almost never has to do with" skepticism about leaders, the success of the media propaganda "probably" didn't stem from an appeal on those grounds. Therefore, **choice (B) is the correct choice.**

(A) The word "psyche" doesn't appear in the passage, but if it relates to issues like boredom and vision (the root causes of youth violence)—and it could—then media may very well have appealed to the youths' psyches. So (A)'s conclusion is not a certainty based on the text.

(C) There's no way to tell whether the cooling down of youth was wholly due to the media influence, or only partly so. We know the media helped because the question says so. But did other factors help? Who knows?

(D) This is far too certain about the way in which the media can cool down youth violence to be deductible, so this is a distortion.

2. A

In summary, the paragraph states that workers earning $30 or $40K a year have more of a burden of work-related expenses than lower-paid employees, while the higher-paid can afford them. The hypothetical "Jenny" is now making a salary identified by the author as particularly burdensome, but she will make more money at grander jobs. So by the author's logic, she will better be able to bear the work-related costs and they'll be less of a burden. **The correct choice is (A).**

(B) This answer is out of scope since future increased benefits are irrelevant.

(C) We don't know how much her subordinates will earn. (Maybe it'll be a healthy six figures, who knows?)

(D) This is also out of scope because her previous job is also irrelevant.

THE ROMAN NUMERAL QUESTION

All kinds of passages can and do contain Roman Numeral questions, and they can be detail, inference, logic, or application-based. Regardless of where and when Roman numeral questions appear, students often greet them with fear and dread. You may remember this question type from the SAT.

Why do so many examinees have trouble with this format? One reason, of course, is lack of familiarity. A second reason is lack of confidence; many people find it tough enough to handle questions where there's *one* right answer, let alone when there's the possibility of two or more. However, these questions can actually be among the most manageable. At the very least they are very amenable to educated guessing.

The Form: Typically three statements or phrases labeled I, II, and III; the answer choices are various combinations of those statements or phrases.

TIPS
- Scan the distribution of the choices before you begin.
- Deal with the Roman numeral statements in any way that makes sense to you—don't automatically start with Statement I.
- Eliminate choices strategically. The moment you decide whether a Roman numeral is "in" or "out," you automatically can discard one or more of the four answer choices, and instantly improve your guessing odds.

And One Really Rare Question Type: Tone

- Tone questions ask you to determine who wrote the passage or in what type of publication it would appear.
- Tone questions ask you to evaluate how the author feels about the topic (not unlike an inference question).

For the first type of tone question, consider the words the author uses. Are they technical? Professional? Specific to art or geology or whatever the topic is? The writer is probably an expert writing to other experts who understand that jargon, and the passage might appear in a professional journal. But if the words are more general or easily understandable, or if the ideas explained in everyday terms, the author is probably writing for a nonprofessional audience reading a general interest book, newspaper, or magazine, such as the science section of a daily newspaper.

For the second type of tone question, the clues are in the answers. Is the author angry, ironic, dismissive, supportive? Review the way the author writes about the subject and his own point of view about it, predict, then match.

Key Points to Remember

- Predicting is important; it focuses you on the answer quickly and correctly.
- Don't spend too much time on any one question.
- The high-yield question types are deduction (for humanities and some social science passages) and detail for science passages.
- Different question types are signaled by different wording; learn to identify question types.
- Use the most efficient strategy for each question type.

Thinking Like the Test Maker

Wrong Answer Pathologies

The MCAT test makers are very nice people. No, really—they are! They don't play tricks on you. They don't, for example, give you a question with no correct answer or more than one correct answer. The test makers give you one, and only one, right answer. One right, three rotten—every time. Test makers are also very consistent in the *kinds* of wrong answers they provide. It's like a pattern. We can predict a pattern because it's consistent, and the same thing applies to wrong-answer patterns. Since we can learn the wrong-answer patterns, we can avoid them. Here's what you need to know about wrong-answer patterns.

> **Key Concept**
>
> Classic wrong answers show up on almost every answer set of every question set of every passage. That's proof of how important it is to recognize them.

FAULTY USE OF DETAIL (FUD)

This will be a detail that is in the passage but is not the right detail for the question asked. If the test maker or your map points you to a particular paragraph, stay there. If you research all over the passage, you may find a nice detail, but it won't be the one you need. You won't be surprised to learn that FUDs show up a lot in science passages in which you can anticipate lots of detail questions. FUDs are also classic wrong answers for main-idea questions. You're looking for an answer that encompasses the entire passage, which a detail can't do. Never choose a detail as the answer to a main idea question.

OUT OF SCOPE (OS)

An out-of-scope answer is outside the parameters of the passage. It may sound good—it may reflect something you know or believe—but if it isn't either in or reflected in the passage, it isn't right. You can be absolutely sure that the correct answer is supported in the passage, so always check your answer with the passage. OS answers are particularly common for inference and deduction questions and also show up in main idea answer choices. Avoid OS answers by remembering that the right answer must be true, at least according to the author, based on what she says in the passage. Unfortunately, what *you* think should be true doesn't count here.

> **MCAT Expertise**
>
> The main reason we include *Scope* in Topic, Scope, and Purpose is to remind ourselves what is and is not in the passage. That helps us stay away from answers that aren't supported in the passage.

DISTORTION (EXTREME)

The MCAT test maker doesn't often give you passages in which the author expresses really extreme ideas, such as "All students always do well on the MCAT Verbal Reasoning section." Consequently, answers using extreme words (*all, always, no, never, impossible*, or *any* word that leaves you nothing in between the extremes) are usually wrong. The only time they're right is when the author is extreme; we already know that's pretty rare. But be careful—don't just look at the word; look at context, too.

MCAT Expertise

Slow down when you read questions and answers. A fast read can lead to a wrong read, and you can't get the right answer if you don't have the right question.

Note, for instance, the difference between the extreme *no* and the possible *almost no*. Train yourself to recognize extreme words and you'll save yourself a lot of wasted time.

OPPOSITE

This is just what you think it is: an answer that's wrong because it's the opposite of what the passage says. It's a common trap for questions that ask you what the author doesn't do ("the author uses all literary devices EXCEPT..."), and it's an easy trap to fall into if you've just skimmed over the question.

Some wrong-answer pathologies will naturally be more common with particular question types. For example, the most common wrong-answer pathologies on Detail questions are Distortion or FUD. You'll always find an Opposite answer choice on "strengthen" or "weaken" questions or LEAST/EXCEPT/NOT questions, since one of the most common mistakes made in Verbal Reasoning is to forget precisely what the question asks.

Avoid the "I Remember" Trap

The test maker always lays a trap for the student who thinks he remembers what he read. There will be at least one answer that is memorable from the passage because it uses a stand-out word, phrase, or idea. The sloppy student says, "Yeah, I remember that, so it must be the right answer." Nope. Relying on your memory is notoriously faulty. Always go back to your map and the passage to check out the possible answers. (Also, practice will show you that it's usually easy to get rid of one or two answer choices, often because they incorporate classic wrong-answer patterns. Eliminate those right away and research the two or three possibilities that remain.)

If you get stuck between two answers, don't compare those two answers because there's no such thing as good, better, best. There's only right and wrong. Instead, challenge yourself to "show me." Go back and see which answer is supported in the passage. The right one is supported; the wrong one isn't. It's that simple.

Right and wrong answers are two sides of the same coin. Knowing the right answer is, of course, the best way to choose correctly. But knowing *why* an answer is wrong allows you to eliminate at least some answers (usually two) and still have time to research the ones that remain. Either way, you're looking at gaining points on Test Day, and that's the name of the MCAT game.

Key Points to Remember

- There is always one right answer and three wrong ones.
- The correct answer is not a guess; it's a matter of which choice is supported by the passage and is relevant to the question.
- Classic wrong answers show up all the time. Learning to recognize them allows you to avoid having to look at all answers carefully and thus saves you time.
- Read questions and answers a bit slower than your passage-reading pace. You don't want to misread or misunderstand them, since they're where the points are.
- Don't nitpick. Even if you don't like a word in the right answer, it's still the one you need to choose if all others are demonstrably wrong.

Self-Evaluation

For students hoping only to "pass" a test, simply taking many practice tests will probably improve their score. But if you're already performing well and want to improve, constant self-evaluation is key. Make this a regular part of your preparation for Verbal Reasoning.

Instead of reviewing the explanations to questions completely, many students stop at seeing why one answer is correct. This is a costly mistake if you want to maximize your score. Learn all you can about your strengths and weaknesses between now and Test Day, then use that information to manage your test-taking. Some people find they make certain mistakes consistently; others only find a tendency toward certain errors. In either case, you can reduce, or even eliminate, the problem if you recognize it.

After practice sets or tests, consider the following questions:

Time Management: Did you spend too much time on any passage?

Kaplan Methods and Strategies: Did you use Kaplan's methods and strategies in the course of this practice session? These should be practiced until they're second-nature.

Fatigue: Did you start to make more mistakes later in the test? If so, you have to build your stamina methodically. Consider, too, taking minibreaks. Periodically put down your pencil, close your eyes and take deep breaths for 10–20 seconds, then go back to work.

Why did you get questions wrong? Get away from the sheer fact of getting a question wrong to learning to reconstruct why and how. The most common reasons for going wrong are:

Misreading the passage: That is, you misunderstood what the passage was saying, or went to the wrong part of the passage.

Misreading the question: Questions that are easy to misread are Reasoning questions, or the questions that employ the words LEAST/EXCEPT/NOT— perhaps you'll find you have a tendency to misread other types. Check the question one last time before settling on a final answer.

Misreading the choices: This is quite common.

Mismanaging time: You ran out of time and became too pressed.

Why did you reject the right answer? When you pick a wrong answer, you reject the right one. Can you see any pattern in what you thought was wrong with the answer that turned out to be the correct one? Often the answer to this is one of the following:

Nitpicked it. Some students object to a preposition or adverb in the credited choice, rather than taking the choice in its totality. Don't fight the test. The right answers are rarely perfect.

Misread it. Hasty test takers are prey to this error. The best defense here is, of course, to read each choice as it's worded.

Never read it. Students often go with the first choice that looks good. This is a bad habit based on false economy.

Some Self-Evaluation Experiments

LOOKING AHEAD AT THE QUESTIONS

Some test takers feel more anchored as they read the passage if they've glanced at the questions first. As a rule, it won't save you time or effort to do so. Most of the questions require a general understanding of the passage. You need to read for meaning and for organization whether or not you've reviewed the questions. However, you may find that a very quick look to identify the subjects of the questions (and any line or paragraph references) helps you to focus on those areas as you read. Experiment with the possible benefits of looking at the questions before you read, and use this technique if it works for you.

One caveat, though: If you decide you can benefit from a preview of the questions, don't look at the choices. The test maker's word for wrong answers is "distracters"—they're designed to confuse and mislead, and you don't want information from the choices clouding your comprehension of the passage.

READING SPEED

Finding your ideal reading pace is essential to maximizing your score in Verbal Reasoning. To do this, try reading a few passages differently. If you believe you tend to get bogged down in passages, try practicing the fastest skimming you can do and still glean the broad outline—that is, the structure. If you believe you tend to skim too quickly, try forcing yourself to slow down; actually read each sentence and paraphrase each paragraph.

Then do the questions and see how your results compare with your usual reading speed. If you do about as well with the radically different speed, your best speed lies midway between the two. If you do significantly better at one extreme than at the other, your best speed lies closer to the former speed.

NOTE-TAKING STYLE

By Test Day you should have developed a note-taking style that works well for you. For some students that means taking copious notes, while others find that the less they note, the better. Your goal is to make as little notation as possible while still establishing and retaining a strong sense of the passage structure. Start with full paraphrases of the ideas in each passage—then strip your paraphrases down until you find a point at which your ability to respond to questions starts to drop, and return to the next higher level of "mapping."

Think Like a Test Maker

You've seen all the AAMC question categories. In their order of frequency, they are: Deduction, Evaluation, Application, Incorporation, Detail, and Global.

Detail and Global questions, of course, are relatively rare and can be drawn from any passage, and your critical reading will arm you to answer them.

But the other types can be asked only if appropriate material is present in the text. Only a finite number of questions can be written for any particular passage, and their type is dictated by the passage itself. Although the AAMC likes to vary the wording of its questions to create the impression that each is unique, they actually translate into a fairly small number of standard questions. Below is a review of the most challenging question types:

Type	Basic Formats
Deduction	Inference: The author most likely would agree that…
	Assumption: In arguing that…, the author implicitly relies on the idea that…
	Definition-in-context: As used in the passage, the expression…most likely means…
Evaluation	Structure: Which of the following best characterizes the author's claim that…?
	Function: The author most likely mentions…in order to:
Application	Hypotheticals: If…, the author would probably advise:
	Analogies: Which of the following is most analogous to…?
	General statements: Which of the following general ideas is most consistent with…?
	Author identity: It reasonably can be inferred that the author of this passage is a:
Incorporation	Effect: Suppose…. What relevance would this information have to the passage?
	Which of the following would most strengthen [or challenge] the argument…?
	Solution: Which of the following would the author consider a solution to [or explanation of] the problem of…?

Reading the Kaplan way means identifying the kinds of information that will appear in those Verbal Reasoning questions: the author's purpose, the expressed and implied Opinions, and the supporting evidence. If you also keep in mind the standard Verbal Reasoning question types, you can take this one step further—you'll start to "see" the questions to expect as you read the passage.

CONTRASTS

Keeping the standard questions in mind, read the following passage excerpt. What questions do you see waiting to be asked in the text?

Panspermia, the hypothesis that life on Earth originated in outer space, has had a number of supporters since the nineteenth century—some of them quite distinguished—but it has never won general acceptance among biologists. However, recent research has found possible support for panspermia. Most of the meteorites that strike the Earth originated in the lifeless wastes of the asteroid belt. A few, though, have been identified as fragments that were torn from the Moon and Mars by comets and asteroids, and eventually drifted to Earth. The Moon and Mars are lifeless, but there is reason to think that, billions of years ago, Mars was warmer and moister than it is now, and capable of supporting life. Indeed, Mars may have been more conducive to the development of life than Earth was at the time. It is feasible that life developed on Mars first, and was carried to Earth on space-borne debris.

This paragraph uses contrasts to structure its argument. The first sentence tells us the theory has some distinguished supporters, but not general acceptance. The next sentence says: However, new research provides some support for it. The rest of the paragraph details that new evidence. The questions you can expect will draw on your abilities to identify the number of different views presented, to see whether and how they are supported, and to determine which, if any, is endorsed by the author. There might be Inference or Evaluation questions such as:

> The author mentions supporters of panspermia in lines 2–4 primarily in order to:

Here's another paragraph offering two views. What types of question are likely?

> There are, broadly, two opposed schools, echoing a conflict that has persisted down the centuries. One side believes that the mind's mental processes are somehow different from the physical stuff of the brain and body, a conviction widely referred to as "mind-body dualism." Opponents of dualism, determined to expel the "ghost in the machine," insist that there is only one sort of reality—material stuff. These "naturalists" maintain that the mind must be explained by explaining it away. Progress in understanding the mind depends on rejecting the idea of an inner self that governs our behavior and adopting a relentlessly reductionist approach to phenomena, reducing everything to its smallest, material, mechanical parts.

In this paragraph, the words "two opposed schools" and the other phrases in quotation marks help identify the different views presented. This is a likely candidate for Deduction or Evaluation questions, such as:

> According to the author, it can be inferred that the "mind-body dualists" would agree that:

> Its opponents criticize dualism by claiming that it:

> Which of the following best describes the structure of the passage above?

Special Vocabulary

Technical terms or other specialized vocabulary might be tested by a Definition-in-context question or an Application question requiring that you determine what new information conforms to the meaning of the term:

According to the author, which of the following would be an example of a "reductionist" explanation of a mental phenomenon?

EXPERIMENTS

Try another passage excerpt:

> REM (rapid eye movement) sleep, also called "paradoxical" sleep because of its neurologically aroused character, is best known as the sleep phase during which intense dreams occur in humans. Monitoring electrical activity in the brain indicates that, in contrast to the slow-wave patterns of dreamless sleep, REM sleep displays high-frequency, low-amplitude waves all but identical to those of wakefulness. It was thought until recently that PGO spikes (short-lived, high-amplitude electrical waves) occurred uniquely in REM sleep and spontaneously (without external stimulus). However when a laboratory worker accidentally struck a cage while a cat's slow-wave sleep was being traced, a PGO spike appeared almost instantly. Subsequent study indicated that both sound and touch produce PGO spikes in either REM or slow-wave sleep. PGO spikes seem to be general alerting responses occurring in several sleep phases.
>
> This finding prompted reevaluation of waves called eye-movement potentials (EMPs) that occur in the waking state. These were believed to depend on environmental levels of light, but in the EEG record they appeared identical to PGO spikes. Researchers seeking to test the validity of this idea eliminated environmental light from a cat's cage and then directed the odor of fish through the cage. They observed EMPs identical to PGO spikes. Sharp noises produced the same result.

A series of experiments provides fertile ground for questions about the reasons for new experiments (Incorporation or Application questions), analogous processes (an Application question), and the evaluation of results (Detail or Deduction questions). Possible questions include:

> Based on the information in the passage, fish odor was directed through a darkened cage in order to determine:

> The author implies that EMPs were reevaluated because:

IMPLICIT STATEMENTS

Wherever arguments are made, there may also be implied evidence or conclusions. You shouldn't spend time trying to identify these while you read—but the more you practice, the more often you'll find you can recognize the presence (though probably not the details) of implicit assumptions and inferences. Now consider this paragraph:

> In her 1929 classic *A Room of One's Own*, Virginia Woolf discusses the exclusion of women from English higher culture. To help explain the absence of female authors in the Elizabethan Age, she imagines what might have happened if William Shakespeare had a sister who possessed all of her brother's genius. "Judith Shakespeare" is one of Woolf's most memorable fictional creations: Scorned by her family and by society at large for attempting to become a professional writer, she ends her days in squalor and misery. This picture influenced feminist thought for decades: If there are few great woman writers in the Western canon, it is because women were prevented from writing. Recent scholarship has shown how misleading this picture is. The oppression of women throughout history is real enough, but even in Shakespeare's England—undeniably a sexist society by modern standards—there were successful women authors.

The author strongly disagrees with Woolf's view, and offers proof for her position. Become alert for inconsistencies. Here, Judith Shakespeare is said to be "attempting to become a professional writer" and the existence of "successful woman authors" is given as proof that she could have become one—does "success" equate with "professional"? When you see the author's reasoning as well as her opinion, look for Evaluation, Deduction, and Incorporation questions:

> In concluding that feminist thought was influenced by Woolf's writing, the author assumes:

> Which of the following would be most useful in disputing the author's argument that successful women writers in Elizabethan England disprove Woolf's conclusion?

Now consider another:

> Although Dorothy Wordsworth was convinced that her journal entries were not literature, they were seamlessly incorporated by her brother William into some of his most famous poems, altered only by his use of the first-person pronoun, the "I." The important question concerning the relationship between Dorothy and William, however, is not whether William's borrowings constituted exploitation, but rather how the relationship contributed to Dorothy's in-

ability to conceive of herself as a writer. Traditionally in literature, the authorial self, the "I," is identifiably masculine; the dominated "other" is feminine. In William's poems, the "other" is usually Nature, often personified as Dorothy. While these literary roles helped to sustain the close relationship between the two in real life, they also reinforced Dorothy's acceptance of the norms that defined her as "other." Thus, her access to authorial self-consciousness was blocked not just by the fact of her gender, but also by her accepted role in her brother's life and poetry.

When the author avoids stating a clearly implicit opinion, you can expect to find it in the questions:

> It can be inferred from the passage that the author believes which of the following about the quality of Dorothy Wordsworth's journal entries?

> It can be inferred from the passage that the author believes which of the following about the relationship between Dorothy Wordsworth and her brother?

You may also have noticed the unusual meaning of "self-consciousness" here—another question waiting to be asked. Now try another paragraph:

> In response to rapidly rising crime rates, legislators in Georgian England initiated a policy of imposing mandatory capital punishment for what to modern eyes is an astonishing range of crimes. Over 200 crimes were punishable by hanging: Not only murder and kidnapping, but also forgery, petty theft, and "posing as a gypsy." Yet, while the number of crimes punishable by death increased, and more and more criminals were brought to trial, the numbers of people who were actually hanged fell. Simple decency alone accounts for many of the instances in which the English chose not to apply their lethal laws. Judges could commute the death sentence for suitably penitent felons. Juries could undervalue stolen goods so as to bilk the prosecution. (Since the law demanded that anyone who stole 40 shillings or more must hang, hundreds of convictions were handed down every year for the theft of goods valued by the jury at 39 shillings.)

When something is stated as being done "in response" to something else (or any paraphrase of this language), the connection between the two is often assumed, leading to a Deduction question:

> In enacting capital punishment legislation, Georgians assumed that:

LISTS AND CATEGORIES

Lists are another frequent source of questions; there might be an Evaluation question about its function, or an Application question about items not mentioned by the author that also belong on the list. "Not only…but also" constructions suggest questions about the distinction between those categories—or perhaps about their similarities.

> The author mentions the crimes of forgery, petty theft, and posing as a gypsy in order to:

Try a final paragraph:

> Sociologist Morton Marks's structural studies of several types of African American music show that the musical event is also a ritual event, defined here as a meaningful structure for social transition between cultures. Marks suggests that the abrupt switch from European to African performing rules in the middle of certain songs signals a transition from conventional "performance" to ritual. In Black American gospel music, for instance, "channel cues"—phrases like going home or feeling the fire—establish the ritual setting and introduce a trance event. Unlike the glossolalia ("speaking in tongues") common in some white churches, trance behavior in African American music takes place within the musical structure, and as such consists of elaborately patterned, linguistically meaningful statements. This transition to African modes, Marks contends, expresses a historical awareness of cultural distinctions between Africa and Europe.

Contrasts and categories established in the passage are frequently the basis for Verbal Reasoning questions:

> Which of the following might the author consider an example of a "channel cue"?

> The author contrasts the trance behavior in African American song rituals with glossolalia primarily to:

As you can see, the elements Kaplan teaches you to look for as you read are the building blocks from which the questions are made. If you train yourself to read each passage critically—and be conscious of the standard questions—there will be few surprises in the questions at the end of each Verbal Reasoning passage.

Verbal Reasoning
Practice Test 1

Let's put all the critical reading strategies together now as we work through a full-length test, all seven passages. We're going to do this test together; that is, we'll walk you step-by-step through the process—how to find what's important in each paragraph, how to map each paragraph, and how to map the entire passage.

We've italicized the important sentences, words, or phrases in each paragraph. Those are the clues to the purpose of the paragraph. We've also placed each map directly under its paragraph so you can read the paragraph and the map together. There are hints and notes for many paragraphs, too. Don't forget to read them.

Your long-term goal will be to finish each passage and its questions in about eight-and-a-half minutes. Read and map each passage in about four to four-and-a-half minutes, leaving about the same amount of time for the questions. The least stressful way to do this is to time yourself for two passages at a time; 17 minutes per passage pair. Right now, though, don't worry about timing. First you want to practice using the Kaplan strategy and making it automatic for you.

There are tips on how to get the right answer for each question, and at the end of all seven passages, you'll find complete explanations for all the right and wrong answers. You'll also find the answers listed just as letters, but don't stop there. You're not going to learn anything from a list of letters. Read the full explanations carefully—that's how you'll learn what makes an answer right or wrong, which kinds of questions are hard for you, and which answer traps you fall for. Once you know that, you can learn how to ace them.

Time—60 minutes

Directions: There are seven passages in this Verbal Reasoning test. Each passage is followed by a set of questions. After reading a passage, select the one best answer to each question. If you are not certain of an answer, eliminate the alternatives that you know to be incorrect and then select an answer from the remaining alternatives.

Passage I (Questions 1–5)

Gautier was indeed a poet and a strongly representative one—a French poet in his limitations even more than in his gifts; and he remains an interesting example of the manner in which, even when the former are surprisingly great, a happy application of the latter may produce the most delightful works. Completeness on his own scale is to our mind the idea he most instantly suggests. Such as his finished task now presents him, *he is almost sole of his kind.* He has had imitators who have mimicked everything but his spontaneity and his temper; and as they have therefore failed to equal him we doubt whether the literature of our day presents a genius so naturally perfect. We say this with no desire to transfer Gautier to a higher pedestal than he has fairly earned—a poor service, for the pedestal sometimes sadly dwarfs the figure. His great merit was that he *understood himself so perfectly and handled himself so skillfully.* Even more than Alfred de Musset (with whom the speech had a shade of mock-modesty) he might have said that, if his glass was not large, as least it was all his own glass.

> Map of Paragraph 1: Gautier was a flawed poet but was nevertheless unique and talented.

There are a host of reasons why we should not compare Gautier with such a poet as Browning; and yet there are several why we should. If we do so, with all proper reservations, we may wonder whether we are the richer, or, at all events, the better entertained, as a poet's readers should before all things be, by the clear, undiluted strain of Gautier's minor key, or by the vast, grossly commingled volume of utterance. It is idle at all times to point a moral. *But if there are sermons in stones, there are profitable reflections to be made even on Théophile Gautier; notably this one: that a man's supreme use in the world is to master his intellectual instrument and play it in perfection.*

> Map of Paragraph 2: Gautier was able to be uniquely himself in his poetry. Compare with others?

He brought to his task a sort of pagan bonhomie which makes most of the descriptive and pictorial poets seem, by contrast, a group of shivering ascetics or muddled metaphysicians.

You Can Do This!

These few lines are all you need to map the entire paragraph. Don't worry about what words you use to map; there's no such thing as a perfect map. Just use the words that make sense to you.

You Can Do This!

To compare or not to compare? Who knows? Just recognize that it's something the author is dealing with.

You Can Do This!

That last line is, perhaps, the easiest to understand of a wildly difficult paragraph. At least you know there are "profitable reflections" to be made, and they are something about playing one's own instrument (read "poetic work") well. Thus, Gautier is unique in his poetry.

He excels them by *his magnificent good temper and the unquestioning serenity of his enjoyment of the great spectacle of nature and art.* His world was all material, and its outlying darkness hardly more suggestive, morally, than a velvet canopy studded with silver nails. To close his eyes and turn his back on it must have seemed to him the end of all things; death, for him, must have been as the sullen dropping of a stone into a well. His observation was so penetrating and his descriptive instinct so unerring, that one might have fancied grave nature, in a fit of coquetry, or tired of receiving but half-justice, had determined to construct a genius with senses of a finer strain than the mass of human family.

Map of Paragraph 3: Gautier was interested in life and nature. Good temper? Pagan bonhomie?

And finally,

Topic: Gautier

Scope: His uniqueness

Purpose: To argue how and why he was unique

1. In the passage, the author suggests that French poet Théophile Gautier's talents included all of the following EXCEPT

   Here's a scattered detail question. You're going to have to look carefully at your map to determine which paragraph holds each answer. Then be even more careful researching the paragraphs. Remember, you're looking for something the author *wouldn't* agree with.

   A. an innovative and unique artistic view of nature.
   B. the ability to compose poetry quickly and immediately.
   C. extensive training in rhetorical and literary techniques.
   D. a strong understanding of his world and himself.

2. For what purpose can it reasonably be concluded does the author reference other writers in this passage, including Musset and Browning?

   This function question is really asking why the author refers to other poets, so it takes us back to that "compare" issue. We may not have understood that the author finally says it isn't worth comparing Gautier to other poets, but we do know the author's conclusion about Gautier: He was unique. So predict that the other poets are here to show that Gautier, as a unique poet, *can't* be compared to others.

   A. To prove that Gautier, as a poet, was unique among his contemporaries
   B. To show that Gautier's poetry was representative of French lyricism at the time
   C. To criticize Gautier's limited talent and creativity
   D. To refute the idea that Gautier's colleagues could easily imitate his style

3. Which of the following, if true, would most WEAKEN the author's conclusion that Gautier's unique artistic gifts more than compensated for his creative limitations?

This is a lovely question because the test maker has given you the author's point of view: Gautier's unique gifts compensated for his limitations. To weaken this, just find some evidence that says no, the gifts don't compensate or, no, Gautier wasn't all that unique.

A. Gautier's poems are still studied more frequently than any of his prose writing.

B. Close study of Gautier's life has revealed that he frequently collaborated with other writers.

C. During the early 1800s, Gautier's primary success came from his critical reviews of art.

D. Numerous later writers acknowledged Gautier's work as an influence on their writing.

4. As used in the passage, the words "pagan bonhomie" (in the first sentence of the last paragraph) refer to

Oops, back to that odd phrase "pagan bonhomie." Didn't you just know that you'd get a question on this? But don't worry. This time you don't have to figure out what it means; you just have to choose from four possibilities. Your map mentions nature and good temper. Look for an answer that has something to do with those attributes.

A. Gautier's extravagant and debauched lifestyle as revealed through his poetry.

B. the unique descriptions of nature that are absent from Gautier's work.

C. Gautier's lack of modesty and his desire for lasting notoriety.

D. a particular attitude toward the world that set Gautier apart from his contemporaries.

5. Without regard for what other critics of the genre might purport, according to the passage, what is the primary reaction a reader should have to poetry?

We didn't actually map a reference to this primary reaction to poetry, so we'll have to scan the passage to find it. As you see, it's in paragraph 2. Now reread and predict.

A. Poetry should produce a strong emotional response within the reader.

B. A reader should enjoy and be entertained by poetry.

C. Readers should learn a moral, social, or political lesson from poetry.

D. Poetry should provide readers with ideas that are relevant to their own lives.

How was that passage for you? Despite the fact that it's about a poet, and is somewhat poetically written itself, the keywords and phrases from each paragraph are enough for you to get a general understanding of the passage and to map it in your own words. Don't forget to use that map to help you locate answers, and don't forget to predict.

Want to try it again? That, of course, is a rhetorical question, since you're about to try your hand at passage II and its questions. Let's do it.

Passage II (Questions 6–12)

The *study of the analog position of mental representation* has many fascinating branches which help illuminate the inner workings of our minds and how we perceive images in our mind's eye. This theory points to the *link between the time it takes to solve mental problems and their complexity.*

> Map of Paragraph 1: Intro analog position idea—how long it takes to solve problems depends on their complexity.

In a now-famous study, *Stephen Kosslyn* asked subjects to imagine an animal, such as a rabbit, next to either an elephant or a fly. When the image was formed, Kosslyn would ask whether or not the target animal had a particular attribute. For example, Kosslyn might say, "elephant, rabbit," and then "leg." He found that it took subjects longer to answer when the target animal was next to the large animal than when it was next to the small animal. Kosslyn interpreted this to mean that subjects had to zoom in on the image to detect the particular feature. Just as one has difficulty seeing details on small objects, so the *subjects could not simply mentally "see" details on the smaller object in their mental image.*

> Map of Paragraph 2: Kosslyn's experiment—mind's reaction to relative sizes of mental images.

Second, Kosslyn and colleagues demonstrated that *the time it takes to scan between two points depends on the distance between the two points in a memorized image.* In one experiment, subjects memorized an array of letters separated by different distances. Kosslyn found that the farther apart the letters were from each other, the longer it took to answer questions about one of the letters. One of the principal hypotheses of the *analog position* of mental representation, which is the idea that mental processing requires one to *move sequentially through all intervening steps* to solve a problem, is that mental images have regular properties. In a similar experiment, Kosslyn had subjects memorize pictures of objects such as a plane or a motorboat. Then he had subjects focus on one part of the object (e.g., the motor) and move to another (e.g., the anchor).

You Can Do This!

Notice how little detail (or how few complete sentences, for that matter) we're putting in the map? You don't need much detail until a question asks you about it, but then your map will tell you where to look.

MCAT Expertise

Again, the question mark here indicates something that seems important but that you don't quickly understand. That's perfectly okay; let it go for now. On the MCAT, you won't have a question asking you to explain this. Whatever question you have on it will be based on the experiment itself, not how much you can explain it.

Map of Paragraph 3: Definition analog position. K's 2nd experiment—longer distance between mental images = longer time to answer questions. Intro experiment 3.

He found that the time it took to determine whether the second part was present depended on the distance between the two parts in the memorized picture. In one of his more famous experiments of this type, Kosslyn and colleagues had subjects memorize the location of various objects (such as a hut or a tree) on a fictional map. Subjects were then told to focus on one object and then scan the image to determine whether another object was or was not on the map. *The amount of time it took to locate objects that were present on the memorized map was linearly related to the distance between the objects.*

Map of Paragraph 4: 3rd experiment—distance in mental images on maps. Same result as 2nd.

Using a completely different paradigm, *Shepard and Feng* tested the amount of time that it would take for subjects to specify whether two *arrows* on unfolded blocks matched up. They found a linear relationship between the *number of folds* between the arrows and the time it took to make this judgment, suggesting that *subjects went through a discrete series of organized steps in order to solve this problem.*

Map of Paragraph 5: Shep/Feng study with folds and arrows. To solve, need to think through a series of steps.

The final type of experiment showing that mental images have regular properties is perhaps the most famous: mental rotation experiments. In 1971, *Shepard and Metzler* tested subjects' abilities to make complex figure comparisons. They presented subjects with a three-dimensional "standard" figure and a comparison figure that was either identical to the standard figure or was its mirror image; the comparison stimulus was rotated, either clockwise or into the third dimension. Shepard and Metzler found that the *time needed* to judge whether the comparison stimulus was identical or a mirror image *depended directly on the size of the angle between the target orientation and the orientation of the standard.*

Map of Paragraph 6: Shep/Metzler. Time needed to mentally compare figures depends on size of angle (?).

Topic: Analog mental imaging
Scope: Experiments supporting theory
Purpose: To describe

6. According to the way it is presented by the author in the passage, the analog position of mental representation argues that

This is a straightforward detail question (the words *according to* tell you that) and should immediately send you back to the map and passage to research the detail. The lovely phrase "analog position of mental representation" screams paragraph 3. Check your map for that paragraph; then predict and match an answer.

    A. mental processing requires one to go sequentially through all intervening steps to solve a problem.

    B. one typically uses shortcuts to solve mental problems.

    C. it should take longer to solve more complex problems.

    D. most problems are not able to be solved by people without help.

7. According to the scanning experiments mentioned in the passage, it should take longer to scan longer distances because the subjects

Distances? Definitely paragraphs 3 and 4. Reread, predict, match.

    A. believe that there is no relationship between distance and time.

    B. have to keep time with a metronome set up by the experimenter.

    C. form a mental picture of the scene and go through all the intervening positions in the picture.

    D. are tricked by the experimenter into taking a longer time.

8. Which of the following conclusions not presented in the passage might be an alternate explanation for the map experiments described by the author?

This is an unusually worded question, so make sure you understand what it's really asking. In the long run, it's asking you to find a different explanation for all those experimental results, essentially weakening the ones given. The word *map* is a giveaway to the answer's location: paragraph 4. What's the conclusion of this experiment? What else would explain the results?

    A. Subjects forget where the objects are.

    B. Subjects know that it should take longer to move longer distances and answer accordingly.

    C. Subjects consult actual maps for the distances, and this takes them more time the greater the distance.

    D. It takes subjects longer to start scanning longer distances and so ultimately takes them longer to finish.

Key Concept

Don't get nervous when you see an unusually worded question. For the most part, all questions on the MCAT will be one of the question types you learned about earlier.

9. According to the passage, why does Kosslyn say it takes longer to identify attributes of objects when they are next to a bigger object than when they are next to a smaller one?

Bigger, smaller, one next to the other—sounds like paragraph 2. Let's reread it.

A. Because one scans objects in order of size from larger to smaller.
B. Because the larger object covers the smaller object and one must move it out of the way.
C. Because large and small objects have all the same features and so interfere with each other.
D. Because one must zoom in to see parts of the smaller object when it is next to a larger object.

10. If it were the case that subjects simply responded as the experimenters encouraged them to do, based on information in the passage, one would expect

Let's see—if the subjects just tried to guess what the experimenters wanted them to say, the experiments wouldn't prove anything. Look for an answer that essentially says that.

A. that the pattern of results would be just as they are.
B. that there would be a nonlinear relationship between distance and reaction time.
C. that the relationship between distance and reaction time would be constant.
D. that the experimenters could create any relationship between distance and reaction time.

11. Based on the passage, which of the following patterns of results would contradict the analog position?

Remember that there are two ways to do this Roman numeral question. Let's start with the answer choices first; in this case, answer I, since it appears in three of the four possible answers.

I. It takes longer to scan longer distances.

II. There is no relationship between scanning time and distance.

III. It takes less time to scan longer distances.

A. I only
B. II and III
C. I and III
D. I, II, and III

12. Other researchers have found that subjects can alter the amount of time it takes to scan images based on the instructions they are given. What implications does this have for the analog view?

This incorporation question is more or less the same as question 10: What would happen if researchers changed what they told people to do? If people change what they do based on what they're told, the findings wouldn't tell us much.

A. It implies that the analog view is more likely to be correct since subjects are scanning as they normally do in non-testlike situations.

B. It implies that the analog view is more likely to be correct since subjects do not have control over the rate at which they scan.

C. It implies that the analog view is less likely to be correct because subjects might be scanning as they believe they should.

D. It implies that the analog view is more likely to be correct since subjects can control the rate at which they scan.

Are you beginning to feel more comfortable with MCAT passages and questions? Keep practicing and staying confident—you can do this!

Passage III (Questions 13–18)

Never accept anything as true that you do not clearly know to be so; that is, carefully avoid jumping to conclusions, and include nothing in judgments, other than what presents itself so clearly and distinctly to the spirit that you would never have any occasion to doubt it. Then, *divide each of the difficulties being examined into as many parts as can be created* and would be required to better resolve them. *Order your thoughts, starting with the simplest ideas*, which are the easiest to comprehend, and advancing little by little, by degrees, to the most complex ideas. Believe that an order exists even among those which do not naturally follow one another. And last, always *make deductions so complete*, and reviews so general, that you are assured of omitting nothing.

Map of Paragraph 1: The four principles of thought

When I was younger, I studied a bit in the fields of philosophy, logic, and math—geometric analysis and algebra. These three disciplines seemed as though they should contribute something to my methodological approach.

Map of Paragraph 2: Author's background studies

While examining these fields, I noticed that, in *logic*, syllogisms and the bulk of other logical theorems *serve only to explain to others the things that one already knows*, or even to speak without judgment of things that one doesn't know, rather

> **Key Concept**
>
> Passages written in the first person are rare. When you do see them, look for a strong author point of view.

than to teach others anything. Although logic contains, in effect, many true and just precepts, there are yet among these so many others which are superfluous or refutable, that it is almost sickening to separate one from the other.

Map of Paragraph 3: Author's problems with logic

As for *geometric analysis and modern algebra*, in addition to the fact that they don't treat anything except *abstract ideas*, which seem to be of no use whatsoever, geometry is always so *restricted to the consideration of figures* that it can't stretch the intellect without exhausting the imagination. Algebra, in contrast, subjects one to certain rules and numbers, to the degree that it becomes a confused and obscure art that troubles the spirit rather than a science that cultivates it.

Map of Paragraph 4: Problems with geometry and algebra

All of this made me think that it was necessary to look for some *other methodological approach* which contained the advantages of these three, while at the same time was exempt from their faults. And, just as the multitude of laws often provides rationalization for vice, such that any State is better ruled if it has but a few closely monitored vices, likewise, instead of following the great number of precepts which compose logic, I thought that I would have enough with *the four preceding*, as long as I made a firm and constant resolution *never*—not even once—to *neglect my adherence to them*.

Map of Paragraph 5: Author's approach—4 principles again

Topic: Thought
Scope: Author's method
Purpose: To argue for

13. As presented within the context of the passage, the first precept of the author's methodological approach is based on the assumption that

As assumption is unstated evidence—something the author must believe is true to support his conclusion but that he doesn't clearly state. For assumptions, try the denial test. Deny the answers and see which answer, when denied, makes the author's conclusion fall apart. That's the necessary assumption.

A. true comprehension depends primarily on rational comprehension and analysis.
B. theories can be accepted as true if they are perceived intellectually and instinctively.
C. relying solely on intellectual prowess is a valid way of determining the validity of a theory.
D. scholars must study philosophy and mathematics in order to understand abstract ideas.

You Can Do This!

Notice how our map is really a simple restatement of the main point of each paragraph? It's as if you were explaining each paragraph to a 10-year-old. That's how to do it!

MCAT Expertise

Each paragraph map centers around the author. Remember what we said in the beginning of this book—it's *all* about the author.

MCAT Expertise

Remember that when you have a main idea question, or one that asks about the author's purpose, read the Topic, Scope, and Purpose backward. In this case, the main idea is to argue for the author's method of thought.

14. Which of the following best expresses the author's attitude toward the existence of vice in a State?

The clue word in this question is *State*. Scan for it quickly; then read what the author says about it.

    A. National vices should be considered equivalent to deductive flaws in logic.

    B. Vices can be justified or excused through legal channels.

    C. An effective government must eradicate all vices in its rulers and citizens.

    D. Certain vices may be unavoidable but can be kept under control through careful observation.

15. According to the passage, which of the following statements is true about geometry?

The paragraph reference is clear. Now which Roman numeral would be best to start with? We think it's II because that shows up in three of the four answer choices.

    I. Geometric analysis is not useful as a logical methodology.

    II. Geometry focuses too narrowly on shapes and lines.

    III. Geometry is largely visual, so comprehension requires both intellect and imagination.

    A. II only

    B. I and II

    C. I, II, and III

    D. III only

16. The author takes time in the passage to describe his study of philosophy and mathematics in an effort to

What's your prediction here?

    A. justify his precepts as being validly based on personal knowledge and experience.

    B. demonstrate the relationship among logic, geometry, and algebra.

    C. provide a scholarly model for his readers so that they can expand their study of logic.

    D. refute prior logicians' theories and indicate their flaws.

17. The author would be LEAST likely to agree with which of the following statements?

The author would be most likely to disagree with anything contrary to what the passage says he agrees with. Look over your map for a quick refresher on his ideas, then make a prediction before going to the answers.

A. Logic is an inappropriate field of research for young scholars.
B. A scholar should always treat the subject of his or her study in its entirety.
C. Orderly study is based on the principle that a whole is the sum of its parts.
D. Teaching is one of the motivations for studying abstract ideas and theories.

18. Based on the point of view taken by the author in the passage, the author's primary concern in developing his method is

It's pretty clear that the author felt the need for a new methodology and, in Paragraph 5, the absolute necessity to stick to it. That's the reasoning behind developing his method, and that's your prediction.

A. objective examination of prior methodologies.
B. thorough grounding in a variety of academic disciplines.
C. consistent adherence to his principles.
D. extensive research in the natural sciences.

MCAT Expertise

If your prediction doesn't match any of the answer choices, eliminate wrong answers instead and see what's left.

Passage IV (Questions 19–23)

With the collapse of the "dot-com" bubble in 2001, and the new trend *toward out-sourcing information technology labor demands,* it becomes *imperative to analyze the state of the economy which has brought us to this place.* With the explosion of the technology industry in the late 1990s, the United States ushered in the so-called "new economy." Based largely on speculation and a "cash-in" mentality, the new economy bustled along until the bottom fell out and it came crashing back to earth. But what set the stage for this collapse to happen was put into motion years earlier.

> Map of Paragraph 1: Intro collapse of dot-com; analyze state of economy leading to it.

The growth of productivity is defined as the rate of growth in product less the rate of growth in the labor used in production. Productivity can be affected by factors such as amount of capital invested in production, methods used in production, educational or demographic composition of the labor force, business climate, global competition, and cost of environmental and safety regulations. Capital investment was booming in the United States in the post-1995 period, nearing a historic peak as a percentage of the United States gross domestic product. Furthermore, that part of capital invested in information technology, including computers, software, and communications equipment, rose to more than fifty times what it had been in 1975. Because of its high gross rate of return in improving methods of production, *capital investment in information technology should have a particularly large impact on overall productivity.*

> **Map of Paragraph 2: Define productivity growth. Big impact from investment in IT.**

For the past five years the big news for the United States economy has been a noticeable productivity growth spurt, which many have attributed to new information and communication technologies. The rate of growth in United States productivity had not been so high since the period extending from the end of World War II through the 1960s. In the early 1970s, productivity growth dropped suddenly. Apart from normal cyclical movements low productivity growth continued until the mid-1990s. Then, performance of the United States economy accelerated to a truly extraordinary level. From 1995 to 1999 real gross domestic product grew at an average rate of about 4 percent per year, and the rate of growth in labor productivity returned to the pre-1970 rate of increase.

> **Map of Paragraph 3: Big spurt of United States econ., some say because of IT.**

The revolution in technology is, at least in some sense, a worldwide phenomenon. Therefore*, one would expect the recent trend in the rate of growth in productivity in the United States to be shared by other developed countries. However,* marked differences exist. Although the United States had the lowest rate of overall productivity growth in the 1981–95 period, in the post-1995 period the United States rate of productivity rose to third among the countries, behind only Ireland and Australia. *In several other developed countries,* including France, Italy, Japan, the United Kingdom, the Netherlands, and Spain, *overall productivity growth slowed quite sharply.* The questions then arise: *Why* are these trends in productivity growth so different; and does this difference illuminate anything about the role of the new technologies? Regression analysis of the rate of growth in productivity in each of these countries in the late 1990s, both as a function of the country's share of spending devoted to information technology and as a function of its number of Internet servers, reveals a positive correlation that passes the test for statistical significance. Therefore, with due deference to the problems of international comparison, *the data appear to reinforce the view that utilization of the new technologies has been important in raising productivity in the United States in recent years.*

> **Map of Paragraph 4: In some countries productivity slowed. United States: IT led to ↑ productivity.**

Topic: Information technology

Scope: Its role in ↑ of American productivity

Purpose: To explain

MCAT Expertise

This is a typical economics passage, filled with dates, numbers, and details. Don't get stuck in those details; stay focused on the main idea of each paragraph.

You Can Do This!

See how little we mapped? It was easier than trying to figure out which of the details was important. We'll go back in the passage when we need to, but meanwhile we've saved a lot of time.

19. According to the passage, a resurgence in productivity occurred in

There's too much information about this in the passage to know exactly where to check, so take a look at the answer choices first. Notice we're dealing with dates and countries. That makes it easier.

    I. the United States in the late 1990s.

    II. Ireland in the late 1990s.

    III. developed countries other than the United States in the 1981–95 period.

    A. I only

    B. II only

    C. III only

    D. I, II, and III

20. In concluding that utilization of new technologies has been important in raising productivity in the United States in recent years, the author assumes all of the following EXCEPT

Again, check out the answers first.

    A. other factors affecting productivity did not become significantly more favorable in this period.

    B. the revolution in technology is a worldwide phenomenon.

    C. the amount of spending on information technology and number of Internet servers are valid measures of utilization of new technologies in production.

    D. the share of spending devoted to information technology and the number of Internet servers are a cause of productivity growth.

21. If the passage were to continue, the next topic the author would discuss would most probably be

This is a pretty rare question type, but it's really just asking you to think about the structure of the passage and predict what would come next. What question was asked but never answered in the passage? We could predict that the passage would go on to answer that question.

    A. what factors caused the drop in the growth of U.S. productivity in the early 1970s.

    B. what factors prevented the productivity growth spurt in the United States from continuing.

    C. the relative importance of other factors in fostering productivity growth in the United States.

    D. why different developed countries invested different shares of total spending on capital investment in new technologies.

22. If given the opportunity to rebut all of the following comments, with respect to the change in productivity growth in the United States in the late 1990s, the author would most probably agree with which of the following statements?

Wow, what an oddly and densely worded question. Stop for a minute and make sure you understand it. In the long run, it's really just asking what the author would agree with (you can forget the "rebut" phrase).

   A. This change is typical of the type of change that is a natural part of the tendency of economies to cycle through periods of higher and lower growth.

   B. This particular change is more remarkable than other changes that have occurred in the last half century and, therefore, warrants a particular explanation.

   C. The factors that caused this change should be identified so that they may be fostered in countries that are not experiencing strong productivity growth.

   D. Investment in information and communication technologies has played a significant role in fostering the productivity gains in the United States.

23. In paragraph 2, the author is primarily concerned with

Be careful here—the most obvious answer isn't always the correct one. You're asked about the author's *primary concern*; in other words, why the author wrote this paragraph. Look to her conclusion, not her evidence.

   A. defining productivity and identifying the types of factors that can affect its growth.

   B. noting a correlation between a peak in capital investment and a peak in the growth of productivity.

   C. emphasizing the impact of the amount of capital invested on the degree of improvement in methods used for production.

   D. introducing an explanation that will then be tested by further investigation.

Passage V (Questions 24–30)

Should the soft spring breath of kind appreciation warm the current chilly atmosphere, flowers of greater luxuriance and beauty would soon blossom forth, to beautify and enrich our literature. If these anticipations are not realized, it will not be because there is anything in our country that is uncongenial to *poetry.* If we are deprived of many of the advantages of older countries, our youthful country provides ample compensation not only in the ways in which nature unveils her most majestic forms to exalt and inspire, but also in our unshackled freedom of thought and broad spheres of action. Despite the unpropitious circumstances that exist, *some true poetry has been written in our country, and represents an earnest hope of better things for the future* and basis to hope that it will not always be winter with our native poetry.

> Map of Paragraph 1: There is some true native poetry written in the author's country and maybe better to come.

Whenever things are discovered that are new, in the records of creation, in the relations of phenomenon, in the mind's operations, or in forms of thought and imagery, some record in the finer forms of literature will always be demanded. *There is probably no country in the world,* making equal pretensions to natural intelligence and progress in education, where the claims of native literature are so little felt, and *where every effort in poetry has been met with so much coldness and indifference, as in ours.*

> Map of Paragraph 2: We need poetry to record new things, but people are indifferent to poetry in his country.

The common method of *accounting for this,* that almost everyone is engaged in the pursuit of the necessities of life, and that few possess the wealth and leisure necessary to enable devotion of time or thought to the study of poetry and kindred subjects, is by no means satisfactory. This state of things is doubtless unfavorable to the growth of poetry; but there are other causes less palpable, which exert a more subtle but still powerful antagonism. Nothing so seriously militates against the growth of our native poetry as *the false conceptions that prevail respecting the nature of poetry.*

> Map of Paragraph 3: Why people are indifferent.

Stemming either from a natural incapacity to appreciate the truths that find their highest embodiment in poetry or from familiarity only with more widely available, but lower forms, of literature, such notions conceive of *poetry as fanciful, contrived, contrary to reason, or lacking the justification of any claim to practical utility.* These attitudes, which admittedly may have some origin in the imperfection that even the most partial must confess to finding in our native poetry, nevertheless also can have the *effect of discouraging native writers of undoubted genius from the sustained application to their craft that is essential to artistic excellence.*

> Map of Paragraph 4: More reasons why: People think it's fanciful, etc. Poets need to work at poetry.

Poetry, like Truth, will unveil her beauty and dispense her honors only to those who

You Can Do This!

Wow, a passage about poetry written in a poetic way. Appropriate, perhaps, but really difficult to understand. Just keep going and map whatever is clear to you.

love her with a deep and reverential affection. There are many who are not gifted with the power of giving expression to the deeper sensibilities, who nevertheless experience them throbbing in their hearts. To them poetry appeals. But where this tongue-less poetry of the heart has no existence, or exists in a very feeble degree, the *conditions for appreciating poetic excellence are wanting.* Let no one, therefore, speak of disregard for poetry as if it indicated superiority.

> **Map of Paragraph 5:** There are people who love poetry, but also conditions for loving it aren't in place.

Rather, it is an imperfection to be endured as a misfortune. Despite prevailing misconceptions, there always remain at least a few who appreciate fine literature. Why do these not provide sufficient nourishment for our native artists? Here, we must acknowledge that so *many of us, as emigrants from the Old Country, cling to memories of the lands we have left, and that this throws a charm around literary efforts originating in our former home. It is indisputable that the productions of our young country suffer by comparison.*

> **Map of Paragraph 6:** We're immigrants and like Old Country poetry, so New Country poetry suffers.

> **Topic:** Poetry
>
> **Scope:** The poor state of poetry in the author's country
>
> **Purpose:** To explain and lament

24. The passage asserts that which of the following is/are reason(s) for the indifference toward native poetry that the author finds in his country?

> Does any one Roman numeral answer look wrong? If so, start there and eliminate all answers with that Roman numeral in them. Don't worry too much about what *edification* means.

   I. There has been insufficient edification of most of the population.

   II. The highest achievements of native poets do not rise to the level achieved by poets of the immigrants' homeland.

   III. Nostalgic feelings orient readers toward the literature of their former home.

   A. I and II only

   B. II and III only

   C. I and III only

   D. I, II, and III

Key Concept

The MCAT test maker always throws in some killer passages that are tough for almost everyone. Your goal is not to spend lots of time on them (spend no more than 10 minutes) but to do carefully the passages you *can* ace and get every one of those questions right.

25. Throughout the passage, the author develops a contrast between

This is a really tough question that is best approached by eliminating wrong answers. One obvious contrast is between the author's claim that poetry is good but not appreciated. If you can get the answers down to two, guess. You have a 50-50 chance of getting it right.

    A. the subtle and the palpable.
    B. false claims and real facts.
    C. the appreciable and the insignificant.
    D. the practical and the impractical.

26. Suppose that the passage does not stand on its own but is excerpted from an introduction to a book. This book would most likely be

This is a bit easier. After all, the author keeps talking about his country and why people don't appreciate its native poetry.

    A. a textbook on the techniques for writing good poetry.
    B. a volume comparing the poetry of two countries.
    C. a volume of recent native poetry.
    D. a volume of essays on poetry and criticism.

27. In the sentence "But where this tongue-less poetry of the heart has no existence, or exists in a very feeble degree, the conditions for appreciating poetic excellence are wanting," the author most probably uses the phrase "tongue-less poetry of the heart" in order to

Research Paragraph 4, but this time read more carefully and put the quote in context. Just before the quote, the author seems to say that some people can't write poetry but nonetheless can feel it in their heart.

    A. emphasize that poetry is more commonly experienced through reading rather than by being heard.
    B. emphasize a defect that exists in those who devalue poetry.
    C. emphasize that appreciation of poetry is not limited to those who can write it.
    D. express compassion for those who lack the gift of writing poetry.

28. The author probably considers which of the following "unpropitious circumstances" (Paragraph 1) most essential to explaining the state of native poetry?

> What are those circumstances? Even though the quoted words are in Paragraph 1, you know that the "whys" are in Paragraphs 3 and 4.

A. Lack of available resources for the study of poetry

B. Failure of native poets to devote themselves to learning their craft

C. Prevalent misconceptions about poetry

D. Nostalgia of emigrants for their home country

29. Which of the following statements, made by poets about the creative process, is closest to the opinions expressed in the passage about what constitutes "true" poetry?

> We may not have understood what "true" poetry is, but we know what it isn't: anything referred to in Paragraph 4. In the same paragraph, we mapped that poets need "sustained application to their craft." That should help find the answer.

A. "Like a piece of ice on a hot stove the poem must ride on its own melting. A poem may be worked over once it is in being, but may not be worried into being."

B. "My method is simple: not to bother about poetry. It must come of its own accord. Merely whispering its name drives it away."

C. "If there's room for poets in this world … their sole work is to represent the age, their own age, not Charlemagne's."

D. "The only way of expressing emotion in the form of art is by finding an 'objective correlative'; in other words, a set of objects, a situation, a chain of events which shall be the formula of that particular emotion; such that when the external facts, which must terminate in sensory experience, are given, the emotion is immediately evoked."

30. By "native literature," the author most probably means

> The author introduces "native poetry" in the first paragraph, but it's in Paragraph 2 where he seems to say that literature is demanded as a record of discoveries, new thoughts, and other phenomena.

A. literature written by the aboriginal people of his home country.

B. literature written by people who make his country their home.

C. literature written by people born in his country.

D. literature produced in and reflecting the circumstances and environment of his country.

Passage VI (Questions 31–35)

We're down to the last two passages. On Test Day, if you don't think you'll have time to do both, you must choose one to do carefully. Briefly look at both passages and their questions. Choose the one you think you can do best. If both look okay, pick the one with the most questions—you have the most to gain here. Before you start work on your chosen passage, answer all questions for the other one; just use your favorite default letter or do it at random. That way, even if time runs out, you'll still have answered all questions in the Verbal section, and odds are at least one of the default answers will be correct. After carefully attacking one of the final two passages, use whatever time you have left to see if you can get one or two more points on the other one. Never give up—even one minute is enough time to get one more correct answer, and one more correct answer can boost your score and percentile.

Without entering now into the *why*, let me observe that the printer may always ascertain when *the dash of the manuscript* is properly and when improperly employed, by bearing in mind that this point represents *a second thought—an emendation*. In using it just now I have exemplified its use. The words "an emendation" are, speaking with reference to grammatical construction, put in *apposition* with the words *"a second thought."* Having written these latter words, I reflected whether it would not be possible to render their meaning more distinct by certain other words.

Map of Paragraph 1: Dash shows a second thought.

Now, instead of erasing the phrase "a second thought," which is of *some* use, which *partially* conveys the idea intended—which advances me a *step toward* my full purpose—I suffer it to remain, and merely put a dash between it and the phrase "an emendation." *The dash gives the reader a choice between two, or among three or more expressions, one of which may be more forcible than another, but all of which help out the idea.*

Map of Paragraph 2: Dashes give readers a choice between ways of saying things, some more forcible than others but all important.

It stands, in general, for the words "or, to make my meaning more distinct." This force *it has* and this force no other point can have; since all other points have well-understood uses quite different from this. Therefore, *the dash cannot be dispensed* with. It has its phases and its variation of the force described; but the one principle of second thought or emendation will be found at the bottom of all.

Map of Paragraph 3: Dashes make things clearer and are important.

That punctuation is important all agree; but how *few comprehend the extent of its importance! The writer who neglects punctuation, or mis-punctuates, is liable to be misunderstood.* This, according to the popular idea, is the sum of the evils arising from heedlessness or ignorance. It does not seem to be known that, *even where the sense is perfectly clear, a sentence may be deprived of half its force—its spirit—its point—by improper punctuation.* For the want of merely a comma, it often occurs that an axiom appears a paradox, or that sarcasm is converted into a sermonoid. There is *no* treatise on the topic, and there is no topic on which a treatise is more needed.

> Map of Paragraph 4: If no dash, idea is less understood and forceful.

There seems to exist a vulgar notion that the subject is one of pure conventionality and cannot be brought within the limits of *intelligible and consistent rule.* And yet, if fairly looked in the face, the whole matter is so plain that its *rationale* may be read as we run. If not anticipated, I shall, hereafter, make an attempt at a magazine paper on "The Philosophy of Point." In the meantime let me say a word more of *the dash*.

> Map of Paragraph 5: Dash can be a consistent rule.

Every writer for the press, who has any sense of the accurate, must be frequently mortified and vexed at the distortion of his sentences by the printer's now general substitution of a semicolon, or comma, for the *dash in the manuscript. The total or nearly total disuse of the latter point has been brought about by the revulsion consequent upon its excessive employment about twenty years ago.* The Byronic poets were *all* dash.

> Map of Paragraph 6: Printers substitute for dashes b/c dashes overused (Byron).

Topic: The dash
Scope: Its use and importance
Purpose: To argue for

31. According to the arguments presented in the passage by the author, which of the following is/are true about the dash?

These are nice, short Roman numeral answers, so you might just want to start with Roman numeral I. It's in three of the four answers anyway.

   I. It is often replaced by printers.

  II. It is overused by some writers.

 III. It serves a unique, necessary function.

  A. I and II only

  B. II and III only

  C. I and III only

MCAT Expertise

This was a much easier passage than the previous one, wasn't it? That's the way the MCAT will go, and that's why you should pick and choose how you order the passages and not necessarily follow the test maker's order.

D. I, II and III

32. According to the passage, the newspaper printers' practice of replacing dashes in authors' manuscripts with other punctuation marks is due to

The question gives us a nice, clear reference to Paragraph 6: the word printers.

A. the overuse of the dash by authors during the period closely preceding the writing of the passage.

B. the widespread ignorance of the importance of punctuation.

C. the fact that the dash serves no function that is not better served by other punctuation marks.

D. the fact that authors seldom have second thoughts about their work.

33. The passage indicates that if given the chance to respond to the following claims, the author is LEAST likely to agree with which of the following statements?

Remember, for this type of question, you're looking for something opposite to the author's stated comments.

A. There is a single ideal way in which any thought can be expressed.

B. The rules of punctuation are simple and rational.

C. Punctuation helps to convey the writer's intended meaning and tone.

D. Most people do not understand the correct use of punctuation.

34. The author most likely mentions his intention to write an article entitled "The Philosophy of Point" in order to

We may wonder why anyone *would write such an article, but at least we know why the author would. Go back to your map for Paragraph 5 and make a prediction.*

A. remind the reader that grammar is a branch of philosophy.

B. indicate the possibility of explaining correct punctuation concisely.

C. furnish his own credentials as an expert on punctuation.

D. emend his statement about punctuation.

35. According to the passage, which of the following is true of the relationship between words or phrases separated by a dash?

Another nice question. Just research the role of the dash.

A. Each word or phrase partially conveys the author's meaning.

B. The second word or phrase renders the first one superfluous.

C. The first word or phrase states the main topic, and the second states the

MCAT Expertise

There were only five questions for this passage, but they were pretty easy ones so your goal would be to get them all right. It doesn't matter if your points come from hard or easy questions; they all count toward your MCAT score.

subtopic.

D. The two words or phrases pertain to separate topics.

Passage VII (Questions 36–40)

Let us consider whether women as a group have unique, politically relevant characteristics, whether they have special interests to which a representative could or should respond. *Can we argue that women as a group share particular social, economic, or political problems that do not closely match those of other groups, or that they share a particular viewpoint* on the solution to political problems? Framing the working *definition of "representable interests"* in this *fashion does not mean that the problems or issues are exclusively those of the specified interest group*, any more than we can make the same argument about other types of groups more widely accepted as interest groups.

Map of Paragraph 1: Define interest group. Women? Different groups can share same issues.

The fact that there is a *labor interest group, for example*, reflects the existence of other groups such as the business establishment, consumers, and government, which in a larger sense share labor's concerns, but often have viewpoints on the nature of, or solutions to, the problems which conflict with those of labor.

Map of Paragraph 2: Example of interest group (labor).

Nor does our working definition of an interest group mean that all of the potential members of that group are consciously allied, or that there is a clear and obvious answer to any given problem articulated by the entire group that differs substantially from answers articulated by others. *Research in various fields of social science provides evidence that women do have a distinct position and a shared set of problems that characterize a special interest.*

Map of Paragraph 3: Women are an interest group but not consciously.

Many of these distinctions are located in the institution in which women and men are probably most often assumed to have common interests, *the family*. Much has been made of the "sharing" or "democratic" model of the modern family, but *whatever democratization has taken place, it has not come close to erasing the division of labor and, indeed, stratification, by sex*. Time-use studies show that women spend about the same amount of time on and do the same proportion of housework and child care now as women did at the turn of the century. To say that women are in a different social position from that of men and therefore have unique interests to be represented is *not, however, the same as saying that women are conscious of these*

MCAT Expertise

When one entire paragraph is simply an example of something, all you need to map is that it's an example.

differences, that they define themselves as having special interests requiring representation, *or that men and women as groups now disagree on policy issues in which women might have a special interest.*

Map of Paragraph 4: One issue of group is family. Differences may be unconscious and don't necessarily lead to disagreement.

Studies of public opinion on the status and roles of women show relatively few significant differences between the sexes, and do not reveal women to be consistently more feminist than men. *On the other hand, law and public policy continue to create and reinforce differences* between women and men in property and contract matters, economic opportunity, protection from violence, control over fertility and child care, educational opportunities, and civic rights and obligations. The indicators generally used to describe differences in socioeconomic position also show that the politically *relevant situations of women and men are different. Women in almost all countries have less education than men, and where they achieve equivalent levels of education, segregation by field and therefore skills and market value remains.*

Map of Paragraph 5: Law/public policy/socioeco. status—reasons why women form an interest group.

Topic: Political interest groups
Scope: Do women represent one?
Purpose: To argue that they do

36. Which of the following would the author be most likely to consider a necessary characteristic of a group having "representable interests" (Paragraph 1)?

The question gives you the paragraph, so quickly review and predict.

A. The problems of the group are unique to its members.
B. The group's proposed solutions to their problems differ radically from those proposed by other groups.
C. Members of the group are not already represented as individuals.

MCAT Expertise

A passage with a nice clear theme throughout is a good one to attack with the intention of getting every question right.

D. Members of the group tend to have similar opinions about the handling of particular political problems.

37. It can be inferred from the passage that which of the following statements is true of men and women as groups?

Recall that an inference question asks about the author's conclusion and restates that conclusion as the correct answer. To answer this question, look at what the author says about men and women.

A. In public opinion polls on women's issues, men's responses do not differ in a consistent way from those of women.
B. Developments in recent years have given men more control over child care issues.
C. Women are becoming more aware of their differences from men than in the past.
D. Men do not wish to recognize the special interests of women.

38. According to the passage, which of the following experiences do modern women have most nearly in common with women who lived in 1900?

Turn of the century, 1900—Paragraph 4, right?

A. They are represented only as individuals and not as a group.
B. They spend about the same amount of time on housework.
C. They experience significant discrimination in employment.
D. The proportion of women among those designated as representatives is lower than among the represented.

39. Based on the passage, of the following issues, the author is most concerned about the problem of

This is just another way of asking a global, or main idea question. Refer to your Purpose, Scope, and Topic, in that order, but stay flexible; the test maker can say the same thing in lots of different ways.

A. the history of women's demands for representation as a group.
B. recent changes in the status of women in society.

    C. opposing views concerning women's awareness of their own special interests.

    D. the criteria that would justify group representation for women.

40. The passage offers the most support for concluding that which of the following is an important problem confronting women today?

Most of the author's evidence is in Paragraphs 4 and 5, so check them over and see which answer choice is reflected there.

    A. Women are in a different socioeconomic position from that of men.

    B. Men differ greatly from women in the answers they propose for women's problems.

    C. Women do not qualify as an interest group because they have not all banded together to pursue common goals

    D. A lack of educational opportunities has inhibited women from voicing their concerns.

There you have it—one complete test with all sorts of notes, tips, and maps. Ideally, you now have a good grasp on what's important in a passage, how to map it, how to understand and predict answers, and what to do when you have no idea what a passage is about.

The next tests—each with seven passages—are your opportunity to practice what you've learned. Remember that all tests have complete answer explanations at the end and you want to go over them very carefully to determine what kinds of passages and questions are the hardest for you. What traps do you fall into? How's your timing? Keeping these questions in mind will help you get the most from each passage you do. Good practice is not a matter of how many passages you can do but what you learn from your approach to each one.

Verbal Reasoning Practice Test 1
Answers and Explanations

ANSWER KEY

1. C	9. D	17. B	25. A	33. A
2. A	10. D	18. C	26. C	34. B
3. B	11. B	19. A	27. C	35. A
4. D	12. C	20. B	28. C	36. D
5. B	13. B	21. B	29. A	37. A
6. A	14. D	22. D	30. D	38. B
7. C	15. B	23. D	31. D	39. D
8. B	16. A	24. C	32. A	40. A

EXPLANATIONS

Passage I: Gautier
Topic: Gautier
Scope: His uniqueness
Purpose: To argue how and why he was unique

Mapping the Passage:

¶1. Gautier was a flawed poet but was nevertheless unique and talented.

¶2. Gautier was able to be uniquely himself in his poetry. Compare with others?

¶3. Gautier was interested in life and nature. Good temper? Pagan bonhomie?

1. C

The presence of the word *suggests* in the question indicates an inference question; you'll be looking for the author's conclusions about Gautier. But since the question has an "All . . . EXCEPT" structure, you want something that doesn't follow from the conclusions, that contradicts them, or that is out of scope. While answer choices that

contradict are much more common, be aware of the other types as well. (C) is out of scope: The passage doesn't discuss Gautier's educational background, and therefore nothing can be inferred about it.

Wrong Answers:

(A) Opposite. We know from the passage that the author thinks Gautier was unique.

(B) Opposite. We can infer that Gautier was able to compose poetry quickly from the author's discussion of Gautier's "spontaneity" in paragraph 1 and his "vast . . . volume of" writing in paragraph 2.

(D) Opposite. This can be inferred from paragraphs 2 and 3, where the author discusses Gautier's self-understanding and keen observation of nature.

2. A

Why does the author mention other poets? Evaluate the examples in the passage individually. At the end of paragraph 1, the author compares Gautier with Musset to say that Gautier was even more distinctive than was Musset, for Gautier, "even more than Alfred de Musset . . . if his glass was not large, at least it was all his own glass." When comparing Gautier to Browning in paragraph 2, the author argues that it's possible to be more entertained by Gautier than Browning, then goes on to say that "a man's supreme use in the world is to master his intellectual instrument . . .," which again suggests Gautier's uniqueness. The author suggests in paragraph 1 that Gautier was unique when he says Gautier was never fully imitated. Finally, in the last paragraph, the author argues that Gautier "excels" other descriptive poets by his personal qualities, which yet again emphasizes uniqueness. Therefore, there is overwhelming evidence for (A)!

Wrong Answers:

(B) Faulty Use of Detail. Though the author suggests this in the first sentence, it has nothing to do with Gautier's comparison to other poets, since French lyricism isn't mentioned again in the passage.

(C) Opposite. Although the passage mentions Gautier's limitations, the author is very complimentary of the poet and never "criticizes" him.

(D) Faulty Use of Detail. Though the author argues in the first paragraph that others have tried and failed to imitate Gautier completely, there is no claim that Gautier's colleagues *could* easily imitate his style to refute in the first place. Did you notice that two wrong answer choices are faulty use of detail (FUD) traps? People fall for FUD answers if they don't research carefully to make sure that the detail they choose really answers the question asked.

3. B

An argument can be weakened by attacks on its evidence, assumptions, or conclusions. Break the question down a bit before predicting. Ask: What are Gautier's artistic gifts? Answer: Mainly his uniqueness, ability to entertain, and powers of observation. If these were the things that overcame his limitations as a poet, you can predict that the right answer will somehow diminish these qualities. (B) does that. If Gautier collaborated with other writers, then his writing may not have been the result of his own uniqueness, and at least one quality that the author uses to justify Gautier's limitations doesn't exist.

Wrong Answers:

(A) Out of Scope. Whether Gautier's poems or prose is studied more has nothing to do with the author's evidence or conclusion.

(C) Out of Scope. Even if this statement were true, Gautier's reviews wouldn't have any effect on the value of his poems.

(D) Opposite. If later writers acknowledged Gautier as influential, the author's conclusion that Gautier overcame his limitations would be strengthened.

4. D

Review the phrase in context. "Pagan bonhomie" apparently makes the other descriptive poets seem not-so-descriptive. Keep reading. Why does Gautier dwarf these poets? Among other things, because of "his magnificent good temper and the unquestioning serenity of his enjoyment of the great spectacle of nature and art." Pagan bonhomie must therefore be some sort of view of life in general that the other poets don't share. (D) comes closest to capturing the author's overall point that Gautier's *attitude* set him apart, not just his descriptions of nature alone.

Wrong Answers:

(A) Out of Scope. The author never claims that Gautier had a wild and excessive lifestyle. Eliminate this choice immediately because it's a classic out-of-scope trap.

(B) Faulty Use of Detail. While this answer is tempting, if you go back to the final paragraph, you'll see that Gautier is unique because of his personality and perspective on the world rather than his "descriptions of nature."

(C) Out of Scope. The author never suggests that Gautier lacked modesty and, in fact, argues the opposite at the end of the last paragraph.

5. B

Where does the author discuss the reader's reaction to poetry? It's buried in paragraph 2; the author says, ". . . we may wonder whether we are . . . the better entertained, as a poet's readers should before all things be. . . ." Therefore, the author believes that the first role of poetry is to bring enjoyment. (B) says the same.

Wrong Answers:

(A) Out of Scope. Though this might be true, the author never discusses the reader's emotional response.

(C) Out of Scope. As in (A), the author never discusses poetry and moral lessons. Though the author discusses a "moral" in paragraph 2, it's not a moral in poetry but rather a lesson to be learned from Gautier in general.

(D) Out of Scope. Though it may be true, the author never argues that poetry should be applicable to the reader's life.

Passage II: Mental Images

Topic: Analog mental imaging

Scope: Experiments supporting theory

Purpose: To describe

Mapping the Passage:

¶1. Intro analog position idea—how long it takes to solve problems depends on their complexity.

¶2. Kosslyn's experiment—mind's reaction to relative sizes of mental images.

¶3. Definition analog position. K's 2nd experiment—longer distance between mental images = longer time to answer questions. Intro experiment 3

¶4. 3rd experiment—distance in mental images on maps. Same result as 2nd.

¶5. Shep/Feng study with folds and arrows. To solve, need to think through a series of steps.

¶6. Shep/Metzler. Time needed to mentally compare figures depends on size of angle (?).

6. A

This question simply asks you to summarize the hypothesis described in paragraph 3. The fastest way to predict here is to read the text. The analog position is "the idea that mental processing requires one to move sequentially through all intervening steps to solve a problem." (A) repeats this almost word for word.

Wrong Answers:

(B) Opposite. This contradicts the argument that mental processing has to proceed step-by-step.

(C) Faulty Use of Detail. Don't get sidetracked by the information in paragraph 1. This follows from the analog position, as supported by the experiments in the passage, but it's not the analog position itself.

(D) Out of Scope. The passage never discusses whether people need help to solve problems.

7. C

What reason would the analog position give for the fact that it takes longer to scan long distances in a mental image? Review the relevant parts of the passage, paragraph 4 in particular. The experiment suggests that people are using a "fictional," or mental, map. Because the analog position suggests that one has to go through steps to solve a problem, it would be reasonable to infer that it takes longer to scan long distances because the person doing the scanning is "looking" at all the intervening space between the two objects. (C) summarizes this.

Wrong Answers:

(A) Out of Scope. The passage never discusses what the subjects believe.

(B) Out of Scope. There is no mention of a metronome in the passage.

(D) Out of Scope. The passage doesn't imply that the experimenter is trying to "trick" or in any way bias the subjects.

8. B

This is an unusual question. What would an alternate explanation do to the conclusions drawn from the experiment? It would weaken them, so this question can therefore be treated as a classic "weaken" question. Look for evidence that would weaken the passage's conclusions. (B) does this: If subjects change an answer based on what they think is expected, the argument takes longer because they're referring to a mental map that is weakened.

Wrong Answers:

(A) Distortion. This choice contradicts the basis of the experiment. Since subjects in the experiments had to memorize the positions of the objects, subjects who forgot the positions wouldn't be part of the experiment's focus.

(C) Out of Scope. The experiment is designed to deal only with "fictional" maps, so any explanation that involves real maps would be implausible.

(D) Out of Scope. The passage states that response times depend on distance, but there's no reason to believe that it would take longer to begin scanning longer distances as opposed to shorter ones.

9. D

Where is Kosslyn's experiment on big and small objects mentioned? It's in paragraph 2, so let's focus on that part of the passage. Review the text to determine why Kosslyn believes it takes longer to identify small objects next to large ones: Kosslyn believes "subjects had to zoom in on the image to detect the particular feature." (D) says the same.

Wrong Answers:

(A) Out of Scope. The passage doesn't discuss the order in which subjects scan the objects.

(B) Out of Scope. Kosslyn's experiment doesn't mention that the objects overlap.

(C) Out of Scope. The features of the two animals are never mentioned in the text.

10. D

Though it's not immediately obvious, this is an incorporation question because you're given new information and asked how it will affect the passage. What would be the case if subjects simply responded in the way they thought the experimenters wanted them to? Predict: The experiment wouldn't prove anything except the experimenters' own biases. (D) restates this: Whatever relationship the experimenters want, they'll get.

Wrong Answers:

(A) Out of Scope. Though this might be true, we don't actually know whether the experimenters would encourage subjects to keep responding the same way.

(B) Opposite. It would make more sense that the subjects would show a *linear* relationship, since the experimenters, in keeping with the analog model, were expecting that.

(C) Out of Scope. As with (A), even though this constant relationship might be reflected, it misses the point that *any* relationship is possible if the subjects are simply following the experimenters' lead.

11. B

Paraphrase the analog position before proceeding to the answer choices to make evaluation easier: Solving a problem requires step-by-step thought, and mental images have properties that can be tested. Start with Statement I, which restates the conclusion of an experiment *supporting* the analog hypothesis. Since you're looking for statements that *contradict* it, you can eliminate (A), (C), and (D). Only (B) is left, and there's no need to evaluate the remaining choices.

Wrong Answers:

II. Opposite. The analog position predicts a direct correlation between distance and time, so an experiment showing that there is no relationship would contradict it.

III. Opposite. This is the opposite of the analog position, which says that questions about longer mental distances require more time to solve.

12. C

This is another incorporation question that asks you to take new evidence and determine how it would affect the passage. Predict the result again: If subjects change their responses based on what they think "should" happen, then the results of the experiment should be called into question, as the subjects are simply reflecting experimental bias. (C) captures this. The same point will often be tested repeatedly throughout a passage's questions. Don't reinvent the wheel! Use your previous work to save time and to maximize your points.

Wrong Answers:

(A) Opposite. If subjects are scanning in the way they think they should, the experiment is more likely revealing experimental bias than the actual mental images it sets out to describe.

(B) Opposite. A lack of subject control over scanning contradicts the information in the question, since it's stated explicitly that subjects *can* alter the time they spend scanning.

(D) Opposite. Even if subjects can control the rate at which they scan, as the question suggests, the analog model would still be weakened by this conscious response.

Passage III: Principles of Thought

Topic: Thought

Scope: Author's method

Purpose: To argue for

Mapping the Passage:

¶1. The four principles of thought

¶2. Author's background studies

¶3. Author's problems with logic

¶4. Problems with geometry and algebra

¶5. Author's approach: 4 principles again

13.   B

Review the author's first precept in paragraph 1: Don't accept anything as true unless it's known to be true. Be sure to look through the rest of the paragraph for evidence and support. The author's first precept depends on the assumption that the author's perception of truth is valid. (B) restates this. If in doubt, try the denial test: Simply put the answer choice in the negative—deny it—and if that makes the author's argument fall apart, it's the necessary assumption. For example, if you denied answer (D)—scholars *do not* need to study . . .—would that affect the argument in any way? No, because the author doesn't mention this one way or the other. But what if (B) were denied? The theory would fall apart since it would undermine the author's ideas. Thus, (B) is a necessary assumption and the correct answer.

Wrong Answers:

(A) Opposite. The author argues that he will believe only what *he* perceives to be true, which means that knowing the truth is ultimately a subjective process. (A) argues that

comprehension is ultimately based on rational analysis rather than personal knowledge, which the author rejects.

(C) Opposite. As above, the author believes that it's necessary to rely on personal opinion in addition to pure intellect.

(D) Distortion. Though the author argues that these disciplines are used for understanding abstract ideas, there's no argument that these things *must* be studied to understand abstract ideas. Even if this were true, it wouldn't have an impact on the author's argument in paragraph 1.

14.   D

Where does the author mention vice in a State? Go back and review the example in paragraph 5. The author says that a "State is better ruled if it has but a few closely monitored vices." Paraphrase: It's best to keep a close eye on the few flaws present. (D) restates this point. Questions and answers that follow complicated paragraphs will often make you earn the points by paraphrasing points in the passage. Get in the habit of restating difficult points in simpler words when predicting answers.

Wrong Answers:

(A) Out of Scope. The author never equates vices and logic.

(B) Faulty Use of Detail. The author argues that many laws can rationalize vices, which is exactly why it's better to stick to just a few rules. This answer captures only the author's introduction to the main point, which is that it's better to have a few rules that are always followed.

(C) Distortion. The author argues that it's best to have only a few vices but never suggests it's advisable or even possible to get rid of all vice.

15.   B

Another detail question. Focus your work in this question on paragraph 4, where geometry is discussed. First tackle statement II, which appears in three choices. The author argues that geometry is "so restricted to the consideration of figures" that it ends up being limited. Statement II paraphrases this, eliminating (D). Statement I states that

geometric analysis is not useful for logical analysis. The author argues that geometry not only deals too much with figures but also doesn't "treat anything except abstract ideas, which seem to be of no use whatsoever," suggesting that it's not useful for logic, almost exactly restating I. Therefore (B) is the correct answer.

Wrong Answers:

III. Faulty Use of Detail. According to the passage, geometry is so "restricted" that it stretches the intellect but exhausts the imagination. From this statement, we can infer that the author believes that geometry needs so much imagination that it leaves no room for an intellectual workout.

16. A

To answer this evaluation question, we need to consider why the author describes his former study of philosophy and mathematics. Predict: He wants to show that they weren't useful by themselves and that he needed new precepts that combined all their advantages (paragraph 5). Look for an answer choice that is similar to this. (A) is reasonable. If the author wanted to create a new system based on the old ones, he'd mention his studies in the other fields in order to show that he had the necessary background to form these new ideas.

Wrong Answers:

(B) Distortion. Though the author wants to combine parts of these fields, he's not concerned with discussing their relationship to each other so much as with describing how they fit into his new way of thinking.

(C) Opposite. The author argues in paragraph 3 that the study of logic by itself is pointless, so he wouldn't want to help readers expand their study of logic.

(D) Distortion. Though the author does argue in paragraph 3 that much logic is flawed, he mentions his own study not so much as to refute specific theories but rather to describe his new method of thinking.

17. B

Since you have no information in the question to narrow your focus, you can be reasonably sure that the right answer will be something with which the author generally disagrees. The shortcomings of traditional systems and the author's four precepts make up the meat of the passage, so look for something that conflicts with the author's negative view of traditional methods of thought and his positive view of his own precepts. The author's second principle states that difficulties should be broken up into many small pieces that can be individually evaluated; (B) argues that subjects should *never* be broken up. The author would clearly disagree.

Wrong Answers:

(A) Opposite. The author argues in paragraph 3 that logic isn't particularly useful.

(C) Opposite. The author would agree that it's possible to understand a big problem by breaking it down into smaller problems.

(D) Opposite. The author argues in paragraph 3 that logical theorems "serve only to explain to others the things that one already knows," which suggests that the author is concerned with teaching abstract ideas in addition to simply learning them.

18. C

Where does the author discuss the reasoning behind his method? Paragraph 5 is concerned almost entirely with this. The author argues that it was enough for him to have four principles as long as he was sure "never—not even once—to neglect my adherence to them." (C) is a close paraphrase of this particular concern about consistency.

Wrong Answers:

(A) Distortion. Though the other methodologies played a role in the author's new system, he doesn't suggest that his *primary* concern is the examination of these old systems. He's more concerned with having a few simple principles.

(B) Distortion. As in (A), though the author suggests that he has this thorough grounding, he believes that it's better to have simple principles that are always followed.

(D) Out of Scope. The natural sciences are not mentioned at all in the passage.

Passage IV: US Economy

Topic: Information technology (IT)
Scope: Its role in ↑ of American productivity
Purpose: To explain

Mapping the Passage:

¶1. Intro collapse of dot-com; analyze state of economy leading to it.

¶2. Define productivity growth. Big impact from investment in IT.

¶3. Big spurt of United States econ., some say because of IT.

¶4. In some countries productivity slowed. United States: IT led to ↑ productivity.

19. A

What is a resurgence? It's a rise to previous levels; if it were just a rise, it would be a surge but not a *re*-surgence. The passage provides enough data only about the United States to infer a resurgence occurred: The author says at the end of paragraph 3 that "the rate of growth in labor productivity returned to the pre-1970 rate of increase." While other nations are mentioned, their previous levels are not mentioned. Therefore, statement I fits, while the other ones don't.

Wrong Answers:

II. Out of Scope. Although paragraph 4 states that Ireland had one of the highest productivity growth rates post-1995, the passage doesn't discuss its economy before this period.

III. Out of Scope. Similarly, the passage does not include any information about other countries before 1981–95, so we cannot classify this growth as a "resurgence."

20. B

An assumption question, but in an "All . . . EXCEPT" format that's rare for this type. Remember that an assumption is an unstated belief bridging evidence and conclusion and that an assumption on the MCAT is always implied—never stated. The conclusion is given: The author believes that information technology has raised American productivity. What is the evidence? Review the map: The author uses data on technology investment in the United States and other developed nations. Look for a choice that is *not* necessary to connect these. (B) fits for a few reasons. Perhaps most obviously, it's explicitly stated: The author says at the beginning of paragraph 4, "The revolution in technology is . . . a worldwide phenomenon." Since an assumption is unstated, (B) must not be an assumption essential to the argument. Furthermore, using the denial test (which here, you want to fail!), if this weren't true and the revolution *were not* a worldwide phenomenon, it would do nothing to diminish the impact of information technology within the United States.

Wrong Answers:

(A) Opposite. The author must assume that other factors aren't significant; if they were, then the author couldn't make the argument that information technology is the major factor responsible for the surge in productivity.

(C) Opposite. The author uses these measures when discussing levels of technology investment in paragraph 4. If these weren't valid measures, the author's point wouldn't mention them.

(D) Opposite. This answer is just another way of saying that the growth of information technology, which includes Internet servers and must assume a fair amount of spending on it, was an important factor in the rise in productivity.

21. B

Review the topic and scope of the passage: The author is concerned with information technology's role in boosting American productivity in the recent past. Look for an answer choice that sticks as closely as possible to topic and scope and is relevant to other information in the passage, such as the "dot-com" bubble mentioned in the first paragraph. (B) does this: It's reasonable to guess that the author would continue the paragraph by talking about the next stage of these trends in the same topic and scope: information technology, its effect on productivity, and why the bubble burst.

Wrong Answers:

(A) Out of Scope. The author discusses the 1970s in paragraph 3 but only as background to discuss the current productivity spurt. It's more reasonable to think that the author will continue by talking about the future trajectory of the productivity gains.

(C) Out of Scope. The author doesn't mention any other possible causes for the increase in productivity and believes that information technology is the primary cause, so it's unlikely that there would be a drastic shift into a discussion of other causes.

(D) Out of Scope. The author only discusses other countries to shed light on *American* productivity gains. Going into greater depth regarding other countries would veer out of scope.

22. D

This odd wording means that you can ignore the entire "rebut" portion of the question stem. You're just looking for the statement with which the author would agree. An inference question: Predict by reviewing the author's main point about U.S. productivity growth in the late '90s. The author believes that it was the result of heavy investment in information technology. (D) says the same thing, simply summarizing the author's main point.

Wrong Answers:

(A) Opposite. The author believes, as argued in paragraph 3, that this particular surge in productivity was "extraordinary" and, therefore, by definition *not* typical.

(B) Out of Scope. The author doesn't discuss other changes, which could encompass any number of subjects, so there's no way to compare how the author feels about this particular change relative to others.

(C) Out of Scope. A classic case of confusing description with prescription: While the author explains a possible cause for the productivity gain, there's no discussion of what should be done with this information.

23. D

This pseudo main idea question asks for the purpose of one paragraph rather than the entire passage. Predict by reviewing your map of paragraph 2. The author's main

intent is to define productivity growth and to suggest that the investment in information technology should have led to a growth in productivity. (D) most closely describes the author's purpose of providing a possible explanation, and it suggests that the explanation is given with the intent of following it up with further evidence, which the author does in fact provide in paragraph 4.

Wrong Answers:

(A) Faulty Use of Detail. Though (A) might be tempting because the author does define productivity and does identify the factors that can affect its growth, this choice neglects the second half of the paragraph about the relationship between productivity growth and IT spending. Since the rest of the passage discusses this hypothesis, it's the author's primary concern here.

(B) Out of Scope. The author describes a correlation between investment and productivity but doesn't describe peaks in either.

(C) Out of Scope. As above, while the author proposes a broad correlation between investment and productivity, there's no specific discussion of how much investment is required for a certain amount of productivity.

Passage V: Poetry

Topic: Poetry
Scope: The poor state of poetry in the author's country
Purpose: To explain and lament

Mapping the Passage:

¶1. There is some true native poetry written in the author's country and maybe better to come.

¶2. We need poetry to record new things, but people are indifferent to poetry in his country.

¶3. Why people are indifferent

¶4. More reasons why: People think it's fanciful, etc. Poets need to work at poetry

¶5. There are people who love poetry, but also conditions for loving it aren't in place.

¶6. We're immigrants and like Old Country poetry, so New Country poetry suffers.

24. C

To answer this detail question, review your map to get a feel for the reasons the author gives for his country's indifference to poetry. Statement I is difficult to decipher because it requires us to know what *edification* means. If you don't know, guess or move on to the next Roman numeral. Taking a quick look at all the answers would show you that II is out of scope, leaving (C) as the only correct answer. By the way, *edification* means "instruction" or "enlightenment", and the author does in fact argue that the country's population is unenlightened, as described at the end of paragraph 2 and the beginning of paragraph 3. There's no need to evaluate statement III at this point unless you skipped statement I. Statement III is correct: Immigrants are reading their homeland's poetry because of nostalgia.

Wrong Answers:

II. Out of Scope. Statement II may be tempting from a quick review of paragraph 6, but it distorts the author's argument. The author argues that *in spite of* the New Country's quality poetry, immigrants read Old Country poetry because of nostalgia. In other words, II is wrong because the author does not give the New Country's "highest achievements" (in poetry), short shift.

25. A

This is a difficult question. One option is to use elimination. Predict a basic contrast in the passage: The author believes that poetry is all sorts of good but that people don't appreciate it as much as they should. Why is poetry not appreciated in the country the author discusses? The author argues that people don't understand poetry as well as they should. Something palpable is easily accessible, and something subtle isn't. Even if you didn't know the definition of *palpable*, you could guess that since the choices are presented as contrasts, it means the opposite of *subtle*. This contrast fits in with the author's general argument made throughout the passage that people simply lack a grasp of poetry's finer points. This claim is made in paragraph 3, when the author says that poetry isn't accepted for "other causes less palpable." In paragraph 4, the author argues that those who don't appreciate poetry are either incapable of

doing so or are more familiar with "widely available, but lower forms, of literature" which again suggests a contrast between the subtle and the less so. In paragraph 5, the author argues that only those who pay careful attention to poetry appreciate it, and in paragraph 1, the author contrasts a "chilly atmosphere" with a more subtle "spring breath." (A) is therefore correct as a contrast made throughout the passage. The other choices are made only in certain parts of the author's argument, while the question refers to the entire passage.

Wrong Answers:

(B) Faulty Use of Detail. The author makes this distinction at the end of paragraph 3 but doesn't mention it throughout the rest of the passage.

(C) Faulty Use of Detail. The author implies in paragraph 4 that some who do not appreciate poetry consider it insignificant, but he doesn't repeat that implication.

(D) Faulty Use of Detail. The author suggests that those who don't appreciate poetry fail to do so because they consider poetry impractical.

26. C

What scope of poetry is the author concerned with? Predict: The author wants to discuss the state of poetry in one particular country. (C) makes the most sense; it's the only answer choice that would justify this focus on the poetry of a single country.

Wrong Answers:

(A) Out of Scope. The author is less concerned with instructing people how to *write* poetry than he is with *appreciating* poetry.

(B) Out of Scope. Though the author compares Old World and New World poetry in paragraph 6, it's not the focus of the passage.

(D) Out of Scope. This statement is too broad; it doesn't include the author's focus on a particular country, which is an integral part of the passage.

27. C

Review the line in context. The author defines the phrase

in the preceding lines when saying that there are "many who are not gifted with the power of giving expression . . . who nevertheless experience [the deeper sensibilities] throbbing in their hearts." Paraphrase: Some people can't write poetry, but they can still appreciate it. (C) says the same thing.

Wrong Answers:

(A) Out of Scope. The author is distinguishing between those who can and cannot create, not between ways of communicating poetry.

(B) Faulty Use of Detail. Although the author discusses people who "devalue poetry" in other parts of the passage, in the quoted line, the author is describing those who *do* value poetry.

(D) Out of Scope. The author speaks about people who lack the gift of writing poetry but doesn't express sympathy toward them. The point is to show that appreciation can exist even when the person can't write poetry.

28. C

Review the phrase in the context of the structure around it. The author says that some true poetry has been written "despite the unpropitious circumstances that exist." It's reasonable to guess that these circumstances are those things that keep true poetry from being written. In paragraph 3, the author gives several reasons for these circumstances, concluding that nothing opposes the growth of poetry as much as "the false conceptions that prevail." (C) repeats this sentiment, almost verbatim.

Wrong Answers:

(A) Faulty Use of Detail. The "lack of available resources" is an argument given in the third paragraph, but it's one that the author considers "by no means satisfactory."

(B) Faulty Use of Detail. The author argues that this does happen, both immediately after this phrase and at the end of paragraph 4, but as the result rather than the cause. The author's position is that native poets don't devote themselves to their craft *because of* misunderstandings about poetry.

(D) Faulty Use of Detail. Though the author mentions this

as one reason for the lack of poetry, it's not the main reason. The author seems to treat this reason with some forgiveness, and therefore it likely would not be one of the negative "unpropitious circumstances" that the author discusses.

29. A

For this application question, predict by reviewing what the author considers true poetry to be. The author argues in paragraph 4 that it is *not* "fanciful [or] contrived" but that it requires "sustained application to . . . craft that is essential for artistic excellence." Look for an answer choice that fits with this idea of poetry. (A) fits the closest, describing poetry that can be edited and made better but that cannot be artificially contrived from the start. This is a good question to answer by eliminating wrong answers; that may be easier than finding the right one.

Wrong Answers:

(B) Opposite. Though the author believes that poetry must be uncontrived, the passage clearly states that good poetry requires a lot of work to perfect. This answer choice suggests the opposite.

(C) Out of Scope. The author discusses poetry that is tied to a particular country but says nothing about poetry tied to a particular time.

(D) Opposite. This description of poetry would likely be something the author would label as contrived and, therefore, more in keeping with misconceptions of poetry than with "true" poetry.

30. D

What is the passage describing when it discusses "native literature"? The author argues that poets within the country should produce more literature for the people in the country, describing phenomena in that country. The author clearly believes that immigrants can be part of this native literature since the country is described as "young" and the author describes himself as part of a group of "emigrants from the Old Country." Furthermore, in paragraph 1, the author focuses on what true poetry should be by discussing the nature of the country itself rather than the nature of the poets. (D) therefore provides the closest fit with what the author is conveying.

Wrong Answers:

(A) Out of Scope. The author is concerned with poetry that comes from and concerns a specific country, but there's no indication that only aboriginal poetry can be considered native.

(B) Distortion. Though this might be an important part of native poetry, the author is more interested in poetry that takes on the characteristics of the country than in poetry written by any particular group of people.

(C) Distortion. As in (B), the author is concerned with a national poetry rather than with the specific origin of the poets themselves.

Passage VI: The Dash

Topic: The dash
Scope: Its use and importance
Purpose: To argue for

Mapping the Passage:

¶1. Dash shows a second thought.

¶2. Dashes give readers a choice between ways of saying things, some more forcible than others but all important.

¶3. Dashes make things clearer and are important.

¶4. If no dash, idea is less understood and forceful.

¶5. Dash can be a consistent rule.

¶6. Printers substitute for dashes b/c dashes overused (Byron).

31.   D

A detail question in Roman numeral format: Let's see what the passage says about each statement. Condition I is stated directly in paragraph 6: the author describes "the printer's now general substitution . . . for the dash." Condition II follows closely afterward; the author argues that this backlash against the dash came as a result of "its excessive employment about twenty years ago." III is supported by paragraph 3, in which the author says that the dash has "force

no other point can have" and "cannot be dispensed with." (D) includes all three statements.

Wrong Answers:

None. Statements I, II, and III are all supported by the passage.

32.   A

Use your work from the previous question to help on this one. In that question, condition II deals with the reason why printers have gotten in the habit of removing dashes. Review paragraph 6: The dash censoring "has been brought about by the revulsion consequent upon its excessive employment about twenty years ago." In other words, writers used it too much, so now it's frowned upon. (A) says the same.

Wrong Answers:

(B) Faulty Use of Detail. Though the author mentions this in paragraph 4, a totally different reason is given for printers' dislike of the dash.

(C) Opposite. In paragraph 3, the author argues vehemently that the dash *does* serve a purpose, one that other punctuation cannot replace.

(D) Out of Scope. Authorial second-guessing is never mentioned in the passage.

33.   A

You're looking for an answer that *isn't* a valid inference. Since the question doesn't provide much information to go on, the answer will probably have something to do with the author's main points. Predict: Punctuation is important, and the dash is unique—it allows multiple expressions of the same thought, something that other punctuation can't accomplish. (A) immediately recommends itself and is clearly supported in paragraph 2.

Wrong Answers:

(B) Opposite. In paragraph 5, the author argues that it's a "vulgar notion" to think that punctuation doesn't follow simple rules. Therefore, the author certainly believes that it does.

(C) Opposite. The author's argument in paragraph 4 is that proper punctuation is necessary if a piece of writing is to be properly understood.

(D) Opposite. This also follows from the author's statement that "few comprehend the extent" of punctuation's importance.

34.   B

Where is "The Philosophy of Point" mentioned? Go back to paragraph 5 and review your map: The author wants to argue that writing can follow clear and consistent rules. It's a good bet, then, that the author mentions the article to reinforce this point. (B) says the same, suggesting that the article would be the author's attempt to explain exactly what the rules of punctuation are.

Wrong Answers:

(A) Out of Scope. Though the author puts the word *philosophy* in the title, there's no suggestion that his text discusses anything philosophical about grammar. Be careful: Don't choose an answer merely because it uses the same word as the text. Match idea for idea, not word for word.

(C) Out of Scope. The author never suggests that the purpose of the proposed magazine article would be to reinforce his credentials.

(D) Opposite. The author is very clear about his position on the dash. There's absolutely no hint that he wants or needs to emend (to edit, change, or modify) it.

35.   A

This detail question asks what the author argues about expressions separated by a dash. Predict: The main point of the dash is to separate multiple thoughts that together explain the meaning "which *partially* conveys the idea intended." (A) says the same.

Wrong Answers:

(B) Opposite. At the end of paragraph 2, the author argues that each phrase helps convey the author's idea.

(C) Out of Scope. Each expression approaches the main thought partially, so there's no subdivision of purpose. Ad-

ditionally, the author never writes about subdivision.

(D) Opposite. The author states that each expression conveys the *same* idea; together they express one idea.

Passage VII: Women Voters

Topic: Political interest groups
Scope: Do women represent one?
Purpose: To argue that they do

Mapping the Passage:

¶1. Define interest group. Women? Different groups can share same issues.

¶2. Example of interest group (labor).

¶3. Women are an interest group but not consciously.

¶4. One issue of group is family. Differences may be unconscious and don't necessarily lead to disagreement

¶5. Law/public policy/socioeco. status—reasons why women form an interest group.

36.   D

Go back to paragraphs 1 and 2, where the author discusses the criteria for "representable interests." The author implies in paragraph 1 that groups with representable interests "share a particular viewpoint on the solution to political problems." (D) paraphrases this.

Wrong Answers:

(A) Opposite. The author states in paragraph 1 that the problems *don't* need to be "exclusively those of the specified interest group."

(B) Opposite. Paragraph 3 states that a legitimate interest group doesn't need to have a view "that differs substantially from answers articulated by others."

(C) Distortion. The author distinguishes between individual and group representation in the first sentence but doesn't suggest that members of a group cannot be represented individually.

37.   A

The author discusses differences between men and women in paragraphs 4 and 5, so focus your search there. The author suggests that notwithstanding all the differences between men and women, there's no evidence that "men and women as groups now disagree on policy issues in which women might have a special interest." (A) follows logically from this.

Wrong Answers:

(B) Distortion. While the author argues in paragraph 5 that differences in child care are being reinforced, there is no indication that this is taking place in a way that gives more control to men.

(C) Opposite. The author argues in paragraph 4 that women are not particularly aware of their differences with men.

(D) Distortion. The author says that women are not "consistently more feminist than men," indicating that men do in fact recognize women's interests.

38.   B

Where does the author mention the year 1900? Though it's not specifically stated, the author mentions the "turn of the century" in paragraph 4. Review the context: Evidence shows that women spend about the same amount of time working around the house as they did around 1900. (B) matches up.

Wrong Answers:

(A) Out of Scope. There's no mention of representation of women, individually or collectively, in 1900.

(C) Out of Scope. The employment of women at the turn of the century is never discussed.

(D) Out of Scope. The passage doesn't talk about the proportion of women as representatives at the turn of the century.

39.   D

This is essentially a global, or main idea, question. Predict by reviewing the author's purpose in writing the passage. The author wants to discuss whether women constitute a politically representative group; (D) summarizes this.

Wrong Answers:

(A) Out of Scope. The main purpose is to determine whether or not women constitute a political group, not what that group's demands would be.

(B) Faulty Use of Detail. In paragraph 5, the author alludes to the changing status of women, but it's less of a concern than the appropriateness of political representation.

(C) Out of Scope. The author never mentions opposing views.

40.   A

Most of the support that the author provides is in the form of evidence listed in the second half of the passage; keep this in mind when evaluating the answer choices. Socioeconomic position is discussed in paragraph 5. The author suggests that the socioeconomic status of women and men is different and provides several reasons for this difference at the end of the paragraph.

Wrong Answers:

(B) Opposite. This contradicts the studies in paragraph 5 that state women and men have few differences in their degree of feminism.

(C) Opposite. In paragraph 3, the author argues that it is not necessary that the members of an interest group be "consciously allied."

(D) Out of Scope. The author never suggests that a lack of education is getting in the way of the voicing of concerns.

Verbal Reasoning
Practice Test 2

Time—60 minutes

Directions: There are seven passages in this Verbal Reasoning test. Each passage is followed by a set of questions. After reading a passage, select the one best answer to each question. If you are not certain of an answer, eliminate the alternatives that you know to be incorrect and then select an answer from the remaining alternatives.

Passage I (Questions 1–6)

The extent to which analysis of social phenomena is compatible with the scientific method is a hotly contested question. Among international relations scholars, historico-deductivist opponents of positivism claim that in the pursuit of objective depictions of the causes, course, and consequences of international phenomena, the character and operation of which are purported to exist independently of the observer, positivists miss or dismiss the implicit attitudes, values, and ideologies embedded in their work, which personalize and subjectivize their conclusions. Positivism, these critics contend, attempts to impose on world politics a coherent facticity akin to that of the natural sciences, but to which the basic nature of world politics is indisposed. As Dougherty put it, "Aristotle warns in the *Nichomachaean* Ethics that the precision of an answer cannot exceed that of its question, but the positivists want clocks and necessity where there are really clouds and contingency."

For historico-deductivists, the problem of *a posteriori* overdetermination is a case in point. In the natural sciences, replicability and verifiability afford the findings of laboratory experimentation potentially nomothetic status. In international relations, however, such lawlike generalizations about cause and effect are rarely if ever possible, not only because events are unique, but also because of the multiplicity of potential causes. Whether World War I resulted from a disequilibrium in the international distribution of power, the ascendancy of government factions committed to aggression, or the accuracy of an assassin's bullet, is, ultimately, unknown. For opponents of positivism, it is better to recognize darkness than to pretend to see light.

While some leading positivists, most notably Pastore, admit as "knowledge" only the sum of all tested propositions, for most it is the very cloudlike nature of political phenomena that requires a clocklike approach. Conceding that their subject does not permit nomothetic propositions, the majority of positivists appear committed to Williams's more moderate rule: "The propensity to error should make us cautious, but not so desperate that we fear to come as close as possible to apodictic findings. We needn't grasp at the torch with eyes closed, fearing to be blinded."

Positivists point to the potential of scientific analysis to yield counterintuitive truths. A frequently cited example is Grotsky's study of the role of nonstate actors in international trade. Published at a time when many scholars were convinced that multinational organizations had effectively "elbowed the traditional sovereign nation-state out of analytical existence in our field," Grotsky's research of the structure, timing, and variance of state expenditures on foreign direct investment effectively restored the state to its position as the dominant unit in international relations scholarship. Despite several efforts, historico-deductivists who had championed the new relevance of nonstate actors have not, as yet, successfully refuted

Grotsky's findings—a consideration that bodes well for those of us who believe that an end to this longstanding debate, which has produced much timely and relevant research, is not necessarily to be desired.

In addition to claiming that critics have mischaracterized their methodological commitments, positivists also contend that the historico-deductivist approach is subject to many of the same criticisms leveled against positivism. For example, on the twentieth anniversary of her seminal article depicting the Peloponnesian War as the archetypal case of power politics in action, Nash, perhaps the exemplar of the historico-deductivist school, revisited her earlier findings, only to conclude that the interaction between the Athenians and Spartans included significant instances of cooperation and reciprocity. Even as Nash's confederates praised the "illuminating evolution" in her thinking, many positivists questioned whether Nash's antipodal findings corresponded to a shift in her initial assumptions over time. The implication, of course, is that if positivists' commitments at the level of proto-theory color their eventual conclusions, then they are not alone in this regard.

1. According to information given in the passage, which of the following is true of *a posteriori* overdetermination?

   I. It presents a challenge to scholars' ability to produce nomothetic statements about world politics.
   II. It exemplifies the analytical confusion created by unique events that often have multiple effects.
   III. It suggests that the historico-deductivism is better suited than is positivism to the study of international relations.

   A. I only
   B. III only
   C. I and II only
   D. II and III only

2. As used at the end of the third paragraph in the statement, "We needn't grasp at the torch with eyes closed, fearing to be blinded," the word "torch" refers to

   A. propensity to error.
   B. nomothetic propositions.
   C. political phenomena.
   D. methodological commitments.

3. As described in the passage, historico-deductivist claims about the problem of *a posteriori* overdetermination in the study of political phenomena depend on the unstated assumption that

   A. positivists' methodological commitments preclude positivists from providing a fully scientific account of the onset of World War I.
   B. complex social occurrences such as wars are ultimately insusceptible to scholarly analysis.
   C. replicability is a more severe obstacle than is verifiability to the scientific study of world politics.
   D. a causal claim that stipulates multiple indistinguishable causes for a certain effect is not likely to be a nomothetic proposition.

4. Which of the following would Dougherty be most likely to describe as "clocks and necessity where there are really clouds and contingency"?

   A. A historico-deductivist study of World War I
   B. A historico-deductivist study of the Peloponnesian War
   C. A positivist study of the nature of reciprocity in the relations among sovereign states
   D. A chemist's study of the behavior of a certain gas under conditions of standard temperature and pressure

5. The principle underlying which of the following is most analogous to "Williams's more moderate rule" (paragraph 3)?

A. A student's estimation of her work is more important than either the grade awarded the work by the student's instructor or the opinion of the work expressed by the student's peers.

B. The proficiency of an expert musician may reflect intelligence different in form from, but nonetheless equal in degree to, that of an accomplished painter or a pioneering physicist.

C. If a worker were certain that he could never earn more than $50,000 per year, this in itself would not be a reason for him to refrain from trying to improve his lot at $20,000 per year.

D. Hazardous road conditions constitute sufficient reason for a motorist to cancel her travel plans, even if the motorist is extremely reluctant to do so.

6. It can reasonably be inferred that the author of the passage is a

A. professor of history.
B. professor of international relations.
C. diplomat.
D. journalist.

Passage II (Questions 7–13)

After being formed deep within the earth, hydrocarbons migrate upward, following a complex path of minute cracks and pore spaces. These molecules will eventually reach the surface and be lost unless they encounter impermeable rocks (such as dense shale) through which they cannot travel. If the rock within which they are trapped is highly permeable (such as sandstone) the hydrocarbons can be extracted by drilling through the impermeable seal and tapping into this permeable reservoir.

Our dependence, as a nation—and as a world—on fossil fuels is only increasing as the global population increases and our reliance on technology expands. There are few things that people in first-world countries do anymore that do not require an external power source of some kind. And in spite of the popularization of renewable sources of energy and nuclear energy, the chief source of power in the world is still derived from fossil fuels.

There are a number of different types of traps, but they can be divided into two broad categories. Structural traps are formed by deformation after the rocks have been formed, for example by folding or faulting. Stratigraphic traps are formed when the loose sediments that will eventually be turned into rocks were laid down. For example if the sea level rises and the permeable sands of a beach are covered with estuarine mud, the buried sediments will, under compression, become sandstone capped by impermeable siltstones, forming an ideal reservoir and trap.

By now the locations of all obvious reserves of oil and gas have been discovered. The need to expand oil and gas reserves therefore brings with it a need to find hydrocarbon reservoirs that are difficult to locate using current geological and geophysical means. To do so, geologists look for rock formations that constitute the seals and reservoirs within which hydrocarbons could be trapped.

Structural traps tend to be easier to locate and are the source of most of the known hydrocarbon reserves. Expanding our reserves therefore means locating more stratigraphically trapped hydrocarbons. The primary means of exploring for oil where there is no surface expression of the underlying geology is by seismology. When a seismic pulse transmitted into the earth encounters an interface where the density changes, typically the surface between two beds or an unconformity with velocity-density contrasts, some of the energy is reflected back upwards. A string of seismophones record these reflections, and after extensive computation, seismologists can build up a visual record of the intensity of each reflection and the time taken for it to reach the surface.

The primary limitation of the seismic method for locating stratigraphic traps is resolution: It is not possible to resolve features that are thinner than a seismic wavelet. The most common stratigraphic traps (with the possible exception of carbonate reservoirs) are in sandstone layers that are much thinner than a seismic wavelet. Seismic wavelets can be narrowed by increasing the frequency of the seismic pulse. However, high frequencies are selectively attenuated as the pulse travels through the earth, so there are limits to how much resolution can be improved by simply generating higher frequency pulses, or by filtering out the lower frequency components of the seismic source. Moreover, the density contrasts between oil-bearing sandstones and the shales that provide stratigraphic seals for the oil are often very small, so that the reflectivities, and hence the strength of the reflection, will be so low that the events may not be observable above background noise.

Recent developments such as zero phase wavelet processing and multivariate analysis of reflection waveforms have decreased noise and increased resolution. In the future it is hoped that these techniques, and greater understanding of stratigraphy itself, will prove fruitful in expanding hydrocarbon reserves.

7. As opposed to other essays written on the same topic, it is likely that the primary purpose of this passage is to

   A. explain how hydrocarbons are formed and trapped within the earth.

   B. detail how seismologists can locate hidden deposits of hydrocarbons.

   C. contrast the relative difficulty of locating structural traps and stratigraphic traps.

   D. discuss the formation of hydrocarbon reserves and how they can be located.

8. According to the passage, it is often difficult to distinguish reflections from the interface between oil-bearing sandstones and the shales that provide stratigraphic seals from background noise because

   A. high frequencies are attenuated as they travel through the earth.

   B. there is little density contrast between the oil-bearing sandstone and the shales that provide stratigraphic seals.

   C. the frequency of the seismic pulse is not high enough.

   D. they are thinner than the seismic wavelet.

9. The example of a stratigraphic trap formed by a rise in sea level (paragraph 3) is brought up to make a certain point. It used by the author of the passage principally to

   A. contrast a typical stratigraphic trap with a typical structural trap.

   B. explain why sandstones covered by siltstones make an ideal reservoir and trap.

   C. illustrate the point that stratigraphic traps were formed when sediments were laid down.

   D. show why stratigraphic traps can be difficult to locate seismically.

10. According to the passage, all of the following are needed if oil is to be extracted from a reservoir EXCEPT

   A. an impermeable seal above the reservoir.

   B. an original source of hydrocarbons below the reservoir.

   C. high-density contrast between the reservoir rocks and the stratigraphic seal.

   D. high permeability within the reservoir.

11. It can be inferred from the passage that, regardless of what angle the author may be trying to present, carbonate reservoirs are

   A. less dense than sandstone reservoirs.

   B. easily located by seismology.

   C. an important type of stratigraphic trap.

   D. at least as thick as a seismic wavelet.

12. Based on the points made throughout the passage, which of the following best describes how the author views seismology as a tool in locating hydrocarbons?

   A. Of limited effectiveness but showing promise

   B. Intrinsically flawed

   C. Effective and profitable

   D. Theoretically useful but ineffectual in practice

13. Which of the following developments in seismic technique would the author view as the greatest aid in the detection of stratigraphic traps?

   A. The discovery of a means of increasing the attenuation of high-frequency seismic wavelets within the earth

   B. The development of a seismic source with an extremely high frequency that does not attenuate over distance

   C. The development of a means of filtering all noise out of seismic sections

   D. Further research into the origin of stratigraphic traps

Passage III (Questions 14–19)

American culture changed forever in the latter part of the 20th century with the advent of pop music. Before the 1950s, music defined its own circles but, at best, only shaded the frame of popular American culture. The birth of rock and roll forever changed that as larger and larger numbers of youth came not only to identify with the music they were listening to but also to identify themselves by that music.

We use pop songs to create for ourselves a particular sort of self-definition, a particular place in society. The pleasure that a pop song produces is a pleasure of identification: in responding to a song, we are drawn into affective and emotional alliances with the performers and with the performers' other fans. Thus, music, like sport, is clearly a setting in which people directly experience community, feel an immediate bond with other people, and articulate a collective pride.

At the same time, because of its qualities of abstractness, pop music is an individualizing form. Songs have a looseness of reference that makes them immediately accessible. They are open to appropriation for personal use in a way that other popular cultural forms (television soap operas, for example) are not—the latter are tied into meanings which we may reject.

This interplay between personal absorption into music and the sense that it is, nevertheless, something public is what makes music so important in the cultural placing of the individual. Music also gives us a way of managing the relationship between our public and private emotional lives. Popular love songs are important because they give shape and voice to emotions that otherwise cannot be expressed without embarrassment or incoherence. Our most revealing declarations of feeling are often expressed in banal or boring language and so our culture has a supply of pop songs that say these things for us in interesting and involving ways.

Popular music also shapes popular memory and organizes our sense of time. Clearly, one of the effects of all music—not just pop—is to focus our attention on the feeling of time and intensify our experience of the present. One measure of good music is its "presence," its ability to "stop" time, to make us feel we are living within a moment, with no memory or anxiety about what has come before us, what will come after. It is this use of time that makes popular music so important in the social organization of youth. We invest most in popular music when we are teenagers and young adults—music ties into a particular kind of emotional turbulence, when issues of individual identity and social place, the control of public and private feelings, are at a premium. What this suggests, though, is not that young people need music but that "youth" itself is defined by music. Youth is experienced, that is, as an intense presence, through an impatience for time to pass and a regret that it is doing so, in a series of speeding, physically insistent moments that have nostalgia coded into them.

14. While there are obviously many differences between the two, the author of the passage suggests that one similarity between popular and classical music is that both

   A. articulate a sense of community and collective pride.
   B. give shape to inexpressible emotions.
   C. emphasize the feeling of time.
   D. define particular age groups.

15. It can be inferred from the passage that the author's attitude toward love songs in popular music is that of being

   A. bored by the banality of their language.
   B. embarrassed by their emotional incoherence.
   C. interested by their expressions of feeling.
   D. unimpressed by their social function.

16. The author probably refers to sport in paragraph 2 primarily in order to

    A. draw a parallel.
    B. establish a contrast.
    C. challenge an assumption.
    D. introduce a new idea.

17. Regardless this passage's purpose as a whole, in the last paragraph, the author is predominantly concerned with

    A. defining the experience of youth.
    B. describing how popular music defines youth.
    C. speculating about the organization of youth movements.
    D. analyzing the relationship between music and time.

18. The author cites which one of the following in support of the argument that popular music creates our identity?

    A. Pop songs are unpopular with older age groups.
    B. Love songs shape our everyday language.
    C. Pop songs become personalized like other cultural forms.
    D. Popular music combines public and private experience.

19. In a debate on the importance of popular music in the social organization of youth, which of the following, if true, would most WEAKEN the author's argument?

    A. Popular songs often incorporate nostalgic lyrics.
    B. Young people are ambivalent about the passage of time.
    C. Older people are less interested in popular music than young people are.
    D. Pop songs focus our expectations on the future.

Passage IV (Questions 20–24)

Tracking seems to contradict the oft-stated assumption that "all kids can learn." If certain students are better in certain subjects, they must be allowed to excel in those areas and not be relegated to an inferior class simply because they have been tracked in another subject in which they don't excel. The major obstacle to the elimination of tracking seems to be scheduling, and tracking has become, in many ways, a means to alleviate difficulties faced by administrators in scheduling their student body for classes.

Tracking has the ability to create divergent experiences, even in identical courses that are meant to be taught at the same level and speed. Administrators who support tracking generally assume that it promotes student achievement, citing that most students seem to learn best and develop the most confidence when they are grouped amongst classmates with similar capabilities. Yet, at least for the lower-level tracks, this method of class assignment can encourage "dumbing down," or teaching to the lowest common denominator of ability within a particular class, rather than accommodating differences and pushing all students equally hard.

Tracking places different students in groups that are usually based on academic ability as demonstrated by their grades and as described in teacher reports. These tracks mean that a student will proceed through every school day with essentially the same group of peers, assigned to classes at a particular level of difficulty. Researcher R. Slavin notes that "students at various track levels experience school differently," depending on their track assignments. There are differences, for example, in how fast a class progresses through material, how talkative and energetic the classroom is, even how stressed or relaxed the teacher appears.

One of the major problems with tracking is that the level in which students are initially placed often determines not only where they remain throughout high school, but also the kinds of courses they are allowed to take. For example, schools that offer Advanced Placement (AP) courses often require that students take the honors-level version of the introductory course before enrolling in the AP course a year or two later. A student who is tracked into the "regular" introductory course, rather than the honors level, may not be able to take the AP course even after doing an exemplary job in the introductory course, simply because the honors course is offered a year earlier than the regular one—allowing honors-track students to complete enough other graduation requirements to have time for the AP course later on. And, even if the "regular"-track student could make it into the AP course, he or she would be at a disadvantage because the introductory course couldn't cover key concepts when the teacher was compelled to slow down the class for the less able students.

20. If it were found that students who were tracked did better overall on standardized tests than those who were not tracked, this would most likely WEAKEN the author's argument that

A. tracking has the ability to create a diversity of student experience in the classroom.
B. tracking encourages teaching to the lowest common denominator.
C. tracking allows administrators to overcome scheduling difficulties.
D. tracking allows students to learn best, as they are grouped with classmates with similar ability.

21. According specifically to the points laid out by the author in the various paragraphs of the passage, the main idea of the passage is that

A. tracking should not be used by schools to try to promote student achievement.
B. tracking may be detrimental to many students' success in school.
C. teachers of tracked classes are often stressed and run their classes at a slow pace.
D. scheduling is a major problem for school administrators.

22. The author's argument that tracking contradicts the assumption that "all kids can learn" would be strengthened by which of the following findings?

   I. Honors-track students almost always have AP classes on their transcripts, while regular-track students do not.

  II. Students in tracked classes do significantly better on standardized tests.

 III. Teachers of the lower math track in a school were unable to cover more than three-quarters of the textbook over the past few years, while their higher-track counterparts have consistently covered the entire book.

  A. I only
  B. III only
  C. II and III only
  D. I and III only

23. According to the arguments made in the passage, students may fall into a particular track because of all of the following conditions EXCEPT

  A. high grades.
  B. learning difficulties.
  C. honors course enrollment.
  D. how talkative and energetic they are.

24. If the author were to encounter a student who was not doing the assigned classwork because he or she claimed to be bored by the material, the author would most likely conclude that

  A. the student has been placed in a track that is too high.
  B. the student is unmotivated and should be disciplined.
  C. the student has been placed in a track that is too low.
  D. the student should be in AP-level classes.

Passage V (Questions 25–30)

The civil rights movement in the United States developed at the same time as the development of pluralist politics. And very much of the latter, especially in the northern urban areas, was infused with a heavy dose of ethnicity. As blacks were coming out of slavery and going into courts, immigrant groups were coming out of Europe, passing through Ellis Island, and going into local political clubs and machines.

The politics of race has been mainly a struggle to restructure constitutional meaning and to establish certain legal claims. This emphasis was necessary precisely because the citizenship status of blacks was defined for a long period as quite different from that of whites. After the abolition of slavery, approximately 100 years ensued—into the 1960s—which were devoted essentially to interpreting the new *constitutional* status of the emancipated black citizens.

A "civil rights" movement developed that saw 95 years (1870–1965) devoted to establishing the privilege of blacks to vote unencumbered by racial barriers. The main arena was the court system. Congress and the presidency were not principal participants, because the political constituencies supporting their elections did not favor such participation. Civil rights advocates went to federal courts to challenge "grandfather clauses," white primaries, and evasive voter registration practices, as well as economic intimidation. These important, tedious battles created a cadre of constitutional lawyers who became in a real sense the focal points of the civil rights struggle. Such was the situation in the famous Montgomery, Alabama, bus boycott from 1955 to 1957, which began when Rosa Parks refused to abide by a municipal law requiring her to sit in the rear of the city bus and ended when the U.S. Supreme Court in *Gayle v. Browder* said she did not have to do so.

But while the politics of race was characterized by a struggle for rights, the politics of plural-ethnicity was characterized by a struggle for resources. The latter was a struggle to capture and control public office and the ability to dispense patronage and divisible and indivisible benefits. Instead of nurturing and training lawyers and plaintiffs, plural-ethnicity focused on precinct captains and patronage. While the black racial political struggle utilized constitutional lawyers as sophisticated interpreters of new constitutional meaning, those focusing on ethnicity utilized lawyers to interpret immigration rules, obtain pushcart licenses, and negotiate the bureaucratic passage from alien to citizen. Both roles were fundamentally critical, but also fundamentally different. The point is the following: when the civil rights struggle evolved from rights to resources, as it certainly did beginning substantially in the 1960s, it took with it the orientation, language, and some of the tactics of the earlier struggle for constitutional rights.

25. According to the passage, how did the struggle for resources differ from the struggle for rights?

   A. It focused on grassroots activism instead of electoral power.

   B. It emphasized control and political representation at a local level.

   C. It was dedicated to effecting changes through election to national political positions.

   D. It cooperated with newly arrived immigrant populations.

26. According to evidence put forth by the author of the passage, why was the executive branch of the government not targeted for civil rights participation in the 1950s?

   A. Early activists had little political clout on a federal level at that time.

   B. Federal policies banned lobbying of Congress by civil rights advocates.

   C. Elected officials acted according to the expressed opinions of their voters.

   D. No members of Congress were interested in enforcing new voting laws.

27. Paying particular attention to the thematic organization of the passage, which of the following statements best describes the structure of the passage?

    A. Two historical developments are described and contrasted.

    B. A historical movement is praised using two closely connected examples.

    C. A general history of a struggle is presented, with a suggestion of how it will be resolved in the future.

    D. Two different approaches to a problem are analyzed and then combined.

28. According to the author, prior to 1965, the civil rights movement on behalf of blacks was characterized by none of the following EXCEPT

    A. an emphasis on removing restrictions on black voting through court cases.

    B. a struggle to overturn the decisions of constitutional lawyers.

    C. the increasing ability of black voters to mobilize and elect black politicians to office.

    D. frequent conflict between the Congress and Supreme Court over controversial issues.

29. In the passage, the author cites the Montgomery, Alabama, bus boycott as an example of

    A. a crucial incident that marked the turn of the civil rights movement toward the goal of controlling resources.

    B. an event that was important because it began the leadership career of Martin Luther King Jr.

    C. one of the better-known battles to assert the civil rights of blacks.

    D. an event whose primary importance was its impact on the enforcement of constitutional rights.

30. According to the author, the "politics of plural-ethnicity" discussed in paragraph 4 differed from the black civil rights movement before 1965 in all of the following ways EXCEPT that it

    A. concentrated more on elections as a way to achieve important goals.

    B. initiated court cases for more sophisticated and theoretical reasons.

    C. was more concerned with the dispensation and control of patronage benefits.

    D. was more based on immigrant ethnicity in northern urban regions.

Passage VI (Questions 31–35)

The first great penal code in the Benthamite tradition, although never enacted, was prepared by an American, Edward Livingston, for the State of Louisiana in 1826. What led to the appearance of this draft code at this time in Louisiana? Many factors, doubtlessly, but conspicuously among them was the commitment of one man to the idea of codification. Livingston was a learned man, well read in Continental as well as English intellectual and social developments. He was captured by the ideas of Bentham and the ferment for legal reform and codification in revolutionary America and France. Earlier in his career as a U.S. Congressman, he sought a revision of the United States' penal law. That his code was drafted for Louisiana may be due simply to the accident that led him to leave New York and to transplant his legal and public career there.

The modern codification tradition to which the Model Penal Code (1962) belongs has its roots in the new rationalism of the 18th-century Enlightenment, which saw reason as the instrument for both understanding and mastering the world. For law, reason provided a lodestar and an instrument for reform. The ideas of the Enlightenment took hold in England as well as the Continent and led to a powerful movement toward codification of law. But it was through the work of one man, Jeremy Bentham, that these ideas had their greatest influence on law reform. Bentham's thinking on codification of criminal law had a powerful influence on every codification effort in the English-speaking world in the 19th and 20th centuries, not excluding the Model Penal Code.

Within Bentham's legacy are such concepts as law defined in advance with clarity and certainty to maximize its potential for guiding behavior; judicial discretion to make or change the law eliminated as product of uncertainty and arbitrariness; the doctrines of the criminal law and the principles of punishment justified only by their service to the purpose of the criminal law to prevent crime; penalties proportioned to the offense; and refusal to punish where it would be "groundless, inefficacious, unprofitable, or needless."

The Penal Code, breathtaking in conception and achievement, included a Code of Procedure, a Code of Evidence, a Code of Reform and Prison Discipline, and a Code of Crimes and Punishments. Livingston's unassisted completion of this task within three years was one of those prodigious, virtuoso performances that is scarcely imaginable today. His Benthamite philosophy was manifested in many of the Code's provisions, notably those relating to the judicial function. Livingston distrusted judges no less than Bentham; consequently, common-law crimes, use of common-law terms, and all means through which judges might infuse their own moral views into the definition of crimes were outlawed. The object of the Code, to leave as little as possible to judicial creativity, is apparent in its preference for exhaustive and detailed specifications of rules. Other notable characteristics of the Code include its rejection of capital punishment, its moderation of punishments, its forceful protection of freedom of speech and the rights of the accused, the prominent place it gave to reform of the offender and its provision of means to accomplish it.

31. If the author read the following statements in an article on the topic of the development of the Penal Code, with which one would she most likely agree?

   A. Edward Livingston's personal commitment to the codification of laws greatly influenced his colleagues, including Jeremy Bentham.

   B. English and Continental lawmakers agreed wholeheartedly on the need for standardization of laws during the 18th and 19th centuries.

   C. Developments in intellectual and philosophical thought during the Enlightenment were a major factor in leading to the establishment of the first penal codes.

   D. The Benthamite concept of penal codes has been highly influential in theory but rarely successful when written into law.

32. The author spends some time discussing Bentham's work on legal reform. Which of the following is NOT attributed by the author to Bentham's work on legal reform?

   I. Making sure the punishment fits the crime

   II. Outlawing unjust and arbitrary penalties

   III. Legalization of capital punishment

   A. II only

   B. III only

   C. I and III only

   D. I, II, and III

33. According to information put forth and argued by the author of the passage, which of the following was one of the primary reasons for the creation of Livingston's penal code?

   A. Influence from previous codification efforts had finally spread from other parts of the country into Louisiana.

   B. American legal figures were impressed by the legal systems in England and wished to emulate them.

   C. Livingston was inspired by intellectual and social changes and progress from abroad.

   D. Colleagues in the legal profession encouraged Livingston to develop a penal code based on the Benthamite tradition.

34. All of the following are strengths of Livingston's penal code EXCEPT

   A. specific protection of defendants' civil rights.

   B. emphasis on reform rather than on punishment.

   C. constraints on judicial discretion to modify rules and legal procedures.

   D. successful implementation and expansion of his code.

35. Assuming that the author was correct and complete in his analysis of Livingston, one of the guiding motivations for Livingston's development of a penal code was

   A. to afford broader rights and less severe punishments to convicted criminals.

   B. to decrease the possibility of judicial misinterpretation of laws.

   C. to define penalties and crimes based on common-law terms.

   D. to protect certain freedoms and civil rights of defendants.

Passage VII (Questions 36–40)

The recognition of exclusive chattels and estates has really harmed and obscured Individualism. It has led Individualism entirely astray. It has made gain, not growth, its aim, so that man has thought that the important thing is to have, and has not come to know that the important thing is to be. The true perfection of man lies not in what man has, but in what man is.

This state has crushed true Individualism, and set up an Individualism that is false. It has debarred one part of the community from being individual by starving them. It has debarred the other part of the community from being individual by putting them on the wrong road and encumbering them. Indeed, so completely has man's personality been absorbed by his trinkets and entanglements that the law has always treated offenses against a man's property with far more severity than offenses against his person.

It is clear that no authoritarian socialism will do. For while under the present system a very large number of people can lead lives of a certain amount of freedom and expression and happiness, under an industrial barrack system, or a system of economic tyranny, nobody would be able to have any such freedom at all. It is to be regretted that a portion of our community should be practically in slavery, but to propose to solve the problem by enslaving the entire community is childish. Every man must be left quite free to choose his own work.

No form of compulsion must be exercised over him. If there is, his work will not be good for him, will not be good in itself, and will not be good for others. I hardly think that any socialist, nowadays, would seriously propose that an inspector should call every morning at each house to see that each citizen rose up and did manual labor for eight hours. Humanity has moved beyond that stage and reserves such a form of life for the people whom, in a very arbitrary manner, it chooses to call criminals.

Many of the socialistic views that I have come across seem to be tainted with ideas of authority, if not of actual compulsion. Of course, authority and compulsion are out of the question. All association must be quite voluntary. It is only in voluntary associations that man is fine. It may be asked how Individualism, which is now more or less dependent on the existence of private property for its development, will benefit by the abolition of such private property. The answer is very simple. It is true that, under existing conditions, a few men who have had private means of their own, such as Byron, Shelley, Browning, Victor Hugo, Baudelaire, and others, have been able to realize their personality, more or less completely.

Not one of these men ever did a single day's work for hire. They were relieved from poverty. They had an immense advantage. The question is whether it would be for the good of Individualism that such an advantage be taken away. Let us suppose that it is taken away. What happens then to Individualism? How will it benefit? Under the new conditions Individualism will be far freer, far finer, and far more intensified than it is now. I am not talking of the great imaginatively realized Individualism of such poets as I have mentioned, but of the great actual Individualism latent and potential in all mankind.

36. The author of the passage most likely mentions Byron, Shelly, Browning, Hugo, and Baudelaire in an effort to

A. give examples of the harmful effect of money on Individualism and art.

B. call attention to the rarity of artistic genius.

C. define what is meant by the phrase "realize their personality."

D. stress the importance of financial independence.

37. Which of the following would the author be most likely to consider an example of "enslaving the entire community"?

I. South Africa under apartheid, where rights of citizenship were denied to the Black majority and granted in full only to the White minority

II. Cambodia under the Khmer Rouge, where the urban population was forcibly deported to the countryside to perform agricultural labor

III. Sweden under the Social Democrats, where all citizens pay high taxes to support extensive social programs

A. I only

B. II only

C. I and II only

D. II and III only

38. As used in the fourth paragraph of the passage, the phrase "the people whom, in a very arbitrary manner, it chooses to call criminals" implies which of the following?

A. All actions should be permitted.

B. Notions of justice are open to question.

C. No one would commit crimes in a socialist society.

D. Criminals are better suited for mandatory labor than other people.

39. Suppose for a moment that Baudelaire was actually not wealthy and that he often had to work to earn money. What relevance would this information have to the arguments posed by the author within the passage?

A. It would refute the author's claim that artists require independent wealth to create.

B. It would refute the author's claim that poets are people who can realize their own personality.

C. It would strengthen the author's claim that the acquisition of wealth leads Individualism astray.

D. The central thesis of the passage would remain equally valid.

40. Based on the information in the passage, we can assume that the author is most likely to agree that

A. most people who have sufficient private property are fully realized individuals.

B. even with sufficient private property, most people never realize their individuality.

C. artists are less likely than others to be dependent on private means to realize themselves.

D. no artist can realize himself except with substantial private means.

Verbal Reasoning Practice Test 2 Answers and Explanations

ANSWER KEY

1. A	9. C	17. B	25. B	33. C
2. B	10. C	18. D	26. C	34. D
3. D	11. D	19. D	27. A	35. B
4. C	12. A	20. B	28. A	36. D
5. C	13. B	21. B	29. D	37. B
6. B	14. C	22. D	30. B	38. B
7. D	15. C	23. D	31. C	39. D
8. B	16. A	24. C	32. B	40. B

EXPLANATIONS

Passage I: Positivism

Topic: Study of international relations
Scope: Positivists versus historico-deductivists
Purpose: To describe the conflict

Mapping the Passage:

¶1. Conflict between historico-deductivists and positivists. Critique of positivism: Tries to be objective when it's impossible.

¶2. Example: Cause of World War I unclear.

¶3. Positivists' defense: They don't pretend to be completely objective, but it's still best to be as objective as possible.

¶4. Another defense: Positivism can lead to unexpected conclusions. Author: The conflict between the two groups is good for research.

¶5. Third defense of positivism: Even if positivists are biased, historico-deductivists are too.

1. A

With a passage this difficult, just map what you can, even if you don't understand it fully. Let the questions help you by focusing on what you need to understand question by question rather than understanding the entire passage. This is a tough question, full of tough words. Since *a posteriori* is in italics, it's easy to spot. Go back to paragraph 2 to review what this is. Immediately after the phrase, the passage says that in natural sciences, lab experiments can have "nomothetic status." What must this mean? Paraphrase: Probably that the findings are assumed to be definitely true. Read on: There's a "however" keyword that contrasts international relations with science, saying that "such law-like generalizations about cause and effect are rarely if ever possible." Therefore, nomothetic status must involve "law-like generalizations," and *a posteriori* overgeneralization must *challenge* positivists' attempts to do this because the historico-deductivists consider it a "case in point." Statement I says the same, and (A) is the correct answer.

Wrong Answers:

II. Opposite. The example of World War I talks about causes, not effects.

III. Out of Scope. There's no suggestion in this passage that historico-deductivism is exempt from the problem of *a posteriori* overdetermination. Therefore, the fact that the positivism is susceptible to this criticism by itself doesn't suggest that the historico-deductivist approach is inherently better.

2. B

Read the word in context. The sentence in which the word appears immediately follows the positivists' "moderate rule," which says that "the propensity to error should make us cautious, but not so desperate that we fear to come as close as possible to apodictic findings." Paraphrase, keeping the main positivist idea of a scientific approach in mind: Just because we can't eliminate error doesn't mean that we shouldn't try to work scientifically. What does the "torch" that the positivists want to grasp represent, then? Predict: The conclusions that they think they'll find. Three choices can be eliminated, leaving you with (B). You know that (B) must be true in any case from the mention of nomothetic propositions in paragraph 2: they're described as absolute scientific findings, exactly the sort of thing that the positivists want. Pay close attention whenever a rule or definition is mentioned. The MCAT loves to test you on things that are clearly defined but in a difficult context.

Wrong Answers:

(A) Faulty Use of Detail. The positivists acknowledge that error can't be eliminated but believe that they can still grasp the "torch": the scientific certainty that they're after.

(C) Distortion. The positivists aren't trying to grasp political phenomena; they're trying to grasp an *understanding* of political phenomena.

(D) Distortion. As above, positivists don't want to get a handle on methodological commitments; they want to use methodology in order to get to the "torch" of understanding.

3. D

Go back to paragraph 2 to review. Historico-deductivists believe that *a posteriori* overdetermination presents some sort of problem for positivists trying to find nomothetic propositions. They also believe that nomothetic propositions, the "lawlike generalizations" used in science, aren't applicable to the study of international relations because one event can have many possible causes. What assumption is necessary to bridge these two beliefs? Predict: Nomothetic propositions can't explain events by relying on multiple causes. If they could, there presumably wouldn't be a problem with applying them to international relations. (D) paraphrases this.

Wrong Answers:

(A) Faulty Use of Detail. While historico-deductivists probably do believe this, it's not an assumption. Try denying it: Even if they didn't believe this, or if they believed that positivists *could* provide a fully scientific account of World War I, their argument about overdetermination wouldn't necessarily fall apart.

(B) Distortion. The historico-deductivists probably believe that complex events aren't susceptible to the scientific analysis that the positivists are trying to use, but they must believe that they can be analyzed somehow—otherwise, they'd be out of work!

(C) Out of Scope. The passage suggests no distinction between replicability and verifiability. Since both of these are part of the scientific method, it's an irrelevant distinction.

4. C

Where is Dougherty mentioned? Go back to the end of paragraph 1. Immediately above the quote in the question is the argument that "the precision of an answer cannot exceed that of its question." The implication is that positivists want certainty where there is none. Tie it back into the metaphor: The "clocks and necessity" represent the certainty positivists want, while the "clouds and contingency" represent the uncertainty that actually exists. Only one answer choice deals with a positivist study, and it's a study of international relations, which the critics of positivists believe is full of uncertainty. (C) must be correct.

Wrong Answers:

(A) Out of Scope. A historico-deductivist study wouldn't be looking for "clocks and necessity," since the approach of the historico-deductivists is fuzzier than that of the positivists.

(B) Out of Scope. As in (A), Dougherty leveled this criticism against "the positivists who want clocks and necessity," not against historico-deductivists.

(D) Out of Scope. While the chemist *would* probably be looking for "clocks and necessity," there's reason to believe, especially from the discussion in paragraph 2, that historico-deductivists would acknowledge natural science as a field where this precision is justified.

5.   C

For this application question, review the "moderate rule" from the third paragraph. Paraphrase the rule: The likelihood of error should make positivists cautious but not so cautious that they give up trying to find scientific explanations as best as they can. Look for a situation that matches with this: (C) fits. Just because a worker can't earn a lot of money doesn't mean he shouldn't try to earn as much as he can.

Wrong Answers:

(A) Out of Scope. The principle behind this seems to be that the opinion of someone who creates a work is more important than that of anyone else judging the work, which is irrelevant to Williams's rule.

(B) Out of Scope. This principle behind this is most likely that different kinds of intelligence can be equal, which has nothing to do Williams's principle of trying to do the best that one individually can.

(D) Opposite. If anything, this is the opposite of what Williams suggests. The principle behind this situation seems to suggest that one should hold back from acting because of possible dangers, while Williams says that one should do as much as one can.

6.   B

A quick scan of the answer choices shows a variety of professions. Who would be most likely to write a passage about a disagreement over how to study international relations? Predict: someone who studied international relations. (B) immediately fits the bill.

Wrong Answers:

(A) Distortion. Though history is mentioned frequently in the passage, it's always in the context of international relations. The author argues that the debate is "among international relations scholars," so a history professor would be less likely to write about it than an international relations professor.

(C) Distortion. While diplomats are *involved* in international relations, they're not necessarily dedicated to the *study* of it. A professor of international relations would be more likely to be interested in the academic side of the topic.

(D) Out of Scope. There's no reason to think that a journalist would be concerned with or so knowledgeable about an academic debate on the study of international relations.

Passage II: Fossil Fuels
Topic: Hydrocarbon reserves
Scope: How they're formed and how to find them
Purpose: To describe

Mapping the Passage:
   ¶1. How hydrocarbons form in pockets underground
   ¶2. Background on global dependence on fossil fuels: constantly increasing
   ¶3. Structural traps and stratigraphic traps
   ¶4. New sources of hydrocarbons difficult to locate: rock formations
   ¶5. Most new oil in stratigraphic traps; method: seismic exploration
   ¶6. Problems with seismic method
   ¶7. New developments: better?

7. D

To answer this global question, use the topic, scope, and purpose to make a prediction (forget about the first part of the question; it's irrelevant). The author discusses how hydrocarbon reserves are formed (especially in paragraphs 1 and 3) and how they can be located (throughout the passage but especially in the second half of the passage). (D) repeats this nearly word for word.

Wrong Answers:

(A) Faulty Use of Detail. This answer says nothing about the location of reserves, which is, after all, the topic of the passage. This is a classic main idea wrong answer; it is too narrow a detail to describe the entire passage.

(B) Faulty Use of Detail. This detail omits reference to how hydrocarbons are formed and the problems of seismic exploration.

(C) Faulty Use of Detail. Although the fifth paragraph states that "structural traps tend to be easier to locate," this is also a detail and not the main idea.

8. B

This is a detail question; "According to the passage . . ." tips you off. Where are difficulties mentioned? Go back to paragraph 6. The last sentence of paragraph 6 states the same thing the question does: that it's difficult to distinguish reflections between the two materials because of the background noise. The beginning of the sentence gives the reason: "the density contrasts between oil-bearing sandstones and the shales that provide stratigraphic seals for the oil are often very small." (B) says the same.

Wrong Answers:

(A) Faulty Use of Detail. While the author mentions this in the same paragraph, it's used in the context of how resolution can be improved, not why it's difficult to distinguish between the sandstone and shale.

(C) Faulty Use of Detail. This is part of the "primary limitation of the seismic method" that the author discusses towards the beginning of the paragraph, not the direct cause of the particular problem in the question.

(D) Out of Scope. Thinness has to do with the primary limitation of the method, not the problem of distinguishing between the different reflections mentioned in the question.

9. C

This is an evaluation question that essentially asks, "Why?" Review the lines in context. Immediately after defining how stratigraphic traps are formed, the author provides the example by stating, "For example . . ." (note the keyword!). Predict the use: The author is simply giving an example of how the traps are formed. That's what (C) says. Note that the word *illustrate* is another way of saying "give an example." When you're looking for an answer that indicates example, focus on this word.

Wrong Answers:

(A) Out of Scope. In the example, the author doesn't provide any contrast to structural traps.

(B) Faulty Use of Detail. The author does explain this but only to explain how stratigraphic traps are formed. This is another part of the example rather than the point of the example.

(D) Faulty Use of Detail. The difficulty of locating stratigraphic traps isn't mentioned until paragraph 6. If you go to the wrong paragraph, you'll get the wrong answer. The problem is not a matter of content but of passage structure.

10. C

A scattered detail question. Either eliminate wrong answer choices or look for a choice that sticks out as correct. (C) should jump out: Since not all traps are stratigraphic, it wouldn't make sense for the author to have said that oil couldn't be extracted without a density contrast between reservoir rocks and a stratigraphic seal.

Wrong Answers:

(A) Opposite. The author states in paragraph 1 that "hydrocarbons . . . will eventually reach the surface and be lost unless they encounter impermeable rocks."

(B) Opposite. The passage begins by saying that "hydrocarbons migrate upward," and the author ties oil reserves to hydrocarbons in paragraphs 1 and 4. So it's reasonable to believe that it's not possible to get oil if an original source of hydrocarbons isn't present.

(D) Opposite. The first paragraph of the text states that hydrocarbons can't be extracted unless they are trapped within highly permeable rocks.

11. D

Where are carbonate reservoirs mentioned? Review the beginning of paragraph 6: "The most common stratigraphic traps (with the possible exception of carbonate reservoirs) are in sandstone layers that are much thinner than a seismic wavelet." What's the implication? Predict: Carbonate reservoirs are in layers that *aren't* much thinner than a seismic wavelet. (D) comes close to this.

Wrong Answers:

(A) Out of Scope. Density has nothing to do with the thickness of the layer, which is what we're concerned with in this part of the passage.

(B) Distortion. While carbonate layers might be *easier* to find than other stratigraphic traps because of their relative thickness, the author gives no indication that they are in fact *easy* to find.

(C) Out of Scope. The author says nothing about the importance (or lack thereof) of carbonate traps.

12. A

What is the author's opinion of seismology? She describes problems with it in paragraph 6, but paragraph 7 discusses new developments that could make it better. Predict an answer that says both, then match it with (A).

Wrong Answers:

(B) Distortion. Though seismology has limitations, there's no indication that it is intrinsically flawed. If it were, the author would not argue for its improvement.

(C) Out of Scope. Nothing at all is said about profitability, and *effective* is too strong a word for a method that the author says is still limited.

(D) Out of Scope. There's nothing in here about theory, and seismology *is* effective, if limited.

13. B

What sort of development would improve seismic exploration the most? Predict: something that overcomes the seismic method's primary limitation. In paragraph 6, the author states that the primary limitation is resolution and that the wavelets are too large to be useful in discovering stratigraphic traps. Therefore, something that allows for higher resolution would be a major development, and if it overcomes the problem of attenuation that the author mentioned, it will sidestep the current problems with high frequencies. (B) fits.

Wrong Answers:

(A) Opposite. While it would be good for the frequency to increase, increasing the *attenuation* of the wavelength only exacerbates the problem with high frequencies that the author mentions.

(C) Distortion. While this would be an improvement, since the author says background noise is a problem, eliminating it wouldn't be as big an improvement as something that overcame the "principal limitation" of seismology.

(D) Out of Scope. The origin of stratigraphic traps has nothing to do with solving the primary problem.

Passage III: Pop Music

Topic: Popular music
Scope: Its social functions
Purpose: To explain and support

Mapping the Passage:

¶1. Intro rock and roll: Youths identify with it.

¶2. Pop creates identity and community.

¶3. Allows individual identification.

¶4. Also helps express and manage feelings.

¶5. Organizes sense of time; important to the definition of youth.

14. C

Where is classical music mentioned in the passage? It isn't! How could we figure out anything about classical music, then? Predict: By relating it to music in general. In paragraph 5, the author notes that "one of the effects of all music—not just pop—is to focus our attention on the feeling of time and intensify our experience of the present." Therefore, both pop music and classical music must focus attention on time, since this is a general quality of music. (C) says the same. Don't panic when a question throws a curve ball in the form of an unfamiliar situation or of terminology that's not in the passage. If it's in a question, it can be related back to the passage; you just need to figure out how.

Wrong Answers:

(A) Faulty Use of Detail. This is a social function of popular music, but the author doesn't suggest that it's a function of other types of music.

(B) Faulty Use of Detail. The author uses this phrase to describe "popular love songs" but not music in general.

(D) Faulty Use of Detail. The author argues in paragraph 5 that pop music defines what youth is, but he doesn't argue a similar function for music in general.

15. C

This is a question about the author's tone. Identifying the author's tone (positive, negative, or neutral) helps narrow down answer choices; with a quick vertical scan, you can look for an answer that matches it. Here the author is positive. In paragraph 4, he says that the love songs "give shape and voice to emotions that otherwise cannot be expressed without embarrassment or incoherence." He also notes that the songs express feeling "for us in interesting and involving ways." Scan the answer choices and note that only (C) is positive and, thus, the right answer.

Wrong Answers:

(A) Opposite. The author argues that love songs are the antidotes to banal language by expressing the same ideas in interesting ways. He certainly doesn't think they're boring.

(B) Opposite. The author argues that popular love songs help us express our feelings. They don't embarrass us.

(D) Opposite. The author clearly believes that popular love songs have an important social function: the management and expression of feelings.

16. A

Here's an evaluation question; more specifically, a function question. Why does the author discuss sports in paragraph 2? Go back to review: The author says that "music, like sport, is clearly a setting in which people directly experience community . . . ." Sport is used as an example of a case in which something similar happens—or, in other words, a parallel, which is exactly what (A) says.

Wrong Answers:

(B) Opposite. Sport is used as a comparison, not a contrast.

(C) Out of Scope. There's no assumption mentioned that could be challenged, and the reference to sport is not used as a challenge but as an analogy.

(D) Opposite. The mention of sport is used to elaborate on the *same* idea, not to introduce a new one.

17. B

What does the author do in the last paragraph? Predict from your map: The author describes the third function of popular music—the organization of time and its relevance to the definition of youth. (B) captures the author's focus on youth.

Wrong Answers:

(A) Distortion. The author briefly discusses the experience of youth but only in the context of how youth relates to popular music, which this choice leaves out entirely.

(C) Out of Scope. This choice tries to capitalize on words familiar from the passage: "organization" and "youth." Time is organized, and youth is defined through popular music, but nothing at all is said about the organization of youth movements. Be careful about matching words. Familiar wording should be used to figure out what part of the passage to review, not to answer the question from the familiarity alone.

(D) Faulty Use of Detail. Though the author does discuss the relationship between music and time, it's done in the context of how music relates to youth, a topic that this choice completely omits.

18. D

Where is the creation of identity discussed? Go back to paragraphs 2 and 3. Review the author's main points: Pop music helps us "directly experience community" and, at the same time, has an "individualizing" effect. The author uses these ideas to show how identity is created through pop music. (D) paraphrases the idea that pop music operates on the communal and individual levels.

Wrong Answers:

(A) Out of Scope. Although the first paragraph states that "larger and larger numbers of youth" began identifying with pop music, the passage doesn't discuss whether pop songs were popular with older listeners.

(B) Faulty Use of Detail. In paragraph 4, the author discusses how love songs affect language but to support the idea that pop music helps to manage feelings, not to support pop music's role of creating identity.

(C) Opposite. The author says that pop songs are "open to appropriation for personal use in a way that other popular cultural forms . . . are not." Pop music is therefore *unique* in this way.

19. D

Why does the author believe that popular music is important for social organization in youth? Go back and review paragraph 5, where he says that it's because good music has the ability to stop time with "no memory or anxiety about what has come before us, what will come after." What would weaken this? Predict: something that said that good music *doesn't* stop time. (D) does just this.

Wrong Answers:

(A) Out of Scope. It may be true that songs incorporate nostalgic lyrics (he mentions "nostalgia" in the last paragraph), but that has nothing to do with what the author says about why the songs are important for social organization.

(B) Opposite. This supports, and in fact paraphrases, the author's argument that "youth is experienced . . . through an impatience for time to pass and a regret that it is doing so."

(C) Opposite. This would also support the author's argument about youth and, in particular, the author's claim that "we invest most in popular music when we are teenagers and young adults."

Passage IV: School Tracks
Topic: Tracking
Scope: Advantages and disadvantages
Purpose: To argue against tracking

Mapping the Passage:
  ¶1. Tracking contradicts the philosophy that all can learn. Administrators like it.
  ¶2. Pros and cons, esp. tracking can "dumb down" lower-level tracks.
  ¶3. Defines tracking; it affects school experience.
  ¶4. Major problem: Students in lower tracks can't enter higher-level classes.

20. B

An incorporation question. How would the author's argument be affected if tracked students did better than their nontracked counterparts? The question tells you that some part of the author's argument would be weakened, so you just need to find an answer choice summarizing an argument the author makes against tracking on the basis of performance. (B) is just such a choice: The author argues in paragraph 2 that tracking encourages "dumbing down."

Wrong Answers:

(A) Faulty Use of Detail. Yes, the author makes this statement, but it's relevant not to student performance but to student experience, so it wouldn't be weakened by the new evidence.

(C) Faulty Use of Detail. Again this is a statement the author makes, but it's in regard to why administrators like tracking—easier scheduling—not related to how students do on standardized tests.

(D) Faulty Use of Detail. This argument, found in paragraph 2, is presented as a belief of proponents of tracking. This is not the *author's* argument, as the author suggests that "dumbing down" is a likely outcome.

21. B

This is a main idea question; go to the purpose as you wrote it. The author argues that tracking in schools leads to disadvantages for the students. Thus, the author is not in favor of tracking. Only (B) accurately encompasses what the author is arguing.

Wrong Answers:

(A) Out of Scope. This oversteps the scope of the passage. The author never actually argues that tracking should be eliminated, only that it has some negative consequences.

(C) Faulty Use of Detail. Stress level is mentioned at the end of paragraph 3, but this is not the main point of the passage. Never choose a detail as the answer to a main idea question.

(D) Faulty Use of Detail. Scheduling is mentioned at the end of paragraph 1, but it's not the main point of the passage.

22. D

Review the argument referenced by the question: At the beginning of paragraph 1, the author argues, "If certain students are better in certain subjects, they must be allowed to excel in those areas and not be relegated to an inferior class." Why does the author believe this is the case? Paraphrase the argument: If students are assigned to a lower track, the school is assuming that they're unable to perform at a higher level, and they might be held back when the teacher has to slow down the class. Look for evidence that would support this, starting with statement III, which appears in three out of the four choices. Statement III would strengthen the author's argument: Lower-track classes that couldn't finish the work they were given would be an example of exactly what the author is discussing at the end of paragraph 4. Eliminate (A). Statement I also supports the author's argument, echoing the argument at the end of paragraph 4 that lower-track students find it hard to take

AP courses. Only (D) remains, and there's no need to check statement II.

Wrong Answers:

II. Opposite. If students in tracked classes scored higher on standardized tests, this data would support the administrators' argument that tracking helps students and would weaken the author's argument that tracking holds some students back.

23. D

Another scattered detail question. Either eliminate or look for a choice that seems wrong. While the first three are mentioned as criteria for tracking in the passage, (D) pops out as being way off base. While the author notes in paragraph 3 that "there are differences . . . in . . . how talkative and energetic the classroom is," depending on tracking, there's no suggestion that students are tracked *based* on how talkative or energetic they are individually.

Wrong Answers:

(A) Opposite. The author mentions grades as a criterion in the opening lines of paragraph 3.

(B) Opposite. The author cites "academic ability" as a criterion for tracking in paragraph 3.

(C) Opposite. The author discusses the way students get locked in to higher tracks (i.e., AP courses) with honors courses (paragraph 4).

24. C

The strategy for many application questions, such as this one, is simply remembering that the author believes his own argument. How would the author respond to a situation in which a student underachieves because of boredom in a way that would strengthen the author's argument? Predict: She'd argue that the student was put in a track that isn't sufficiently challenging, a problem discussed at the end of paragraph 4. (C) rewards the careful prediction.

Wrong Answers:

(A) Opposite. The author doesn't address the possibility that students might be tracked too high; she's far more concerned with the "dumbing down" of classrooms.

(B) Out of Scope. There's nothing in the passage to suggest that the author considers lack of motivation in students a particular problem that requires disciplining.

(D) Distortion. Though the author might agree that the student should be in a higher track, the higher track doesn't necessarily need to include AP classes, which represent a very specific situation mentioned in paragraph 4.

Passage V: Civil Rights

Topic: Civil rights movement
Scope: Its origin and relation to pluralist politics
Purpose: To compare and contrast the methods used in civil rights movement with those in pluralist politics

Mapping the Passage:

¶1. Civil rights movement began near the same time new immigrants banded together (plurality politics).

¶2. Importance of constitutional interpretation to race politics.

¶3. Civil rights movement fought through courts; ex: Parks.

¶4. Civil rights movement vs. plural-ethnicity politics (struggle for resources thru politics).

25. B

Resources is the keyword that tells you to research the immigrant rights method and how it differed from the civil rights one. The author clearly tells us that while the civil rights movement worked through the courts, the immigrant movement focused on involvement in "local political clubs" (paragraph 1), "public office," "patronage," and "precinct captains" (paragraph 4). Only (B) and (C) incorporate this idea of politics, and of these, only (B) focuses on the local politics that the author suggests when discussing "local political clubs and machines" and "precinct captains and patronage."

Wrong Answers:

(A) Opposite. The author argues that the immigrants' fight for resources *did* involve electoral power.

(C) Opposite. While this choice does include a focus on politics, it specifically mentions national politics, while the author discusses "local political clubs and machines."

(D) Faulty Use of Detail. It was the newly arrived immigrant population that struggled for resources, so it doesn't make sense to say immigrants "cooperated" with themselves.

26. C

Review the author's discussion of the executive branch, which appears in paragraph 3. The author argues that the presidency and Congress didn't get involved in the civil rights movement "because the political constituencies supporting their elections did not favor such participation." Paraphrase: The president and Congress didn't help with the civil rights movement because it was politically unpopular. (C) is another way of saying this, since "politically unpopular" would mean that voters didn't like it.

Wrong Answers:

(A) Out of Scope. The national clout of activists is not discussed.

(B) Out of Scope. Lobbying is not discussed, and the author is clear that members of the legislative branch failed to act because their voters didn't want them to, not because of lobbyists.

(D) Distortion. Although the author indicates that Congress represented its voter base in not supporting civil rights, he doesn't support the extreme statement that "no members of Congress were interested."

27. A

This is a rare question that asks about the structure of the whole passage. Use your map to refresh your memory of how the passage is put together, then predict. Paragraphs 2 and 3 describe attempts to gain rights through the courts in the civil rights movement, while paragraph 4 contrasts this effort with attempts to gain resources through politics of various ethnicities. (A), though lacking in specifics, closely matches the structure of the prediction.

Wrong Answers:

(B) Out of Scope. The author doesn't praise the movements, and he describes two completely different movements, not a single movement with two examples.

(C) Out of Scope. The author gives a general history of the civil rights struggle but gives no indication of how it will play out in the future. This answer choice also leaves out the political struggle discussed in the passage.

(D) Distortion. The author discusses two different approaches, but they're different approaches to *different* problems, not the same problem.

28. A

Notice the unusual wording of this question: "none of the following EXCEPT." What exactly are we looking for? We want the one statement that *does* characterize the civil rights movement prior to 1965. This is a detail question, so start by finding where 1965 is mentioned in the passage. The author says in paragraph 3 that "a 'civil rights' movement developed that saw 95 years (1870–1965) devoted to establishing the privilege of blacks to vote unencumbered by racial barriers." Paraphrase: Before 1965, the civil rights movement was primarily interested in giving blacks the right to vote freely. (A) fits the bill. Make sure you read questions carefully and even reword them if you need to. You can't get a correct answer if you don't know the correct question.

Wrong Answers:

(B) Opposite. The author argues that the movement "created a cadre of constitutional lawyers who became in a real sense the focal points of the civil rights struggle." In other words, the author likely believes that constitutional lawyers were the ones struggling to overturn unjust decisions, not the other way around.

(C) Faulty Use of Detail. This characterizes the civil rights movement using the language the author reserves for the plural-ethnicity's struggle for *resources* in paragraph 4.

(D) Out of Scope. The author never discusses any conflict between Congress and the Supreme Court.

29. D

Go back to the third paragraph, which discusses the Montgomery bus boycott started by Rosa Parks. This situation is an example of what? Answer: An important civil

rights "battle" in which Constitutional lawyers and a court case "became in a real sense the focal points." That's pretty much what (D) says, though in a more general way.

Wrong Answers:

(A) Faulty Use of Detail. Rosa Parks represents a struggle for rights rather than resources.

(B) Out of Scope. Martin Luther King Jr. isn't mentioned in the passage; this choice tries to play on your outside knowledge. Remember to stick only to what is said and is necessarily implied by the passage.

(C) Out of Scope. Though it may very well be one of the better-known battles, the author doesn't suggest anywhere that this is the case, and the example isn't making this point.

30. B

Since this scattered detail question deals with the main contrast in the passage, review the basics: The civil rights movement fought for rights through the courts, while the movement of "plural ethnicity" fought for resources through politics. While three answer choices fit with the summary and with details from paragraphs 1 and 4, (B) says that the plurality (immigrant) movement used the courts to advance its ends, while the author says that this was a trait of the *civil rights* movement. In scattered detail questions such as this, be on the lookout for an answer that contradicts the author's point of view or distorts a detail from another part of the passage.

Wrong Answers:

(A) Opposite. This is exactly what the pluralistic movement did; therefore, it is a way in which the two movements differed.

(C) Opposite. This answer paraphrases the author's point that "plural-ethnicity focused on precinct captains and patronage," which the civil rights movement didn't do.

(D) Opposite. Paragraph 1 specifies that pluralist politics, "especially in the northern urban areas, was infused with… ethnicity." Nevertheless, the main reason (D) is wrong is because the black civil rights movement was more based in the South.

Passage VI: Penal Code

Topic: Model Penal Code
Scope: Origins, especially Livingston and Bentham
Purpose: To describe

Mapping the Passage:

¶1. Introduce Livingston's background and penal code.
¶2. Intellectual tradition leading to the Model Penal Code; Bentham
¶3. Bentham's concepts
¶4. Details of Livingston's penal code

31. C

For this broad inference question, review the author's main ideas: The author spends most of the passage discussing the traditions and people that led to the Model Penal Code. The beginning of paragraph 2 says that "the Model Penal Code . . . has its roots in . . . Enlightenment." (C) paraphrases this closely, echoing the author's point.

Wrong Answers:

(A) Out of Scope. The author never suggests that Livingston influenced his colleagues, and this answer reverses the order of influence between Livingston and Bentham. Bentham came before Livingston and influenced Livingston's work.

(B) Distortion. The author says in paragraph 2 that there was a "powerful movement toward codification of law" in both of these places but doesn't mention lawmakers specifically, nor is it suggested that they agreed wholeheartedly—a rather extreme statement.

(D) Opposite. The Model Penal Code is based on the law reforms that stemmed from Jeremy Bentham's ideas. The Penal Code has certainly been successful.

32. B

Where will ideas attributed to Bentham's work be found? Predict: Probably in the monster of a sentence that is paragraph 3, which starts out, "Within Bentham's legacy are such concepts as. . . ." Statements I and II are mentioned in the list. Statement III is not mentioned in the third

paragraph and runs counter to Livingston's prohibition of capital punishment in his code, which was presumably borrowed from Bentham's ideas. (B) must be correct.

Wrong Answers:

I. Opposite. According to the passage, one of Bentham's legacies is "penalties proportioned to the offense," so this choice would be attributed to him.
II. Opposite. The passage also states that Bentham eliminated judicial discretion to remove "uncertainty and arbitrariness."

33. C

Where are the reasons for Livingston's creation of his penal code described? Review paragraph 1. The author says that "many factors" were responsible and then describes Livingston's commitment to the idea. Choice (C) paraphrases the author's point that Livingston "was captured by the ideas of Bentham and the ferment for legal reform and codification in revolutionary America and France."

Wrong Answers:

(A) Out of Scope. There's nothing in the passage about ideas spreading to Louisiana. In fact, the author suggests that the only reason Livingston developed his code in Louisiana is that he happened to be living there at the time.
(B) Out of Scope. How can you get to "American legal figures" from the very specific question about Livingston?
(D) Out of Scope. The author emphasizes that the code came about as "the commitment of one man to the idea of codification" and states in paragraph 4 that Livingston's creation of the code was "unassisted," which means that Livingston's colleagues had nothing to do with it.

34. D

A scattered detail question—though not too scattered, since you know that the strengths of Livingston's code are mentioned in the second half of paragraph 4. All are mentioned except (D), which is specifically contradicted in paragraph 1 by the author's note that Livingston's code was "never enacted."

Wrong Answers:

(A) Opposite. The author notes that protection of "the rights of the accused" is part of Livingston's code.

(B) Opposite. The author also mentions "the prominent place [Livingston's code] gave to reform."

(C) Opposite. The author states that "Livingston distrusted judges no less than Bentham" and notes that the point of the code was "to leave as little as possible to judicial creativity."

35.   B

Why did Livingston want to create the code? The author gives several reasons, so review the basics in paragraphs 1 and 4 and look for an answer that fits. (B) echoes paragraph 4: The point of the code was "to leave as little as possible to judicial creativity" and to ensure that "all means through which judges might infuse their own moral views into the definition of crimes were outlawed."

Wrong Answers:

(A) Faulty Use of Detail. While the rights of criminals was a characteristic of the code, there's no indication that it was one of the guiding motivations. The author states explicitly that restricting judges' latitude was *the* object of the code.

(C) Opposite. The author notes that "use of common-law terms" was outlawed in Livingston's code.

(D) Faulty Use of Detail. Though these are also described as characteristics of the code, like (A), they're not explicitly mentioned as reasons for creating the code.

Passage VII: Individualism

Topic: Individuality and private property
Scope: How private property reduces individuality
Purpose: To argue for abolishment of private property

Mapping the Passage:

¶1. Private property has harmed Individualism.

¶2. State crushed true individualism, created false one? Law protects property, not person (Note: The question mark says you don't really understand the paragraph so will just note interesting words.)

¶3. Socialism won't work—no freedom.

¶4. Compulsion won't work.

¶5. Socialism entails authority, compulsion (not good); associations must be voluntary; abolish private property? Ex. of people who were individuals although had private property.

¶6. Argues that individualism will benefit from the elimination of personal property.

36.   D

Where are these individuals mentioned? Look over your map of paragraph 5. These were all individuals who were able to maximize their individuality because they were so rich that they didn't have to work. Only (A) and (D) involve money, and (D) alone fits with the author's overall point in the paragraph.

Wrong Answers:

(A) Opposite. While this choice does talk about money, and while the author's overall point is that property should be abolished, in this paragraph the author is giving examples of artists who had an "immense advantage" by being rich. In those artists' cases, money must be *helpful* to Individualism.

(B) Out of Scope. While the author might believe that genius is rare, the scope of the paragraph is money and its advantages to Individualism.

(C) Distortion. The author does define this; it's simply Individualism. The focus of the paragraph is on money, however.

37.   B

Where does the author use the phrase mentioned in the question? It's in paragraph 3, where the author is arguing against compulsory socialism. Instead, the author argues that "every man must be left quite free to choose his own work." Look for choices that exemplify compulsory socialism. Start with statement II, which appears in three choices: In this example, part of the population is forced to perform a certain type of labor, which certainly would qualify as compulsory socialism. Look at statement I: No socialism is suggested in this example, only segregation.

Statement III represents socialism, but there's no suggestion that it's *compulsory* socialism. (B) must be correct.

Wrong Answers:

I. Distortion. In this example, the white minority still has a life of freedom, meaning the "entire community" has not been enslaved.

III. Out of Scope. The author equates being forced to do a particular type of work, not paying high taxes, with slavery.

38. B

Find the phrase mentioned in the question: it's in paragraph 4. Review the context: The author argues that "humanity has moved beyond" enforced manual labor, which is saved for the criminals, who are labeled as such "in a very arbitrary manner." He clearly thinks that the definition of "criminal" is far from precise. That's your prediction, and it matches (B) very nicely.

Wrong Answers:

(A) Out of Scope. Though the author thinks that the label of "criminal" might be arbitrary, he doesn't say anything about permitting all actions.

(C) Out of Scope. The author never suggests that a socialist society would eliminate crime.

(D) Distortion. The author says that society reserves compulsory labor for criminals, but he doesn't go so far as to say that criminals are better suited for it than are others.

39. D

Baudelaire is used as an example of what? Answer: Someone who was able to cultivate his genius because he didn't have to hold down a day job. If Baudelaire *had* needed to work, this would weaken the author's idea of wealth as an advantage to attaining individuality. However, since he's one of five examples, it wouldn't weaken the idea all that much; the author would have plenty to fall back on. With or without Baudelaire, the argument is still valid.

Wrong Answers:

(A) Distortion. As already noted, losing Baudelaire would weaken the argument by one, but the author would still have Byron, Shelley, Browning, and Hugo as evidence.

(B) Out of Scope. Even if Baudelaire had needed to work, he would still be a poet who recognized his own personality.

(C) Faulty Use of Detail. Baudelaire doesn't tie into this part of the argument.

40. B

This is an inference question with no hint as to specifics, which means that the answer will probably tie into the author's main idea. Predict: Compulsory socialism is bad, but private property should be eliminated because it gets in the way of individuality. (B) fits most closely. The author believes that though a few people are able to achieve individuality with the help of wealth, "mankind generally" is a different matter.

Wrong Answers:

(A) Distortion. While the author mentions a few artists who were exceptions to the rule, for most people, private property (i.e., wealth) impedes individuality.

(C) Opposite. The author only mentions artists who *were* dependent on private means to achieve their individuality.

(D) Distortion. The extreme word *no* should raise a red flag in your mind, since such answers are almost always wrong. In any case, the author doesn't say that the only way to self-realization is through wealth.

Verbal Reasoning
Practice Test 3

Time—60 minutes

Directions: There are seven passages in this Verbal Reasoning test. Each passage is followed by a set of questions. After reading a passage, select the one best answer to each question. If you are not certain of an answer, eliminate the alternatives that you know to be incorrect and then select an answer from the remaining alternatives.

Passage I (Questions 1–7)

Suspicious as they are of American intentions, and bolstered by court rulings that seem to give them license to seek out and publish any and all government secrets, the media's distrust of our government, combined with their limited understanding of the world at large, damages our ability to design and conduct good policy in ways that the media rarely imagine.

The leak through which sensitive information flows from the government to the press is detrimental to policy insofar as it almost completely precludes the possibility of serious discussion. Leaders often say one thing in public and quite another thing in private conversation. The fear that anything they say, even in what is construed as a private forum, may appear in print, makes many people, whether our own government officials or the leaders of foreign countries, unwilling to speak their minds.

Must we be content with the restriction of our leaders' policy discussions to a handful of people who trust each other, thus limiting the richness and variety of ideas that could be brought forward through a larger group because of the nearly endemic nature of this problem? And along with the limiting of ideas, we have less reliable information to analyze. It is vitally important for the leaders of the United States to know the real state of affairs internationally, and this can occur only if foreign leaders feel free to speak their minds to our diplomats. This cannot occur when leaders are fearful of finding their private thoughts published in newspapers, and therefore they do not share their real beliefs (let alone their secrets) unless they are certain that confidences will be respected.

Until recently, it looked as if the media had convinced the public that journalists were more reliable than the government; thus, many citizens came to believe that the media were the *best* sources of information. When the media challenged a governmental official, the public presumed that the official was in the wrong. However, this may be changing. With the passage of time, the media have lost their luster. They—having grown large and powerful—provoke the same public skepticism that other large institutions in society do. A series of media scandals has contributed to this. Many Americans have concluded that the media are no more credible than the government, and public opinion surveys reflect much ambivalence about the press.

While leaks are generally defended by media officials on the grounds of the public's "right to know," in reality they are part of the Washington political power game, as well as part of the policy process. The "leaker" may be currying favor with the media, or may be planting information to influence policy. In the first case, he is helping himself by enhancing the prestige of a journalist; in the second, he is using the media as a stage for his preferred policies. In either instance, it closes the circle: the leak begins with a political motive, is advanced by a politicized media, and continues because of politics. Although some of the journalists think *they* are doing the work, they are more often than not instruments of the process, not prime movers. The media must be held accountable for their activities, just like every other significant institution in our society, and the media must be forced to earn the public's trust.

1. Based on the information in the passage, with which of the following statements would the author most likely agree?

   A. Keeping the public uninformed is warranted in certain situations.
   B. The public has a right to know the real state of foreign affairs.
   C. The fewer the number of people involved in policy discussions, the better.
   D. Leaders give up their right to privacy when they are elected.

2. The passage suggests that press exposés of the private thoughts of foreign officials do NOT result in U.S. leaders having a better grasp of foreign affairs because

   A. U.S. leaders are already privy to the private thoughts of foreign leaders.
   B. foreign officials begin to view their American counterparts as untrustworthy.
   C. foreign officials do not reveal their secrets to the press.
   D. the information that reaches the press about policy discussions is unreliable.

3. Imagine you are an opponent of the author and disagree with her conclusions. In an upcoming written rebuttal, you want to address the author's best-supported claims first. For which of the following claims does the passage provide some supporting evidence or explanation?

   A. The media rarely understand that their actions damage America's ability to conduct foreign policy.
   B. Leaks can be an intentional part of the policy process.
   C. Every significant institution in society besides the media is held accountable for its activities.
   D. The media is suspicious of the intentions of the American government.

4. Implicit in the author's argument that leaks result in far more limited and unreliable policy discussions with foreign leaders is the idea that

   A. leaks should be considered breaches of trust and therefore immoral.
   B. leaks have occurred throughout the history of politics.
   C. foreign and U.S. leaders discussed policy without inhibition before the rise of the mass media.
   D. leaders fear the public would react negatively if it knew the real state of affairs.

5. In the context of the fifth paragraph, the term "prime movers" would most accurately refer to

    A. U.S. officials who pass on sensitive information to the media.

    B. journalists who are attempting to enhance their own prestige.

    C. media executives who use their own journalists to further political causes.

    D. the unwritten rules that govern the flow of leaked information in Washington.

6. Leaked information typically comes to journalists anonymously since the government official leaking the information fears reprisal. What relevance does this have to the passage?

    A. It supports the claim that the "leaker" plants information to influence policy.

    B. It supports the claim that journalists are more reliable than the government.

    C. It weakens the claim that the media can be used as a stage for an official's preferred policies.

    D. It weakens the claim that a "leaker" can curry favor with a journalist.

7. Based on the passage, when the media now challenge the actions of a public official, the public assumes that

    A. the official is wrong.

    B. the media are always wrong.

    C. the media may be wrong.

    D. the official and the media may both be wrong.

Passage II (Questions 8–13)

The person who, with inner conviction, loathes stealing, killing, and assault, may find himself performing these acts with relative ease when commanded by authority. Behavior that is unthinkable in an individual who is acting of his own volition may be executed without hesitation when carried out under orders. An act carried out under command is, psychologically, of a profoundly different character than spontaneous action.

The important task, from the standpoint of a psychological study of obedience, is to be able to take conceptions of authority and translate them into personal experience. It is one thing to talk in abstract terms about the respective rights of the individual and of authority; it is quite another to examine a moral choice in a real situation. We all know about the philosophic problems of freedom and authority. But in every case where the problem is not merely academic, there is a real person who must obey or disobey authority. All musing prior to this moment is mere speculation, and all acts of disobedience are characterized by such a moment of decisive action.

When we move to the laboratory, the problem narrows: if an experimenter tells a subject to act with increasing severity against another person, under what conditions will the subject comply, and under what conditions will he disobey? The laboratory problem is vivid, intense, and real. It is not something apart from life, but carries to an extreme and very logical conclusion certain trends inherent in the ordinary functioning of the social world. The question arises as to whether there is any connection between what we have studied in the laboratory and the forms of obedience we have so often deplored throughout history. The differences in the two situations are, of course, enormous, yet the difference in scale, numbers, and political context may be relatively unimportant as long as certain essential features are retained.

To the degree that an absence of compulsion is present, obedience is colored by a cooperative mood; to the degree that the threat of force or punishment against the person is intimated, obedience is compelled by fear. The major problem for the individual is to recapture control of his own regnant processes once he has committed them to the purposes of others. The difficulty this entails represents the poignant and in some degree tragic element in the situation, for nothing is bleaker than the sight of a person striving yet not fully able to control his own behavior in a situation of consequence to him.

The essence of obedience is the fact that a person comes to view himself as the instrument for carrying out another's wishes, and he therefore no longer regards himself as culpable for his actions. Once this critical shift of viewpoint has occurred, all of the essential features of obedience—the adjustment of thought, the freedom to engage in cruel behavior, and the types of justification experienced by the person (essentially similar whether they occur in a psychological laboratory or on the battlefield)—follow. The question of generality, therefore, is not resolved by enumerating all of the manifest differences between the psychological laboratory and other situations, but by carefully constructing a situation that captures the essence of obedience—a situation in which a person gives himself over to authority and no longer views himself as the cause of his own actions.

8. Suppose that a pilot in the Rimland Air Force initially contests an order to bomb a city but eventually agrees to carry it out willingly. How would this scenario affect the author's view of obedience to authority?

   A. It would support the author's view.
   B. It would contradict the author's view.
   C. It would support the author's view only if it could be shown that the pilot had a history of carrying out orders that he did not initially support.
   D. It would contradict the author's view only if it could be shown that the pilot had a history of refusing to carry out orders.

9. Which of the following would be considered "acts of disobedience" as this term is used in paragraph 2?

   A. A nurse who administers a drug to a patient, even though the patient's doctor knows that the drug may kill the patient
   B. An employee who refuses to work overtime, even though the employee's boss has told the employee that a certain project must be finished as soon as possible
   C. A soldier who refuses to harm a civilian, even though the soldier's commanding officer has ordered that the civilian be shot as a spy
   D. An engineer who certifies a building as safe, even though the engineer knows that his construction company has not adhered to all government safety codes

10. In the context of the points being made by the author in the passage, the phrase "absence of compulsion" (paragraph 4) refers to

    A. the lack of punishment in psychological experiments.
    B. obedience that is willingly given to one's superior.
    C. the freedom to disobey the orders of those in authority.
    D. one's ability to consider the moral implications of an act.

11. Which of the following findings would serve most to WEAKEN the author's claim in the passage about obedience to authority?

    A. A study that concludes that most obedience to authority is motivated by fear
    B. A study that demonstrates that most authority figures in government behave immorally
    C. A study that shows that most people do not have strongly held ethical values
    D. A study that asserts that people with a college education are less likely to obey authority figures than are those with only a high school education

12. For which of the following statements does the passage provide some explanation or evidence?

    A. A laboratory experiment can be made to simulate real-world behavior.
    B. The subject of obedience has not received the attention it deserves from the field of social psychology.
    C. It is unfortunate that people are often not in full control of their own behavior.
    D. People in positions of authority tend to have lower moral standards than people who are not in positions of authority.

13. Suppose that a person who is not in a position of authority kills a person who is in a position of authority. Would this information be relevant to the author's view of obedience to authority?

    A. It would be relevant under any set of circumstances.
    B. It would not be relevant under any set of circumstances.
    C. It would be relevant under a certain set of circumstances.
    D. It would be relevant only if the two had no prior relationship.

Passage III (Questions 14–19)

Most diseases or conditions improve by themselves or are self-limiting. Even if fatal, they seldom follow a strictly downward spiral. In each case, intervention can appear to be quite efficacious. This becomes all the more patent if you assume the point of view of a knowing practitioner of fraudulent medicine.

To take advantage of the natural ups and downs of any disease (as well as of any placebo effect), it's best to begin your treatment when the patient is getting worse. In this way, anything that happens can more easily be attributed to your wonderful and probably expensive intervention. If the patient improves, you take credit; if he remains stable, your treatment stopped his downward course. On the other hand, if the patient worsens, the dosage or intensity of the treatment was not great enough; if he dies, he delayed too long in coming to you.

In any case, the few instances in which your intervention is successful will likely be remembered (not so few, if the disease in question is self-limiting), while the vast majority of failures will be forgotten and buried. Chance provides more than enough variation to account for the sprinkling of successes that will occur with almost any treatment; indeed, it would be a miracle if there weren't any "miracle cures."

Even in outlandish cases, it's often difficult to refute conclusively some proposed cure or procedure. Consider a diet doctor who directs his patients to consume two whole pizzas, four birch beers, and two pieces of cheesecake for every breakfast, lunch, and dinner, and an entire box of fig bars with a quart of milk for a bedtime snack, claiming that other people have lost six pounds a week on such a regimen. When several patients follow his instructions for three weeks, they find they've gained about seven pounds each. Have the doctor's claims been refuted?

Not necessarily, since he might respond that a whole host of auxiliary understandings weren't met: the pizzas had too much sauce, or the dieters slept sixteen hours a day, or the birch beer wasn't the right brand. Number and probability do, however, provide the basis for statistics, which, together with logic, constitutes the foundation of the scientific method, which will eventually sort matters out if anything can. However, just as the existence of pink does not undermine the distinction between red and white, and dawn doesn't indicate that day and night are really the same, this problematic fringe area doesn't negate the fundamental differences between science and its impostors.

The philosopher Willard Van Orman Quine ventures even further and maintains that experience never forces one to reject any particular belief. He views science as an integrated web of interconnecting hypotheses, procedures, and formalisms, and argues that any impact of the world on the web can be distributed in many different ways. If we're willing to make drastic enough changes in the rest of the web of our beliefs, the argument goes, we can hold to our belief in the efficacy of the above diet, or indeed in the validity of any pseudoscience.

14. In the context of the passage, its discussion of various medical conditions, and the particulars of those conditions, the term "self-limiting" (paragraph 3) refers to medical conditions that

    A. run a definite course that does not result in the patient's death.

    B. impair the patient's ability to engage in everyday activities.

    C. have a very high rate of mortality.

    D. never shows improvement.

15. Suppose that in order to demonstrate the legitimacy of his work, a faith healer compiles a book of interviews with people who swear that he has cured them just by blessing them. The author would most likely respond by asserting that

    A. eyewitness testimony of emotional events tends to be unreliable.

    B. the interviewees would have gotten better without the healer's intervention.

    C. the ability to cure people does not justify shameless self-promotion.

    D. the interviewees have been deluded into thinking that they have improved when they have not.

16. According to the passage, which of the following would best determine whether a practitioner's intervention is worthwhile or not?

    A. Keeping a record of the time it takes for a patient to respond to the practitioner's treatment

    B. Keeping a record of the number of patients the practitioner has treated successfully

    C. Keeping a record of the dosage that the practitioner employs in his treatment

    D. Keeping a record of both the successes and failures of the practitioner

17. Based on the information in the passage, which of the following opinions could most reasonably be ascribed to the author?

    A. Too often nothing truly effective can be done to ameliorate the illness of a patient.

    B. There is no way that pseudoscience will ever be eliminated.

    C. Beliefs can be maintained even in the absence of strong supporting evidence.

    D. Experience never forces one to reject any particular belief.

18. Doctors and scientists continue to debate whether certain types of alternative medicine are scientific or pseudoscientific. How is this information relevant to the passage?

    A. It weakens the claim that one can hold on to whatever pet theory one fancies.

    B. It weakens the claim that the scientific method is useful in sorting science from pseudoscience.

    C. It strengthens the claim that there is a fundamental difference between medicine and science.

    D. It strengthens the claim that science and pseudoscience cannot always be distinguished.

19. The author of the passage would most likely agree with an individual who argues that W. V. O. Quine's philosophical views are

    A. extreme, because some beliefs can be proven to be either true or false.

    B. insightful, because any set of beliefs has to be as valid as any other.

    C. flawed, because they do not explain why anyone would reject any belief.

    D. bankrupt, because they do not apply to any particular situation.

Passage IV (Questions 20–24)

In the decades following World War II, American business had undisputed control of the world economy, producing goods of such high quality and low cost that foreign corporations were unable to compete. But in the mid-1960s, the United States began to lose its advantage, and by the 1980s, American corporations lagged behind the competition in many industries. In the computer chip industry, for example, American corporations had lost most of both the domestic and foreign markets by the early 1980s.

The first analysts to examine the decline of American business blamed the U.S. government. They argued that stringent governmental restrictions on the behavior of American corporations, combined with the wholehearted support given to foreign firms by their governments, created an environment in which American products could not compete. Later analysts blamed predatory corporate raiders who bought corporations, not to make them more competitive in the face of foreign competition but rather to sell off the most lucrative divisions for huge profits.

Still later, analysts blamed the American workforce, citing labor demands and poor productivity as the reasons American corporations have been unable to compete with Japanese and European firms. Finally, a few analysts even censured American consumers for their unpatriotic purchases of foreign goods. The blame actually lies with corporate management, which has made serious errors based on misconceptions about what it takes to be successful in the marketplace. These missteps involve labor costs, production choices, and growth strategies.

Even though labor costs typically account for less than 15 percent of a product's total cost, management has been quick to blame the costs of workers' wages for driving up prices, making American goods uncompetitive. As a result of attempts to minimize the cost of wages, American corporations have had trouble recruiting and retaining skilled workers.

The emphasis on cost minimization has also led to another blunder: an over-concentration on high-technology products. Many foreign firms began by specializing in the mass production and sale of low-technology products, gaining valuable experience and earning tremendous profits. Later, these corporations were able to break into high-technology markets without much trouble; they simply applied their previous manufacturing experience and ample financial resources to the production of higher quality goods. American business has consistently ignored this very sensible approach.

The recent rash of corporate mergers and acquisitions in the United States has not helped the situation either. While American firms have neglected long-range planning and production, preferring instead to reap fast profits through mergers and acquisitions, foreign firms have been quick to exploit opportunities to ensure their domination over future markets by investing in the streamlining and modernization of their facilities.

20. The passage makes certain comparisons of American workers to Japanese workers. It suggests that compared to Japanese workers, American workers are often considered

A. more content and more efficient.
B. more content but less efficient.
C. less content and less efficient.
D. less content but more efficient.

21. With which of the following general statements would the author most likely NOT agree?

A. American business has been hurt by the inability to plan for the long term.
B. Cutting production costs always leads to increased competitiveness.
C. American consumers are not the prime cause of the decline of American business.
D. Initial analysis of the decline of American business yielded only partially accurate conclusions.

22. Which of the following would most WEAKEN the author's argument about the over-concentration of high-technology products?

A. Producing low-tech products is not as profitable as producing high-tech products.
B. Manufacturing high-tech products is a completely different process than manufacturing low-tech goods.
C. Most of the low-tech products purchased by Americans are made by foreign firms.
D. Most of the high-tech products purchased by Americans are made by foreign firms.

23. A reader of this passage is asked to decide whether or not she stands behind the author's arguments. Adopting the author's views as presented in the passage would most likely mean acknowledging that

A. it should be the goal of American business to regain control of the market.
B. the major blunder of American businesses was to alienate skilled workers.
C. the future of American business would appear to be hopeless.
D. the foreign market is more important for business survival than the domestic market.

24. The author of this passage would probably give his strongest support to which of the following actions by the corporate management of an American company?

A. Acquiring a smaller company in order to gain financial resources
B. Considering the option of paying the most skilled workers a higher wage
C. Imitating the general management strategy of foreign firms
D. Paying for television advertisements that will win back American consumers

Passage V (Questions 25–30)

From the outset of his dramatic poem *Samson Agonistes* (1671), John Milton establishes and expands upon a hero/antihero dichotomy that has its roots in the Book of Judges. Samson is the "epic hero," a tragic figure who falls despite tremendous personal strength. In prison, Samson's thoughts and words are melancholy and self-effacing. He compares his body to a vessel, tragically steered off course and consequently wrecked by his lust for Dalila.

The chorus of friends visiting him in prison does not allow their hero to take full blame, but placates him with the androcentric consolation: "wisest Men/Have err'd, and by bad women been deceiv'd." In this, the chorus's trope of woman-as-deceiver (and thus logical repository for blame) is much more simplified and essentialist than is Samson's view. While he clearly despises Dalila for leading him into such a trap ("That specious Monster, my accomplisht snare"), he also implicates himself in his capture.

Samson's confession of his culpability is, in a way, analogous to the scene in Milton's more widely read *Paradise Lost* in which Adam takes partial responsibility for the Fall. However, despite the similarities of the "falls" in *Samson Agonistes* and *Paradise Lost,* the overall gender relations in the two texts are not so simply analogous. Adam and Eve are co-creators of the Fall; Eve is not the deceiver but rather the deceived. She beseeches Adam to taste the fruit not out of malice or hope for worldly gain, but instead in an attempt to share the "wisdom" that she falsely believes she has acquired. Dalila, on the other hand, is much more cognizant of her deception; in fact, she revels in it as a means of gaining wealth and renown. She receives the forgiveness of neither her husband, Samson, nor her author, Milton. Samson may be aware of his culpability, but his anger toward and hatred of Dalila are not quelled by this self-awareness.

When Dalila first approaches Samson in the prison, she feigns contrition, telling Samson that she did not realize her deed would cause him so much agony—that she wishes to make amends for her "rash but more unfortunate misdeed." It is, however, difficult to believe that someone heretofore positioned as the deceiver would do anything *but* deceive. Samson rebukes her, regretting the lust that drew him to her side; he no longer wishes to be "entangl'd with a posynous bosom snake." This imagery calls to mind not only the deadly asp of another femme fatale, Cleopatra, but also Satan as the serpent in the Garden. This identification links Dalila more explicitly with the serpent than with Eve. Eve and Dalila, though both responsible to some degree for a "fall," are, in Milton's eyes, two very different women.

It is interesting to note that, while Milton avoids the fallacy of overt stereotyping, by describing Dalila as a certain "type" of woman, Dalila herself *employs* essentialism to relieve herself of some culpability and ingratiate herself with Samson. She attempts to pass off her treachery as common to all women, saying, "it was a weakness/In me, but incident to all our sex." She uses antifeminist rhetoric to exonerate herself in the same way Samson uses it to incriminate her. In both instances, the fallacy of sexual essentialism is clear.

When Samson rejects her advances, Dalila quickly reverts to the cold persona that the reader has come to expect. She gloats over the downfall of the great Samson and her "public marks of honor and reward," self-aggrandizing glee that certainly does not endear Dalila to Samson, to Milton, or to the reader, but does re-emphasize her cleverness and power.

25. The primary purpose of this passage is to

    A. provide a detailed comparative study of gender roles in two of Milton's dramatic poems, *Samson Agonistes* and *Paradise Lost*.

    B. examine the motivations and actions of a sometimes oversimplified character.

    C. advocate a feminist reading of the character of Dalila in *Samson Agonistes*.

    D. compare and contrast Milton's version of the Samson and Dalila story with that found in the biblical Book of Judges.

26. The passage suggests that which of the following is NOT a tactic employed by Dalila in order to manipulate Samson?

    A. Appropriating patriarchal stereotypes in order to further her argument

    B. Deceiving under the guise of romantic and sexual interest

    C. Arguing the superiority of the female intellect to the male

    D. Giving false apologies in order to win back Samson's trust

27. The author most likely mentions the serpent (paragraph 4) in order to

    A. make a comparison between Milton's portrayal of Dalila and Shakespeare's portrayal of Cleopatra.

    B. remind the reader of the similar dichotomy between Adam/Eve and Samson/Dalila.

    C. emphasize Milton's view of Dalila by comparing her to a creature traditionally associated with deception.

    D. differentiate between the asp in the story of Cleopatra and the serpent of biblical tradition.

28. According to the passage, *Samson Agonistes* and *Paradise Lost* share all of the following characteristics EXCEPT

    A. the "fall" of a male character as the result of a decision made by a female character.

    B. a similar gender hierarchy in which the woman wields the power of deception.

    C. an acceptance of culpability by the male character.

    D. the literary expansion of a biblical story.

29. Which of the following, if true, would be LEAST consistent with the author's claim that Milton views Eve and Dalila as two clearly different "types" of women?

    A. The introduction of textual evidence that proves Samson's punishment was as devastating as Adam's

    B. Evidence from *Paradise Lost* that proves Eve made Adam taste the fruit so that she might have some amount of power over him

    C. The introduction of evidence that, in the Judges version of the story, Samson was neither as intelligent nor as self-reflective as he is in Milton's retelling

    D. The introduction of evidence that, at the beginning of both the Judges story and *Samson Agonistes*, Dalila was in love with Samson

30. It can be reasonably inferred that the author of this passage is

    A. a biblical scholar doing comparative research on the similarities and differences between an Old Testament story and a literary retelling.

    B. a feminist scholar researching examples of feminist characters in English literature.

    C. a historian researching societal attitudes toward strong female figures.

    D. a literary scholar exploring the personality and motivations of a significant female character.

Passage VI (Questions 31–35)

The planned expansion of the North Atlantic Treaty Organization (NATO) into Eastern Europe has been compared by one sour critic to the behavior of a couple in a crumbling marriage who, instead of going to a marriage counselor, try to save their relationship by having a baby, or possibly even several babies. NATO itself is in the middle of a very confused debate about its identity and role, and partly as a result, it is difficult to detect any honest, coherent discussion in the West of the necessity for expansion and of how it will affect relations with Russia, the security of Ukraine and the Baltic States, and the peaceful integration of Ukraine into Europe.

The official Western line at present is that NATO expansion is meant to "strengthen European security," but not against Russia or against feared Russian aggression. Nevertheless, all public discussion in Poland—and much of it in the United States—has been conducted in terms of the need to contain a presumed Russian threat and to prevent Russia from exerting influence on its neighbors, influence that is automatically viewed as illegitimate and threatening to the West.

The overwhelming majority of Russian politicians, including most liberals, now believe it is necessary that most of the former Soviet Union excluding the Baltic States be within a Russian sphere of influence. They see this not as imperialism but as a justifiable defense of Russian interests against a multiplicity of potential threats (radical Islam, future Turkish expansionism), of Russian populations outside Russia, and of areas in which Russia has long maintained a cultural presence—Ukraine, for example.

This does not necessarily involve demands for hegemony over Russia's neighbors, but it certainly implies the exclusion of any other bloc's or superpower's military presence. In justification, Russians point to the Monroe Doctrine and to the French sphere of influence in Africa. Most educated Russians now view Western criticism as mere hypocrisy masking Western aggrandizement.

The attitude of the entire Russian political establishment to the expansion issue is now strongly and unanimously negative, though the government hopes for the moment to continue exerting influence against expansion by cooperating with NATO—hence its agreement to join the Partnership for Peace. The reasons for Russian opposition are these: NATO expansion is seen as a betrayal of clear though implicit promises made by the West in 1990–91 and a sign that the West regards Russia not as an ally but as a defeated enemy. Russians point out that Moscow agreed to withdraw troops from the former East Germany following unification after NATO promised not to station its troops there.

Now NATO is planning to leapfrog over eastern Germany and end up 500 miles closer to Russia, in Poland. Western arguments that the 1990 promise to Mikhail Gorbachev referred only to East Germany, not to the rest of Eastern Europe, though strictly speaking correct, are not unnaturally viewed by Russians as purely Jesuitical.

Russian officials say that the NATO expansion would lead to a reversal of the previous pro-Western policy of the Yeltsin and Gorbachev governments. Also, Russians fear that NATO expansion will ultimately mean the inclusion of the Baltic States and Ukraine within NATO's sphere of influence, if not in NATO itself—and thus the loss of any Russian influence over these states and the stationing of NATO troops within striking distance of the Russian heartland. The West's inability publicly to rule out the possible future incorporation of any country in NATO makes it very difficult to assuage Russian fears.

31. In the context of the analogy in the first paragraph, the couple is to the baby as

    A. NATO is to Russia.
    B. Russia and NATO together are to an Eastern European country.
    C. NATO is to an Eastern European country.
    D. Eastern Europe is to NATO.

32. If the author of this passage were asked in an interview about his feeling regarding potential action that NATO might take with regard to the passage, he would probably give his greatest support to which of the following actions by NATO?

    A. Admitting officially that NATO expansion is meant to contain the Russian threat
    B. Halting expansion once Poland has been absorbed into NATO
    C. Stating publicly that Ukraine will never be included in NATO's sphere of influence
    D. Reconsidering plans to establish a presence in Eastern Europe

33. Judging from the passage, the "clear though implicit promises" made by the West to Russia in 1990–91 were promises that

    A. the West would allow Russia to station troops in Poland.
    B. the West would not station troops in any East European country.
    C. the West would withdraw its troops from East Germany following unification.
    D. the West would leapfrog over East Germany into Poland.

34. Based on the passage, which of the following could be considered true beliefs of the majority of Western diplomats?

    I. Any expansion of Russia's influence on its neighbors would endanger the West.
    II. Ukraine is not in any danger of being absorbed by NATO.
    III. Russia would not be justified in regaining control of former Soviet territories.

    A. II only
    B. II and III only
    C. I and III only
    D. I, II, and III

35. Based on the passage, which of the following could one most reasonably expect of a country that is attempting to expand its sphere of influence?

    A. A complete cessation of communication with potential enemies
    B. A declaration that the purpose of expansion is greater security
    C. A stubborn refusal to admit defeat when it has in fact been suffered
    D. A prolonged period of careful planning and diplomatic negotiation

Passage VII (Questions 36–40)

The original Hellenistic community was idealized, the Greeks' own golden dream—a community never achieved but only imagined by the Macedonian Alexander, who was possessed of the true faith of all converts to a larger vision. The evolving system of city-states had produced not only unity with a healthy diversity, but also narrow rivalries. No Hellenic empire arose, only scores of squabbling cities pursuing bitter feuds born of ancient wrongs and existing ambitions. It was civil strife made possible by isolation from the great armies and ambitions of Asia.

Greek history could arguably begin in July of 776 BCE, the First Olympiad, and end with Theodosus's ban on the games in 393 CE. Before this there had been a long era of two tribes, the Dorians and Ionians, scarcely distinguishable to the alien eye, but distinctly separate in their own eyes until 776. After Theodosus's ban, most of the Mediterranean world was Greek-like, in fact, but the central core had been rendered impotent by diffusion.

During the eventful Greek millennium, the Olympics reflected not the high ideals of Hellenes but rather the mean reality of the times. Its founders had created a monster, games that twisted the strategists' aspirations to unity to fit the unpleasant reality of the Hellenistic world. The games not only mirrored the central practices of the Greek world that reformers would deny, they also imposed the flaws of that world. Like the atomic theory of the Greek philosophers, the Greek gamers' theories were far removed from reality; they were elegant, consistent, logical, and irrelevant.

Part religious ritual, part game rite, in the five-day Olympic Games various athletes came together under the banner of their cities; winning became paramount, imposing defeat a delight. As Greek society evolved, so, too, did the games, but rarely as a unifying force. Athletes supposedly competing for the laurel of accomplishment in the name of idealism found that dried olive leaves changed to gold. Each local polis (city-state) sought not to contribute to the grandeur of Greece, but to achieve its own glory. As in the real world, in the games no Greek could trust another, and each envied rivals' victories. The Olympic spirit was not one of communal bliss but bitter lasting competition institutionalized in games.

36. In the context of the passage, the phrase "dried olive leaves changed to gold" (paragraph 4) refers to

   A. the peace achieved by Greek city-states during Olympic years.

   B. the benefits that athletes could expect to derive from Olympic victories.

   C. the political unification of Dorian and Ionian tribes in 776 BCE.

   D. the spread of Greek culture during the period from 776 BCE to 393 CE.

37. For which of the following statements does the passage provide some evidence or explanation?

   I. Alexander united ancient Greece through a series of military conquests.

   II. The divisions among Greek city-states were reflected in the Olympics.

   III. The Olympic Games could not have occurred without a city-state system.

   A. II only

   B. III only

   C. I and II only

   D. II and III only

38. Suppose that a Greek wrestler had just won the Olympic wrestling contest. Which of the following rewards would he have been LEAST likely to receive?

A. A sense of pleasure in defeating an opponent
B. A grant of land from his own city-state
C. A political office in his own city-state
D. A monetary prize from another city-state

39. Which of the following, if true, would most strengthen the author's claims about the Olympic Games in ancient Greece?

A. Contested outcomes of Olympic events sometimes caused wars between city-states.
B. The Olympic Games began long before Alexander united all of the city-states.
C. Most city-states regularly applauded the Olympic victories of athletes from other city-states.
D. Each city-state was only allowed to send one athlete per Olympic event.

40. The statement "The Olympic spirit was not one of communal bliss but bitter lasting competition institutionalized in games" (paragraph 4) indicates that the author believes that

A. the Greeks were more internally divided than other Mediterranean civilizations.
B. the Greek millennium was a period of constant warfare.
C. the Olympic Games did not serve a beneficial national purpose.
D. the First Olympiad in 776 BCE began the decline of Greek civilization.

Verbal Reasoning Practice Test 3 Answers and Explanations

ANSWER KEY

1. A	9. C	17. C	25. B	33. B
2. B	10. B	18. D	26. C	34. C
3. B	11. C	19. A	27. C	35. B
4. D	12. A	20. C	28. B	36. B
5. A	13. C	21. B	29. B	37. A
6. D	14. A	22. B	30. D	38. D
7. C	15. B	23. A	31. C	39. A
8. A	16. D	24. C	32. D	40. C

EXPLANATIONS

Passage I: Media Leaks

Topic: The media

Scope: Media leaks and negative effects

Purpose: To argue that media leaks have negative effects

Mapping the Passage:

¶1. The media's suspicion of government and lack of knowledge about the world harm government policy.

¶2. Leaks make leaders afraid to speak their minds.

¶3. Leaks limit ideas, are bad for foreign policy b/c beliefs not shared.

¶4. Media was trusted by the public, but now public is skeptical.

¶5. Why leaks occur.

1. A

Check your map to review the author's main arguments; she'll agree with anything she already said, but stay flex-ible. (A) recalls the author's point in paragraph 2: "Leaders often say one thing in public and quite another thing in private conversation." The author explains why this occurs (fear of media leaks) and clearly opposes such leaks. Therefore, the author must agree with (A)'s contention that keeping the public in the dark is sometimes warranted.

Wrong Answers:

(B) Opposite. This is the opposite of the author's argument; he argues that revealing the inner workings of the government has negative consequences for the country.

(C) Opposite. The author argues in paragraph 3 that involving more people in policy discussions brings a "richness and variety of ideas."

(D) Opposite. The author's point in decrying leaks is that privacy is a necessary component of leadership.

2. B

Scan back in the passage to find the author's mention of foreign officials. In paragraph 3, the author argues that foreign officials fear leaks and are less inclined to speak their minds if they think that their private thoughts will be revealed. So it makes sense that foreign policy would be harmed because the foreign leaders would be less likely to confide in American officials. (B) summarizes this point.

Wrong Answers:

(A) Opposite. If U.S. leaders already know what foreign leaders think, the author wouldn't argue that foreign leaders "do not share their real beliefs (let alone their secrets)."

(C) Faulty Use of Detail. The point of the paragraph about foreign leaders is not that they don't share with the press but that they're afraid to share with U.S. leaders.

(D) Out of Scope. The passage doesn't discuss whether the published information is reliable or not, and anyway, this isn't relevant to leaks of foreign officials' thoughts.

3. B

This is a long question, but the only relevant part is the last sentence: Which claim is supported by evidence? When looking for a claim supported by evidence, search for an answer choice that summarizes an entire paragraph. Unsupported claims will usually be secondary claims that don't directly tie into the main points of the passage and often appear at the end of a paragraph. Review the author's main points before looking for an answer choice that is both a claim made in the passage *and* supported by evidence. This question is harder than some of the same type because *all* the answer choices are claims made by the passage. However, three claims are simply made with no support. (B) alone is a claim made (in paragraph 5) and supported by explanation that makes up the bulk of the paragraph.

Wrong Answers:

(A) Faulty Use of Detail. While this claim is made in paragraph 1, where the author says that the media cause "damage . . . in ways [they] rarely imagine," it's given no support before the author moves on to discussing leaks.

(C) Faulty Use of Detail. The author makes this claim in the end of the last paragraph but provides no support.

(D) Faulty Use of Detail. This is a claim made in paragraph 1, again without support.

4. D

The word *implicit* tells you this is an assumption in the argument. Look for evidence with which the author must agree but that she doesn't explicitly state. In paragraph 2, she writes that leaks harm discussions with foreign leaders. The author argues that foreign leaders don't want their private thoughts to be made public, so she must assume that leaders have some reason for not wanting their views to be made public. (D) provides a possible reason. If unclear, use the denial test: If leaders didn't have this fear, why would they hide their personal views?

Wrong Answers:

(A) Distortion. The author dislikes leaks, but she never argues that they're immoral.

(B) Out of Scope. This is possibly true but has no relevance to the author's argument.

(C) Out of Scope. The author never suggests that there were no barriers to discussion before the press, only that there are far more barriers now that the press is in the habit of receiving leaked information about these discussions.

5. A

Here's a nice question with a direct paragraph reference, so go back to the context to review what the author is saying: She's arguing that journalists are used as tools rather than being the ones in charge. Therefore, the "prime mover" must refer to whoever *is* in charge, which the author suggests is the official doing the leaking. (A) says just this.

Wrong Answers:

(B) Opposite. The author says just the opposite: The journalists are "instruments of the process, not prime movers."

(C) Out of Scope. Media executives aren't mentioned in the situation at all.

(D) Out of Scope. The author refers to the primer movers as the officials angling for power, not abstract rules that govern leaks.

6. D

How do anonymous leaks affect the author's argument? Paragraph 5 argues that officials use leaks as a way of either currying favor with the media or planting information to influence policy. How does anonymity affect each of these? While it would have no effect on the policy aspect, it would negate the possibility of currying favor. Therefore, if most leaks are anonymous, the author's argument about favor currying must be weakened.

Wrong Answers:

(A) Out of Scope. As previously explained, anonymity would have no effect on this motivation. Leaks can influence policy even if the person leaking the information isn't named.

(B) Out of Scope. It would have no bearing on the issue of reliability, and in any case, the author never argues that journalists are more reliable.

(C) Opposite. As explained above, the policy aspect isn't affected by anonymity of the source.

7. C

Go back to paragraph 4 to review what the public thinks of the media. The author says that in the past, the public always assumed the media was right when it challenged the government but that "this may be changing." Therefore, the public *might* now consider the possibility that the media, rather than the government, is wrong. While the wrong answer choices distort this, (C) rewards careful and methodical thought.

Wrong Answers:

(A) Opposite. The author argued that in the past, the public assumed the official was wrong but that is no longer necessarily the case.

(B) Distortion. The author suggests that the public might believe that the media is wrong, but he never says that the media is *always* considered wrong in a showdown with government.

(D) Out of Scope. Although the passage says "many Americans have concluded that the media are no more credible than the government," it does not suggest there are times when both are wrong.

Passage II: Obedience Experiments

Topic: Obedience

Scope: What determines when we obey

Purpose: To argue that it's a matter of obeying authority vs. controlling own actions

Mapping the Passage:

¶1. People do things they otherwise wouldn't when ordered by authority.

¶2. To study obedience, have to turn theory into real experience.

¶3. Laboratory-tested obedience is effective.

¶4. Obedience is influenced by the desire to cooperate or fear—person obeying has trouble controlling own behavior.

¶5. Lab can effectively simulate real-world conditions that lead to obedience.

8. A

The situation involves someone who doesn't want to do something, presumably against his morality, but who finally does it because he's ordered to. How does this fit in with the author's argument? It matches closely with the point made in paragraph 1 that people will do things they don't really want to because an authority tells them to do so. Therefore, it supports the author's argument without qualification; (A) is correct.

Wrong Answers:

(B) Opposite. For the reasons described, the pilot's actions would support the author's argument. In other words, this is the opposite of the author's argument.

(C) Out of Scope. While the author's argument would be supported, there's no reason to believe this would be the case only if the pilot had a history of obeying orders he disliked. This example, even if isolated, is enough by itself to support the author's argument.

(D) Opposite. The fact that the pilot, under compulsion, followed an order he initially resisted supports the author's argument, regardless of what happened previously.

9. C

Review the phrase in context: Who is defying what? The author seems to be referring to a general case in which someone defies an order he doesn't want to obey, presumably for moral reasons. Looking for a situation that reflects this turns up (C): Someone is disobeying an authority on principled grounds. The other choices do not explicitly defy orders at all.

Wrong Answers:

(A) Opposite. There's no defiance of orders; though the doctor "knows" the drug is potentially dangerous, there is no indication that the doctor has ordered the nurse not to administer the drug.

(B) Opposite. There's no *direct* defiance of orders here. The employee wasn't ordered to work overtime but simply to finish the project as soon as possible. There's also no element of principle in this situation.

(D) Opposite. No orders are being defied in this example. If anything, the engineer is disobeying his own conscience.

10. B

Review the lines in context. The author argues that when there is no compulsion present, obedience relies more on a "cooperative mood," which suggests that the person is obeying of his or her own free will. With the word *willingly*, (B) says the same.

Wrong Answers:

(A) Faulty Use of Detail. In the fourth paragraph, the author compares two sets of conditions. On one side is the "absence of compulsion" and on the other the "threat of force or punishment." Therefore we can conclude that the first case lacks a *threat* of punishment, not a "lack of punishment."

(C) Distortion. While the person who has an absence of compulsion presumably is free to disobey, the phrase is more concerned with those who *do* obey—willingly.

(D) Out of Scope. Moral implications aren't discussed or hinted at anywhere near this phrase.

11. C

The first thing to do with a weaken (or strengthen) question is to review quickly the author's claim. In this case, it's that people do things they don't want to do because they feel compelled to by authority. Look for something that challenges this point: If (C) is true, the author's point about not wanting to do things, most clearly expressed in paragraph 1, makes no sense. If people have no strong ethical values, then they wouldn't consider actions either good or bad, so nothing is necessarily against their ethical will.

Wrong Answers:

(A) Opposite. This would support the author's point about fear made in the final paragraph.

(B) Distortion. We don't know if the author would say "most authority figures" behave immorally, but he does refer to "obedience we have so often deplored throughout history." Either way, his argument would not be weakened.

(D) Out of Scope. Education does not play any role in the author's argument.

12. A

Keep the author's major point in mind while reviewing the choices. (A) is the subject of paragraph 3 and is referred to again in the last paragraph.

Wrong Answers:

(B) Out of Scope. The passage does not comment on the amount of attention psychology has given to obedience.

(C) Faulty Use of Detail. The author inserts this at the end of paragraph 4 but without support.

(D) Out of Scope. The author doesn't compare the moral standards of people in authority with those of people who are not.

13. C

How would someone who is not an authority figure killing someone who *is* an authority figure affect the author's argument? It would probably weaken the author's argument that obedience is usually an overriding factor in decision making *if* the authority figure had authority over the other person. On the other hand, the two could be working in two totally separate chains of command. Therefore, the situation will have relevance *only* if there is an authoritarian relationship between them. (C) is the best restatement of this prediction.

Wrong Answers:

(A) Distortion. "Any set of circumstances" takes in just about anything that could possibly happen.

(B) Distortion. As in (A), we need more information.

(D) Out of Scope. Prior relationships don't figure at all into the author's argument.

Passage III: Fraudulent Medicine

Topic: Pseudoscience
Scope: Example of quack medicine
Purpose: To explain it and why we believe pseudoscience

Mapping the Passage:

¶1. Most diseases go away on their own, but quacks take advantage of this.

¶2. How quacks take advantage of disease ups and downs.

¶3. Why quacks can convince people of their pseudoscience claims.

¶4. Example of quack medicine.

¶5. Difficulties of refuting false claims and distinguishing between real and pseudoscience.

¶6. Quine: Why people believe false claims.

14.   A

The author uses the term "self-limiting" to discuss diseases that are limited in their progression, in which the patient is likely to recover; these diseases more or less keep themselves in check (like a cold). (A) matches perfectly.

Wrong Answers:

(B) Faulty Use of Detail. The term *self* refers to the disease, not the patient.

(C) Opposite. If the disease ends with the patient's death, it's not doing much self-limiting; it's going as far it can go.

(D) Distortion. Be skeptical when you see the word *never*. Also, if the disease is self-limiting, the author says, any treatment will likely seem to be successful, which means that there must be natural improvement.

15.   B

This question is simply asking how the author would respond to a medical charlatan, which is essentially the scope of the first half of the passage. Some pseudoscience appears to work because the body naturally improves. Look for the predictable answer choice: The "cure" didn't do the trick; the body's natural tendency to heal itself did so. (B) jumps out with this prediction in mind.

Wrong Answers:

(A) Out of Scope. The passage never discusses the validity of eyewitness testimony.

(C) Out of Scope. The author may not like charlatans, but he doesn't say anything about "shameless self-promotion."

(D) Opposite. Obviously the interviewees *had* improved—the question refers to cures. The issue here, though, is that the patients think the quack doctor's treatment did the trick.

16.   D

What does the author say is needed to evaluate scientific claims? "Statistics . . . with logic." To zero in on the answer, combine this with the author's argument that people usually only remember successes. (D) covers it all.

Wrong Answers:

(A) Out of Scope. Measuring the time of response does nothing to distinguish between treatments that work and those that don't.

(B) Distortion. The author argues that people only remember the successes. But what about the failures? They need to be recorded, too, for a statistical determination of the "doctor's" claims.

(C) Out of Scope. Dosages have no necessary link to success, particularly if the success has nothing to do with the treatment.

17. C

For this inference question, quickly review your map to see what the author agrees with, then jump to the answer choices. While each of the wrong answer choices can be knocked out quickly as not necessarily following from the author's argument, (C) is essentially a paraphrase of the argument made in paragraph 5.

Wrong Answers:

(A) Distortion. Though quackery might not be effective, the author doesn't say that as a general rule *nothing* can be done.

(B) Distortion. Even though Quine argues that we often can continue to hold an untenable belief (paragraph 6), it's not the view of the author. And watch out for the phrase *no way*.

(D) Faulty Use of Detail. This is Quine's opinion again. It's crucial to distinguish between what Quine believes and what the author believes. Always be sure to distinguish the author's opinion from opinions of other people to whom the author refers, and read the question carefully to be sure you know to whom the question is referring.

18. D

A quick scan of the answer choices shows that this is a weaken/strengthen question. Where does the author talk about distinguishing between science and pseudoscience? Target the final paragraph and summarize the argument: There is a difference, but it's sometimes tough to tell. A debate over whether a type of medicine is one or the other would support the idea that the line is fuzzy. (D) rewards the careful logic.

Wrong Answers:

(A) Out of Scope. It's a weakener, for one, and without relevance to the question as well.

(B) Distortion. The author *does* believe that the scientific method is useful for distinguishing, but she acknowledges

that there's a fuzzy middle ground. This evidence would support the idea that there are two sides—the issue is fuzzy.

(C) Opposite. As with (B), two sides of a debate mean two ways of thinking about it—still fuzzy. If there's a fundamental difference, it's not yet clear.

19. A

In paragraph 5, the author states that there are "fundamental differences between science and its imposters." Furthermore, logic and statistics—the bases of the scientific method—will eventually distinguish the difference between science and pseudoscience, if such a difference can ever be made. Quine, in contrast, "ventures even further" than the author. Thus, unlike Quine, the author's views are more moderate: We *can* prove things one way or the other. (A) matches nicely.

Wrong Answers:

(B) Opposite. The author would strongly disagree with the idea that all beliefs are equally valid since she feels that the scientific method can determine if something is valid or not. This, of course, indicates the probability that *some* beliefs will turn out to be not valid.

(C) Out of Scope. While the author would consider Quine's ideas flawed, there's nothing in the passage dealing with the reason listed afterward.

(D) Out of Scope. "Bankrupt" is far too extreme a word, and there's no reason to believe that Quine's views couldn't apply to some situations.

Passage IV: U.S. Business
Topic: American business
Scope: Decline
Purpose: To explain possible reasons, support one

Mapping the Passage:

¶1. Outlines decline of American business.

¶2. Reasons: Gov't./corporate raiders.

¶3. More reasons: Labor/consumers. Author: reason is management.

¶4. Management's problems with labor.

¶5. American business's fixation on high-tech products.

¶6. Mergers a problem, also lack of long-term planning.

20. C

A quick scan of the answer choices shows that you have to compare the workers of the two nations on two criteria: contentedness and efficiency. Search for a part of the passage that touches on this. Paragraph 3 is the only one that cites Japan, and it mentions that analysts consider American workers as less productive and as makers of labor demands, a sign they are less content. (C) it is.

Wrong Answers:

(A) Opposite. This is the flip side of the correct answer.

(B) Faulty Use of Detail. Less efficient yes, but not more content.

(D) Faulty Use of Detail. Same as (B) but turned around.

21. B

This is an inference question; make sure that you're clear on the main points of the author's argument. The author will agree with three answer choices but will disagree with the correct answer. The three wrong answers can be easily eliminated, leading to (B). You could also reason that since management has suffered by cutting labor costs, cost cutting doesn't always result in increased competitiveness.

Wrong Answers:

(A) Opposite. In the last paragraph, the author says that "American firms have neglected long-range planning."

(C) Opposite. The author mentions that "a few analysts even censured American consumers for their unpatriotic purchases of foreign goods," but then says that the real blame "lies with corporate management" (paragraph 3). Therefore the author agrees.

(D) Opposite. This is the focus of paragraphs 2 and 3.

22. B

Paraphrase the author's argument about high technology: It's better to start out with low-tech products, get experience, and then use this knowledge to switch to high-tech goods. Search the answer choices for something that would

contradict this. (B) clearly does; if the processes are completely different, why start with low-tech? That experience wouldn't help in producing a completely different product.

Wrong Answers:

(A) Out of Scope. Although this might be true, it wouldn't affect the author's chain of reasoning.

(C) Faulty Use of Detail. Although the third paragraph says that some analysts blame "American consumers for their unpatriotic purchases of foreign goods," this has nothing to do with the author's argument (in the fifth paragraph) about high-tech products.

(D) Opposite. This statement strengthens the idea that starting out with low-tech products makes the high-tech business easier, since this answer says that the products are made by foreign firms and starting low is exactly what those producers do.

23. A

This is just a fancy way of asking what the author would agree with and therefore is a question requiring a deduction. Keep the author's main points in mind while determining whether an answer choice has to follow from them. If the author believes that America has stumbled by losing market share, it follows that regaining that control would be a good thing. If the author didn't believe this, there would have been no real reason to make his argument. (A) it is.

Wrong Answers:

(B) Distortion. While American business has had trouble keeping skilled workers, the passage also faults these companies for focusing on the high-tech sector and neglecting long-term planning. None of these three mistakes is singled out as *the* major blunder.

(C) Distortion. The outlook may be bleak, but "hopeless" is far too extreme.

(D) Out of Scope. The author's argument is all about American business, not markets.

24. C

We're looking for a business action that would presumably fix one or more of the problems that the author sees in

American business. The author's major point is problems with management, so it makes sense that he would agree with some action that improves management. While (C) offers no detailed prescriptions, we know that the author believes foreign models of management to be superior across the board—in their handling of labor costs, production choices, and growth strategies. If American business followed their lead, the author would probably give his support.

Wrong Answers:

(A) Opposite. In the last paragraph, the author cites acquisitions as yet another problem, not an action he would agree with.

(B) Out of Scope. The author does argue that businesses should stop trying to minimize wages, but he says nothing about wage fairness between groups of workers, only wage fairness as a whole. In fact, the author would probably say that more money should be funneled to lower-skilled workers making low-tech products.

(D) Out of Scope. There's nothing to suggest that the author would agree with this strategy, especially given the fact that he considers the American business model rotten at the core. Simple advertising won't cut it.

Passage V: Milton's Dalila

Topic: Milton's *Samson Agonistes*
Scope: Character and actions of Dalila; compare with Eve
Purpose: To describe their effects on Samson

Mapping the Passage:

¶1. Intro Milton's *Samson Agonistes* and hero/antihero dichotomy.

¶2. Friends try to convince Samson that he is blameless; Samson explains his blame.

¶3. Compares *Samson Agonistes* and *Paradise Lost*; differences between Eve and Dalila.

¶4. Examines Dalila's motives; different from Eve's, similar to serpent's.

¶5. Dalila's antifeminist argument to explain her actions.

¶6. Dalila not a nice character for anyone.

25. B

Clearly this main idea question is going to have something to do with Dalila; she's all over our map. Predict such an answer, however it might be worded, and match it. (B), though not mentioning Dalila by name, is the only answer that focuses on one character and her motivations.

Wrong Answers:

(A) Faulty Use of Detail. *Paradise Lost* is discussed but only for the span of one paragraph; the passage is not a thorough comparison of gender roles in *Paradise Lost* and *Samson Agonistes* because it looks primarily at the two women.

(C) Distortion. We're told in paragraph 5 that Dalila employs sexual essentialism and antifeminist rhetoric.

(D) Faulty Use of Detail. While the biblical Book of Judges is mentioned, it's included merely as a reference point for the original Samson and Dalila story; it is neither discussed at length nor compared to Milton's version.

26. C

Let's see. In paragraph 4, Samson rebukes Dalila for using lust, so sex and romance are in. In the same paragraph, she apologizes. In paragraph 5, she blames the female sex in general, and in paragraph 6, she gloats. What doesn't she do? (C) is it.

Wrong Answers:

(A) Opposite. This is not an easy answer to understand so you might want to just keep it and look at the others. In the long run, (C) is obvious. By the way, "patriarchal stereotypes" refers to the stereotypes of women ("a weakness/In me, but incident to all our sex") in a male-dominated society. Furthermore, Milton refers to her as a "certain *type* of woman."

(B) Opposite. In paragraphs 1 and 4, we learn that Samson felt he had been ensnared by his lust for Dalila.

(D) Opposite. We see Dalila apologize to Samson in paragraph 4, and the author clearly mistrusts her sincerity.

27. C

This is a function question asking why the author refers to something in the passage; in this case, the serpent. In paragraph 4, the serpent shows up as "posynous" and reminds Milton of the equally poisonous asp that killed Cleopatra and the treacherous snake in the Garden of Eden. Clearly the serpent and its associated lethal cohorts are bad news all around. The serpent must represent something really bad, and (C), deception, fits the bill. Did you use your map to find where the author mentioned "serpent"? It would have saved you time.

Wrong Answers:

(A) **Faulty Use of Detail.** While the author mentions Cleopatra and the asp, this is only to give a nod to a common association.

(B) **Faulty Use of Detail.** In mentioning the serpent in such close affiliation with Dalila, the author is making the point that Milton associated Dalila more with the serpent than with Eve.

(D) **Faulty Use of Detail.** While the asp in the story of Cleopatra is mentioned, there's no real comparison of it to the serpent of biblical tradition.

28. B

You're asked to compare two of Milton's works: *Samson Agonistes* and *Paradise Lost.* Check your map, and you'll be directed to paragraph 3. If you missed mapping it, using those title clue words should make it fairly easy to locate where the author compares the two poems. Remember, you're looking to eliminate three answers that *are* part of the comparison. The right answer isn't, and that's (B). Eve beseeches Adam to taste the fruit not out of deception but out of an honest desire for him to gain the knowledge that she believes she has gained.

Wrong Answers:

(A) **Opposite.** Both Adam and Samson experience a "fall" because of a decision made by a female character.

(C) **Opposite.** To differing degrees, both Adam and Samson accept the blame for their situation.

(D) **Opposite.** Both stories are expansions upon biblical passages.

29. B

Again we are asked to compare Dalila and Eve. Dalila, we know, acted mostly out of malice, deception, and the desire for personal gain. Eve, on the other hand, acted out of an almost innocent desire to share "wisdom." What would be inconsistent with (weaken) that view? (B) says that Eve acted not out of a desire to share but as a power play. That would make her fit the same mold as the deceptive and treacherous Dalila, weakening the author's claim.

Wrong Answers:

(A) **Out of Scope.** Samson's punishment has nothing to do with Eve's or Dalila's character types.

(C) **Out of Scope.** Even if Milton has given his Samson a few more positive characteristics than are granted to the biblical Samson, this has no effect on the way Dalila treats him or on the way Eve treats Adam.

(D) **Out of Scope.** Even if Dalila were once genuinely in love with Samson, it has no real bearing on her later decision to betray and deceive him, and it doesn't bring her closer in personality type to Eve.

30. D

The author builds her argument using three sources: *Samson Agonistes, Paradise Lost,* and the Bible—each one a literary text. Predict that the author has a focus on literature, and you'll come up with (D).

Wrong Answers:

(A) **Distortion.** The passage does not include enough comparisons between *Samson Agonistes* and the Old Testament to conclude that the author is a biblical scholar.

(B) **Opposite.** Because Dalila uses antifeminist rhetoric, she would most likely not be included in research of feminist characters.

(C) **Out of Scope.** Nowhere does the author mention general societal attitudes toward figures such as Dalila.

Passage VI: NATO Expansion

Topic: NATO

Scope: Expansion

Purpose: To argue that it will cause diplomatic problems with Russia

Mapping the Passage:

¶1. Expansion of NATO reflects internal confusion and may create problems.

¶2. Perceived purpose of expansion is to combat Russian aggression.

¶3. Why Russians feel they have a right to exert influence over former Soviet states.

¶4. Russia believes the West shouldn't control its neighbors.

¶5. Why Russia opposes NATO expansion.

¶6. More of . . .

¶7. Another reason: Potential encroachment on Russia's sphere of influence.

31. C

Go back to the first paragraph to review the analogy. NATO itself is compared to the couple; its new members are compared to the baby; in this case, the addition of an Eastern European country. (C) matches the prediction.

Wrong Answers:

(A) Out of Scope. The author describes NATO as adversarial toward Russia, which a couple wouldn't be toward their baby.

(B) Out of Scope. "The couple" refers to NATO alone.

(D) Faulty Use of Detail. This answer confuses the pieces of the analogy.

32. D

Review what the author wants NATO to do: not solve its internal problems by adding members, avoid threatening Russia's sphere of influence, and keep implicit promises. It seems likely he would support any action that agrees with these points, as (D) does.

Wrong Answers:

(A) Distortion. While the author wouldn't mind this, admitting publicly that it views Russia as a threat doesn't solve the main problems of NATO expansion.

(B) Distortion. Though the author wouldn't argue against this, the author would rather that there be no NATO expansion at all.

(C) Distortion. Though the author wouldn't consider this unwelcome, it doesn't go far enough. The author would support NATO's declaring that *all* countries in Russia's sphere of influence are out of bounds for NATO.

33. B

Where does the author mention these promises? Go back to paragraph 5. In the second half of the paragraph, the author argues that promises to stay out of East Germany were in the same spirit as "implicit promises" to stay out of Eastern Europe. (B) rewards reading in context.

Wrong Answers:

(A) Out of Scope. The paragraph never mentions anything about Russia stationing troops in Poland.

(C) Faulty Use of Detail. *Russia* withdrew its troops, not the West. The West promised not to *station* troops there.

(D) Opposite. The author argues that the promises implied just the opposite: NATO would not station troops any nearer to Russia than it already had.

34. C

Take a moment to separate what the author argues the diplomats *say* from what he believes they *mean*. In the second paragraph, the author states that NATO's true goal is to "contain a presumed Russian threat." Additionally the author says that any Russian influence "is automatically viewed as illegitimate and threatening." Look for choices that fit with this, reading back in the passage as needed. Statement III would fit this view: The West would consider this unjust aggression. Eliminate (A). Statement I fits with the author's opinion of the unstated goal of NATO: to contain a threatening Russia. However, NATO clearly desires "the peaceful integration of Ukraine into Europe" (paragraph 1) and therefore most likely believes that the Ukraine will eventually become part of NATO (as Russia fears, paragraph 7). Eliminate statement II, and (C) is your answer.

Wrong Answers:

II. Opposite. As stated above, Western diplomats would agree that Ukraine will likely be added to NATO.

35.   B

Consider spheres of influence in the context of the passage. Both NATO and Russia want to expand their spheres of influence. What do the two have in common in doing so? The author argues that both claim to be doing so in the name of national security. (B) rewards the prediction instantly.

Wrong Answers:

(A) Out of Scope. The passage says nothing about stopping all communication with perceived enemies.

(C) Distortion. Although the fifth paragraph says Russia believes the West views it as "a defeated enemy," there is no implication in the passage that this assessment is actually true.

(D) Out of Scope. The passage doesn't discuss either Russia or the West being involved in "diplomatic negotiations" to expand its sphere of influence.

Passage VII: Greek Olympics

Topic: Hellenistic period
Scope: Example: The Olympic games
Purpose: To argue that Games mirrored Greek city-state competition, not cooperation

Mapping the Passage:

¶1. Hellenic period was tumultuous, not the idealized community Alexander desired.

¶2. Time frame for the Greek civilization and the Olympic Games.

¶3. Games reflected negative Greek culture.

¶4. Games reinforced disunity instead of unity.

36.   B

Go back to review the phrase in context. The author argues in this paragraph that in theory, the competition was "in the name of idealism" and for "the grandeur of Greece." In reality, each competitor strove to "achieve its own glory." The phrase must therefore mean that athletes competed not for idealistic reasons but for personal gain. (B) uses the term "benefits," which has the same meaning as the passage.

Wrong Answers:

(A) Out of Scope. The phrase is referring to athletes, not Greek society. In any case, the author would probably argue that peace did not, in fact, increase during Olympic years.
(C) Faulty Use of Detail. This detail appears in paragraph 2 and has nothing to do with the phrase.
(D) Out of Scope. This phrase is referring to the Olympics, not the spread of Greek culture.

37.   A

Take a moment to remind yourself of the author's main point about the Games and look at the layout of the choices before trying to answer. Statement II is the most frequent, so hit that first. Statement II restates the author's main argument, and the passage itself is explanation and example for this. Eliminate (B). Statement I offers a point not made by the passage: The author argues that Alexander never truly unified Greece (and he offers no evidence for this). Eliminate (C). The author never makes the claim in statement III, so (D) can be eliminated. (A) alone is left.

Wrong Answers:

I. Out of Scope. Although this may be true, the only mention of Alexander in this passage refers to his vision for an idealized Hellenistic society.
III. Distortion. While the Olympic Games did occur within a city-state system, the passage doesn't suggest that city-states were necessary.

38. D

Paragraph 4 discusses the rewards associated with victory; take a second to reread it before looking for an answer choice that doesn't match. While the wrong answer choices are all perks awarded by an athlete's home city, (D) jumps out as a sign of cooperation and friendship between city-states, which the author would argue didn't exist.

Wrong Answers:

(A) Opposite. The author argues that "imposing defeat [was] a delight."

(B) Opposite. A reward from his own city-state would fit with the economic value the author says was associated with winning.

(C) Opposite. Political office would constitute one of those dry, golden leaves; it would be a tangible perk of winning.

39. A

Review the author's main point about the Games in Greece: they reflected and exacerbated the disunity among city-states. Look for a fact that would reinforce this point: (A) is an example of disunity specifically triggered by the Games themselves.

Wrong Answers:

(B) Out of Scope. When the Games began would have no effect on the author's argument that the Games fostered unproductive competition.

(C) Opposite. This would *weaken* the author's claim that city-states were at each other's throats during the games.

(D) Out of Scope. The number of athletes would probably have little effect on how the city-states regarded each other.

40. C

This statement certainly reinforces the author's main point that the Games made a bad national situation worse. That's another way of saying that they didn't help the situation, and (C) says the same thing. The author clearly believes that the Games made the Greeks' internal tensions worse than they already were.

Wrong Answers:

(A) Out of Scope. The author doesn't discuss the divisions in other civilizations.

(B) Distortion. The author argues that the Greeks were constantly divided, but she doesn't claim that they were always at war as a result.

(D) Opposite. The author argues in paragraph 2 that this marked the *beginning* of Greek history and so surely couldn't also represent the point of decline.

Verbal Reasoning
Practice Test 4

Time—60 minutes

Directions: There are seven passages in this Verbal Reasoning test. Each passage is followed by a set of questions. After reading a passage, select the one best answer to each question. If you are not certain of an answer, eliminate the alternatives that you know to be incorrect and then select an answer from the remaining alternatives.

Passage I (Questions 1–6)

Originally published in 1861, *Incidents in the Life of a Slave Girl Written by Herself* was long regarded as a powerful argument for the abolition of slavery in the United States. Recently, however, its meaning and relevance have changed. Thanks to the work of historian Jean Fagan Yellin, it has become clear that the work is not a novel, as was initially believed, but a true account by Harriet Jacobs of her own life—a primary source on the realities of an African-American woman's life under slavery.

Circumstances initially led 19th-century readers to receive the book as a work of fiction in the tradition of *Uncle Tom's Cabin*, written as a thinly veiled political tract in the Abolitionist cause. *Incidents* was published anonymously. The title page provided no name other than that of its editor, Lydia Maria Child, a noted abolitionist and novelist, whose previous novels had included plotlines and themes similar to those in *Incidents*, fueling speculation that she was the author. Since the first-person narrator of the book, in consideration of others, had "concealed the names of places and given persons fictitious names," there was no way to trace the authorship of the text beyond Mrs. Child, whose denials served only to deepen the mystery surrounding the book's provenance.

But perhaps the most important reason they insisted *Incidents* was a novel was an inability to accept that the woman depicted in the book—who endured the brutality of slavery, hid from her owners in a garret for seven years, and then escaped to the North—could write a work so rooted in the melodramatic literary tradition popular among female readers and authors of the time. In fact, deeply ingrained racial prejudices held by most white Americans (even the abolitionists) made it difficult for them to acknowledge that an African-American was capable of such a powerful and dramatic work under any circumstances.

In the 1980s, Jean Fagan Yellin, struck by the book's attempt to create a sense of sisterhood between white and black women, decided to re-examine the claims of its authenticity made by the narrator and Lydia Maria Child. While others had voiced similar arguments as early as 1947, Yellin went one step farther, meticulously documenting the existence of people and events in the book. Studying the papers of Lydia Maria Child and others in her circle, Yellin found among them Jacobs's letters and other documents that led to general recognition of Jacobs as the writer.

Answering the charge that a former slave could not possibly have been familiar with the literary tradition the book reflected,

Yellin demonstrated that Harriet Jacobs had access to the extensive libraries of abolitionist women. She found that Jacobs's daughter, Louisa, had been educated as a teacher and had transcribed the manuscript in preparation for its publication. Harriet Jacobs's own letters show considerable literary ability; Louisa standardized her mother's spelling and punctuation. And the author's insistence on anonymity was explained in large part by the fact that the book discussed the unique and difficult situation faced by slave women: the sexual predations of male slave owners and their powerlessness to exert on their own behalf society's standards of chaste womanhood. Such matters would be deemed inappropriate for a woman to discuss publicly in 1861, but Jacobs saw the necessity of reaching out to her female readership in this manner. *Incidents in the Life of a Slave Girl* is now recognized as a record of harrowing experiences in slavery.

1. The author probably refers to *Uncle Tom's Cabin* (paragraph 2) primarily in order to

   A. illustrate the racial stereotyping that is also present in *Incidents*.
   B. argue that it is a poorly written novel in comparison with *Incidents*.
   C. assert that precedent existed for the type of book readers believed *Incidents* to be.
   D. provide an example of another novel that was confused with nonfiction.

2. With which of the following statements would the author of the passage most likely agree?

   A. Harriet Jacobs should not have included discussions of sexuality in her book.
   B. American standards of behavior were easy to achieve for most men who were slaves.
   C. *Incidents* was most popular among women readers when it was published.
   D. Novels can provide valuable insights into the history and politics of an era.

3. Each of the following is used by Yellin to support the idea that Harriet Jacobs wrote *Incidents in the Life of a Slave Girl* EXCEPT

   A. her daughter was educated as a teacher.
   B. Lydia Maria Child was listed on the title page as its editor.
   C. discussions of sexuality were deemed inappropriate for a woman in 1861.
   D. the people and events cited in the book did in fact exist.

4. Which of the following ideas is most analogous to the situation described in the passage?

   A. A public figure who is identified with an important political issue writes a novel that dramatizes the issue.
   B. Thanks to the use of new technology, an oil well is discovered on land that was formerly the site of a plantation house.
   C. The value of work by a scientist who was poorly regarded during his lifetime is increasingly recognized in the years after his death.
   D. A painting that was thought to be a forgery turns out after careful analysis to be the work of a well-known artist.

5. Suppose that it was a common convention in 19th-century literature for former slaves to dictate their memoirs to whites, who then edited the memoirs for publication. What effect would this information have had on the arguments about the authorship of *Incidents*?

A. It would provide additional support to the idea that Lydia Maria Child wrote the book.
B. It would lend support to the idea that the book could be a work of nonfiction.
C. It would weaken Jean Fagan Yellin's contention that Jacobs wrote the book by herself.
D. It would make the author's choice to remain anonymous less credible to the modern reader.

6. Claims for the authenticity of *Incidents* were made as early as 1947, but its status as nonfiction was not established until the 1980s. Based on evidence in the passage, the best explanation for this delay is

A. the identification of characters and locations in the book was not done until the 1980s.
B. Jacobs's frank discussion of sexuality brought great criticism on the book.
C. the book was forgotten for many years after slavery was abolished.
D. the libraries of the abolitionists who befriended Jacobs had not yet been discovered.

Passage II (Questions 7–13)

The theory of moral reasoning advanced by Lawrence Kohlberg holds that the thought processes of an individual contemplating a moral dilemma are more revealing than the person's actual behavior in a real situation. On the basis of thousands of interviews attempting to probe such thought processes, Kohlberg concluded that every person passes through three distinct stages of moral reasoning—each divided into two substages. According to Kohlberg, the evidence shows that more persons at "higher" stages of moral reasoning are found in older age groups and that persons observed over a period of years typically advance to a higher level. Having studied subjects in the United States and many other countries, Kohlberg claims cross-cultural validity for his findings.

Within Kohlberg's most basic stage of moral reasoning, the "preconventional" stage, the first substage is that of "punishment-obedience." An individual at this substage will justify a course of action on the basis of tangible consequences such as incurring or avoiding trouble or punishment. A more advanced but still preconventional attitude, the "instrumental relativist orientation," involves reasoning on the basis of satisfying one's own desires and needs. Preconventional reasoning is most commonly observed among young children and preteens.

The next, or "conventional," stage is initially marked by an "interpersonal concordance" orientation and, later, by an orientation toward law and order. The former is characterized by a comprehension of "good" or "bad" motives for a particular action; the latter is concerned not with intent but with authority as an absolute—the law must be respected at all times. Adolescents and young adults are usually conventional reasoners.

Kohlberg's final, "postconventional" stage is more independent of prevailing social mores and stresses the individual's personal values. In the "social contract orientation" substage, a person takes social standards into account but not as absolutes: they are valid because agreed on by society, but they apply only within a pertinent sphere and may be disregarded in appropriate circumstances. In the higher substage of "universal ethical principle orientation," abstract ideals such as human rights, justice, or equality are invoked to justify behavior; deviation from socially accepted standards—even breaking one's own rules—is justifiable if one remains true to one's own underlying ethical ideals. Kohlberg asserts that most adults reason at one of the two postconventional substages.

There appears to be some correlation between the level of moral reasoning attained by an individual and that person's level of cognitive development; Kohlberg's theory is thus regarded as an extension of Piaget's views, which regard cognitive development as occurring in successive stages from the earliest sensorimotor coordination through mastery of "concrete operations" and finally "formal operations." Piaget believed age and external stimuli pushed an individual to higher levels of cognitive development; Kohlberg similarly claims that individuals are capable of such longitudinal movement, although he attributes advances to social development. It is important to realize, however, that Kohlberg's stages are not directly correlative to behavior; what develops is not the degree to which one engages in acts one considers "right" or "wrong," but the kinds of justification offered for doing so.

7. Which of the following most accurately describes the passage?

   A. An analysis of the ways in which moral reasoning differs from behavior in real-life situations

   B. A critique faulting Kohlberg's theory for not accurately predicting real behaviors

   C. A description of Kohlberg's theory of the stages of moral reasoning

   D. A consideration of that which distinguishes moral thought from immoral behavior

8. The passage suggests that an individual displaying an "interpersonal concordance" orientation would reason on the basis of

   A. an understanding of law and order.

   B. comprehension of good and bad.

   C. respect for the concept of the social contract.

   D. consideration of the values of justice and equality.

9. Which of the following best describes Kohlberg's conception of the development of moral reasoning, as implied by the passage?

   A. Moral reasoning usually moves from concrete justifications to more abstract and personal ideals.

   B. Human behavior generally becomes increasingly moral in older age groups.

   C. People are increasingly guided by their own personal needs and desires as they mature.

   D. In general, human beings become more conservative in their moral judgments with the passing of time.

10. According to the passage, a difference between Kohlberg's views and those of Piaget is that

   A. Kohlberg describes moral behavior, while Piaget catalogues cognitive development.

   B. Piaget's stages regard actual behavior, while Kohlberg's regard thought processes.

   C. Kohlberg's theory concerns cognitive development through adulthood, while Piaget focuses on the development of children.

   D. Kohlberg attributes development of thought processes to social development, while Piaget attributes it to age and external stimuli.

11. Which of the following would most seriously WEAKEN Kohlberg's theory?

   A. A study that shows "postconventional" reasoners sometimes decide to act against socially accepted norms

   B. A study that concludes that infants and toddlers are not capable of grasping the concept of altruism

   C. An experiment that reveals individuals reason at all three levels of Kohlberg's typology throughout life

   D. A study that strongly suggests that the development of moral reasoning and cognitive development coincide

12. The author most likely uses the phrase "longitudinal movement" (paragraph 5) to mean a(n)

A. advancement to progressively higher levels of reasoning.

B. lateral motion between different substages.

C. exhibition of increasingly moral behavior.

D. alternation between moral and cognitive development.

13. Which of the following might be indicative of a person in the "conventional" stage of moral reasoning?

A. A driver who runs a red light in order to reach an appointment in good time

B. A clerk who witnesses but doesn't report an impoverished woman's shoplifting

C. A person who believes that police should use whatever means necessary to maintain order

D. A counterfeiter who flees the country when his scheme is brought to light

Passage III (Questions 14–18)

Sixty-five million years ago, something triggered mass extinctions so profound that they define the geological boundary between the Cretaceous and Tertiary periods (the K-T Boundary). Approximately 75 percent of all animal species, including every species of dinosaur, was killed off; those species that survived lost the vast majority of their numbers. The Earth exists in a region of space teeming with asteroids and comets, which on collision have frequently caused enormous environmental devastation, including extinctions of animal species. Yet few traditional geologists or biologists considered the effect these impacts may have had on the geologic and biologic history of the Earth. Since gradual geologic processes like erosion or repeated volcanic eruptions can explain the topographical development of the Earth, they feel there is no need to resort to extraterrestrial explanations.

An important theory proposed in 1980 by physicists Luis and Walter Alvarez challenges this view. The Alvarezes argue that an asteroid roughly 6 miles in diameter collided with the Earth at the K-T Boundary. Although the damage caused by the meteorite's impact would have been great, the dust cloud that enveloped the planet, completely blotting out the sun for up to a year—the result of soil displacement—would have done most of the harm, according to this theory. Plunged into total darkness—and the resulting drastically reduced temperatures—plant growth would have been interrupted, cutting off the food supply to herbivorous species, the loss of which in turn starved carnivores. Additional species would have perished as a result of prolonged atmospheric poisoning, acid rain, forest fires, and tidal waves, all initiated by the asteroid's impact.

Subsequent research has not only tended to support the Alvarez theory, but has suggested that similar impacts may have caused other sharp breaks in Earth's geologic and biologic history. Research in the composition of the Earth has revealed a 160-fold enrichment of iridium all over the world in a thin layer of sediments corresponding to the K-T Boundary. The presence of this element, which is extremely uncommon in the Earth's crust but very common in asteroids and comets, suggest that a meteorite must have struck Earth at that time. Additional physical evidence of such a strike has been found in rock samples, which contain shocked quartz crystals and *microtektites* (small glass spheres)—both by-products of massive collisions.

Observation of the lunar surface provides further evidence of the likelihood of a massive strike. Since the moon and the Earth lie within the same swarm of asteroids and comets, their impact histories should be parallel. Although some lunar craters are of volcanic origin, over the last 4 billion years at least five impact craters ranging from 31 to 58 miles in diameter have marred the lunar surface. By extrapolation, over the same time span Earth must have experienced some 400 collisions of similar magnitude. Although such an impact crater has not been found, Alvarez supporters don't consider finding it necessary or likely. Geologic processes over 65 million years, like erosion and volcanic eruptions, would have obscured the crater, which in any case probably occurred on the ocean floor.

Traditional biologists and geologists continue to deny the validity of the Alvarez theory. They point to the absence of any impact crater; to the fact that iridium, while rare at the Earth's surface, is common at its core and can be transported to the surface by volcanic activity; and to the fact that the Alvarezes, though eminent physicists, are not biologists, geologists, or paleontologists.

14. The views of those scientists who oppose the Alvarez theory would be strengthened if

   I. major deposits of iridium were found in the lava flows of active Earth volcanoes.

   II. iridium was absent in sediments corresponding to several episodes of mass extinction.

   III. iridium was absent in fragments of several recently recovered meteorites.

   A. I only
   B. I and II only
   C. III only
   D. I and III only

15. The passage suggests that the author would characterize those who hold the traditional views about the topographical development of the earth as

   A. detrimental to scientific progress.
   B. unrivaled at the present time.
   C. correct in challenging alternative views.
   D. unreceptive to new evidence.

16. The author discusses the Alvarezes' description of environmental conditions at the end of the Cretaceous period in order to

   A. demonstrate that an immense meteorite hit the earth.
   B. explain why no trace of an impact crater has yet been found.
   C. argue that Earth is vulnerable to meteorite collisions.
   D. clarify how a meteorite may account for mass extinctions.

17. The author's statement that "Earth exists in a region of space teeming with asteroids and comets," is most consistent with

   A. the Alvarezes' claim that an asteroid's impact caused atmospheric poisoning, acid rain, forest fires, and tidal waves.
   B. the Alvarezes' view that the resulting dust cloud, rather than the impact of the meteorite, did most of the harm.
   C. Alvarez supporters' argument based on extrapolation from the numbers of craters on the surface of the moon.
   D. traditionalists' view that topographical development of the Earth can be explained by gradual geologic processes.

18. Suppose new evidence is found establishing irrefutably that the impact of an asteroid 6 miles in diameter on the moon would result in a crater 500 miles in diameter. What effect would this information have on the arguments made in the passage?

   A. It would strengthen the Alvarez theory, because the moon and earth lie within the same group of asteroids and comets.
   B. It would weaken the Alvarez theory, because the craters that have been measured on the moon are too small to represent the impact of such a meteorite.
   C. It would contradict the traditional view, because craters that large would certainly have catastrophic effects on earth's environments.
   D. It would have no effect on any arguments made in the passage, because the size of a crater on the moon isn't relevant to the size of a crater on earth.

Passage IV (Questions 19–23)

Gender-based trends in labor are of great interest to historians and sociologists, since these shifts mark a transition in the nation's economic prosperity and are linked to the ever-changing concepts of what constitutes "men's" and "women's" work. Perhaps one of the most significant labor transitions in American history occurred in the evolution from the Colonial era, during which most families farmed or ran small "cottage industries" in their homes, to the Industrial Revolution, when a large segment of the population earned wages in mills and factories. Though both eras were patriarchal, the pre-industrial colonists enjoyed a degree of economic egalitarianism that would all but disappear with industrialization.

While the Colonial era is certainly not an example of gender equality, its economic system did allow women some power. The family was a self-sufficient economic unit, and all necessary goods and services were available either within or just beyond the home. Work was considered a civic duty for women, integral to the family's economic survival, and wasn't confined to the home: many women were also shopkeepers, midwives, and even blacksmiths. Instead of being embarrassed by their wives' participation in labor-intensive activities, husbands encouraged and relied on it.

With the advent of the Industrial Revolution came stricter definitions of men's and women's roles. The move from a subsistence economy to a market economy all but obliterated the family-based "cottage industries" so prevalent during the Colonial era. The gap between the genders widened, as men and women occupied different social realms and physical workspaces. Thus developed the "doctrine of two spheres"—to men the realm of public visibility and economic opportunity, to women private, domestic responsibility. Women felt themselves further demoted in an already patriarchal society.

While Colonial women had the satisfaction of contributing to the family's economic well-being, the society of the Industrial Revolution, on the whole, appreciated neither their presence in, nor their contributions to, the labor force. Instead of encouraging women to help catalyze industrialization, mainstream society endorsed the disempowering phenomenon known as the "Cult of True Womanhood." Women's roles were both idealized and restricted; women were held to the highest standards of piety, purity, domesticity, and submissiveness. The "moral authority" given to women was nominal in comparison to the *actual* authority that their husbands possessed. While many middle- and upper-class families had the luxury—at least ostensibly—to fulfill these requirements, this was simply not an option for the working class, whose women had to leave the home to put food on the table. This experience could be both personally frustrating and socially limiting.

Men felt the pressure and anxiety created by the Cult of True Womanhood as well, each afraid of letting social status and credibility decrease. The "good-provider role," a position shared by men and women during the Colonial era, was now assigned solely to the man of the household. Many men, for a variety of reasons, could not successfully maintain the position of breadwinner. Some overperformed the good-provider role at the expense of emotional intimacy with their wives and children; others refused the burden and abandoned their families. Caught between these two extremes were the everyday male workers who tried their best to maintain social status and strong familial ties—dual goals that were often unattainable.

19. Which of the following general theories is best supported by the passage?

    A. A sharp economic downturn at the end of the Colonial era prompted a move toward the gender-segregated labor system of the Industrial Revolution.
    B. The Colonial era in America was characterized by a social egalitarianism that disappeared with the advent of the Industrial Revolution.
    C. The Industrial Revolution, while known as a time of great progress in American history, caused significant socioeconomic strain for men and women alike.
    D. The beginning of the women's movement in the early 20th century was a backlash against the Cult of True Womanhood created during the Industrial Revolution.

20. The author most likely mentions the status of the working class during the Industrial Revolution in order to

    A. compare the economic standing of working class families of the Industrial Revolution and the Colonial era.
    B. examine a section of the population for which socially ideal gender roles were not easily attained.
    C. emphasize the negative attitudes the middle and upper classes had toward the lower class.
    D. discuss a social class that didn't view the Cult of True Womanhood as its ideal.

21. The author would be most likely to make which of the following claims about the difference between the Colonial period and the Industrial Revolution?

    A. The Industrial Revolution was a time of marked prosperity, while the Colonial era was characterized by economic struggle.
    B. Colonial men were more accepting of women's participation in the labor force than were men during the Industrial Revolution.
    C. Men in the Colonial era found it more difficult to maintain the "good-provider role" than did men in the Industrial Revolution.
    D. Children were less likely to be forced into labor during the Colonial era than during the Industrial Revolution.

22. Which of the following situations would the author be most likely to consider an example of adherence to the Cult of True Womanhood?

    A. A woman works in a garment factory all day and then returns home to clean the house, bathe the children, and cook dinner for the family.
    B. A woman sacrifices the financial advantages of taking a job in a factory so that she can tend to the children and participate in church activities.
    C. A woman opens a clothes-tailoring service in her home so that she can contribute to the family's income without having to work outside the house.
    D. A woman's husband becomes overwhelmed with the pressure of providing for his wife and children and eventually abandons the family.

23. The passage indicates that the author is LEAST likely to agree with which of the following statements?

A. The Industrial Revolution introduced new social and economic standards to American life that proved to be both helpful and harmful.

B. The financial contribution of working-class women during the Industrial Revolution was similar to that of Colonial women, but Colonial women received more recognition.

C. Both the Colonial era and the Industrial Revolution were characterized by gender inequality.

D. The role a woman played in society was much less important during the Colonial era.

Passage V (Questions 24–30)

The Augustan Age has been called "The Great Age of Satire," since almost all its major writers produced satirical works. They also wrote *about* satire, and often disagreed with each other. Addison was strongly against the use of satire, claiming that the unkind writers who used it inflicted irreparable harm on their scorned victims. Pope, in contrast, called satire a "sacred weapon" that permitted oblique criticism in his *Epilogue to the Satires*. In his own mock epic, *The Rape of the Lock,* Lady Belinda's tresses are cropped by a suitor while she lingers over her coffee. Samuel Johnson called this a questionable topic for poetic treatment: "below the common incidents of common life." Yet the frivolous story was ideal to lambaste traditional epic machinery and romantic conventions.

Swift had a mixed opinion of satire. On the one hand, he believed it could instruct—that those who were influenced neither by the rebuke of clergy nor by fear of punishment would dread to have their misdeeds and peccadilloes published to their neighbors. On the other hand, as P. K. Elkin writes, Swift is the only major Augustan writer who questioned the efficacy of satire on a hardened heart. In the preface to *A Tale of a Tub,* for example, the Tubbian says satirists should give up remonstrating with the notorious, who are insensible to verbal lashes.

In spite of this ambivalence, many of Swift's most famous works—like *An Argument Against the Abolishing of Christianity* and *A Modest Proposal*—are satires. Given his mixed feelings, we might question why he chose to satirize such serious subjects as religion and the politics of famine. Perhaps Swift thought satire effectively conveyed strong opinions. The ironic personae adopted in these works—unreliable narrators—are vital to the force of his message because in questioning the narrator's mind and morals, the reader questions what the narrator says. The juxtaposition of the literal and the veiled meaning of the narrators' words effect complicated, subtle operations on the mind of the reader. Unless his readers are fools or knaves, they read with increasing discomfort as they sense the seriousness behind the wit and their own complicity in the guilt.

The ironic personae used in these two works are not the same. The narrator of the *Argument* occupies the middle of the road, sharing his society's goals, but disagreeing with the means most people would use to attain them. The author of the *Proposal*, by contrast, is so extreme that some critics have called him mad—a plausible characterization since the Proposer takes literally the abstract economic principle that people are the riches of a nation: People, the riches of Ireland, can be raised, sold, butchered, and eaten like cattle. There is a difference, too, in the narrators' methods. The Arguer admits the possibility, however slight, that the reader may disagree with him. The Proposer, on the other hand, is obsessed with the perfection of his solution. The Arguer argues the right cause for the wrong reasons; the Proposer posits a solution that can't be reasonably entertained.

The Arguer and the Proposer share some characteristics, though. Both display Swiftian concern for reason gone awry. Both are outwardly rational, but like the Laputians on the Flying Island, they attempt to see everything one way. The Proposer "can think of no one Objection, that will possibly be raised against this Proposal." The reader, by this time aware of the Proposer's fixation, can and will raise objections. Less obsessive than the Proposer, the Arguer states and refutes objections to his argument, but dismissively, only to forestall demur.

24. The information in the passage supports which of the following conclusions concerning Augustan satire?

   I. Satirists could focus both on the foibles of individuals and on larger, societal ills.

   II. Satire could be used to mock literary conventions.

   III. Satire could serve as a formidable weapon for personal revilement.

   A. I only
   B. III only
   C. I and III only
   D. I, II, and III

25. Based on the information provided in the passage, which of the following might be an Augustan satire?

   A. A polemic decrying Lockean ethics
   B. An exposé of patronage at the court of Charles II
   C. A fanciful description of a mythical land
   D. A cleverly disguised attack on a pedantic academic

26. Based on the passage, we can reasonably assume that the author believes Johnson's criticism of *The Rape of the Lock* represents

   A. an overly narrow perception of the appropriate content of poetry.
   B. fixation on a minor flaw inhibiting enjoyment of the work as a whole.
   C. a failure to appreciate that the work is intentionally humorous.
   D. a conviction that the work mocks the dignity of everyday life.

27. The passage implies that, in the opinion of the author, during the period before the Augustan Age

   A. satire dealt only with subjects of political and religious importance.
   B. the conventions of heroic poetry were considered above criticism.
   C. satire was seen as only one among several important literary genres.
   D. greater political freedom allowed writers to express political ideas directly.

28. The author most probably includes details from the "plot" of *The Rape of the Lock* in order to

   A. argue that Pope had captured the ideal context for Augustan satire.
   B. contrast Pope's view of satire with Addison's strong objection to its use.
   C. demonstrate a dispute between Augustan writers about the proper subject of satire.
   D. show how frivolous Pope's satire was, as compared to the serious satire of Swift.

29. An assumption apparently made by Addison in his criticism of satire as a genre is that

   A. satire was potentially beneficial but not generally effective.
   B. any instructional value of satire was outweighed by its harm to individuals.
   C. most readers were unable to comprehend the indirect significance of satire.
   D. the subject matter of satire was the "below the common incidents of common life."

30. The author concludes that Swift chose to write on such serious subjects as religion and politics in the form of satire because

   A. he believed that satire was effective even on the hardened hearts of the notorious.
   B. satire was the only genre in which he could use his favorite persona, the unreliable narrator.
   C. the ironic personae used in these satires both display Swift's concern for reason gone awry.
   D. it juxtaposed absurd literal ideas with hidden subtext that was especially effective at involving the reader.

Passage VI (Questions 31–35)

Despite the falling popularity of smoking in the United States, the increase in smoking among young women continues. Whereas older teenage males appear to have reached a plateau in the early 1970s, with approximately 19 percent smoking, over 26 percent of older teenage females are now regular smokers.

A 1989 study examined smoking habits among young women as reported by approximately 600 undergraduate women at four Maryland colleges. Researcher Mary Smith and colleagues examined the respondents' description of parental and peer smoking behavior to determine whether these factors were correlated with their smoking behavior.

The researchers first analyzed the effects of parental smoking on the initiation of smoking. Smith views the initiation of smoking as a function of psychosocial rather than physiological influences since the physical effects of nicotine are not felt until later in life. Smoking behavior of the respondents' mothers was significantly associated with the college women's own early smoking behavior. Among respondents with mothers who smoked, 56.9 percent of the daughters had smoked or did smoke, while 43.1 percent had never smoked. Of respondents with nonsmoking mothers, 46.5 percent had smoked or did smoke, while 53.3 percent of such respondents had never smoked. The smoking behavior of the father during the initiation stage appears to have little or no effect upon the respondents' smoking behavior.

The next stage of the smoking career, the maintenance of smoking habits, was less significantly related to the smoking behavior of the primary socialization agents. The smoking behavior of the respondents' fathers seemed to have no effect on their smoking maintenance, while the smoking behavior of the mother was related only to the frequency of smoking, but not the duration of the habit. Of much greater importance to the maintenance of smoking habits of respondents was the smoking behavior of particular members of her proximal social environment—her closest female friends. Interestingly, smoking habits of even the closest male members of the respondent's social network seemed to have no bearing upon the frequency and duration of the respondents' smoking behavior.

According to Smith, cessation constitutes the third stage of an individual's smoking career; in the Maryland study, cessation was measured by the respondents' categorizations of perceived or actual difficulties associated with giving up cigarettes. Her parents' smoking behavior was not taken into consideration, but the relationship between cessation of smoking and the smoking behavior of members of the respondent's social network was similar to that cited above: only the smoking behavior of female friends was significantly correlated with the respondent's perceived or actual difficulty in breaking her own habit. Smith and her associates concluded that same-sex relationships are important in every phase of a woman's smoking career.

31. According to the passage, a young woman's closest female friends

A. have little effect on her smoking habits.
B. encourage her to smoke heavily.
C. determine whether she will start smoking.
D. influence the duration of her smoking habit.

32. The passage suggests that male smoking behavior

A. helps to explain female smoking behavior.
B. influences the smoking habits of other males.
C. affects women's decisions to stop smoking.
D. does not account for female smoking habits.

33. Which of the following would most seriously WEAKEN Smith's basic argument?

    A. Mothers have influence over the earliest stages of their daughters' smoking careers.

    B. Close female friends influence the duration, but not the frequency, of young women's smoking.

    C. The maintenance of one's smoking habits is heavily influenced by one's economic status.

    D. The smoking habits of both parents significantly influence a daughter's initial decision to smoke.

34. Which of the following most accurately describes the passage?

    A. A refutation of an earlier hypothesis

    B. An explanation of a popular theory

    C. A summary of recent research findings

    D. A description of a controversial study

35. According to the passage, in the early 1970s, the percentage of male smokers

    A. leveled off at 26 percent.

    B. decreased to 19 percent.

    C. increased to 26 percent.

    D. leveled off at 19 percent.

Passage VII (Questions 36–40)

Muzak, the intentionally unobtrusive music that most people associate with elevators and dentists' waiting rooms, represents the paradoxical success story of a product designed to be ignored. Although few people admit to enjoying its blandly melodic sounds, Muzak reaches over 100 million listeners in 14 countries and has played in the White House; the Apollo lunar space-craft; and countless supermarkets, offices, and factories. This odd combination of criticism and widespread acceptance is not surprising, however, when one considers that Muzak is not created for the enjoyment of its listeners: rather; its purpose is to modify physiological and psychological aspects of an environment.

In the workplace, Muzak is credited with increasing both productivity and profitability. Research into the relationship between music and productivity can be traced to the earliest days of the Muzak Corporation. Developed by a military officer in 1922 as a way of transmitting music through electrical wires, Muzak blossomed in the 1930s following a study that reported that people work harder when they listen to certain kinds of music. Impressed by these findings, the BBC began to broadcast music in English munitions factories during World War II in an effort to combat fatigue. When workers assembling weapons increased their output by 6 percent, the U.S. War Production Board contracted the Muzak Corporation to provide uplifting music to American facto-ries. Today, the corporation broadcasts its "Environmental Music" to countless businesses and institutions throughout the world. And while most people claim to dislike Muzak's discreet cadences, it seems to positively influence both productivity and job satisfaction.

Researchers speculate that listening to Muzak and other soft music improves morale and reduces stress by modifying our physiology. Physiological changes such as lowered heart rate and decreased blood pressure have been documented in hospital studies testing the effect of calming music on cardiac patients. In addition, certain kinds of music seem to affect one's sense of emotional, as well as physical, well-being. It is just this sort of satisfaction which is thought to result in increased per-formance in the workplace. In a study of people performing repetitive clerical tasks, those who listened to music performed more accurately and quickly than those who worked in silence; those who listened to Muzak did better still. Moreover, while Muzak was conceived as a tool for productivity, it also seems to influence a business's profitability. In an experiment in which supermarket shoppers shopped to the mellow sounds of Muzak, sales were increased by as much as 12 percent.

What makes Muzak unique is a formula by which familiar tunes are modified and programmed. Careful instrumentation adds to an overall sound that is neither monotonous nor rousing. But it is the precisely timed programming that separates Muzak from other "easy listening" formats. At the core of the programming is the concept of the "Stimulus Progression." Muzak programs are divided into quarter-hour groupings of songs, and are specifically planned for the time of day at which they will be heard. Each composition is assigned a mood rating between 1 and 6 called a stimulus value; a song with a rating of 2, for example, is slower and less invigorating than one with a value of 5. Approximately six compositions with ascending stimulus values play during any given quarter hour; each 15-minute segment ends in silence. Each segment of a 24-hour program is carefully planned. Segments that are considered more stimulating air at 11 A.M. and 3 P.M. (the times when workers typically tire), while more soothing segments play just after lunchtime and toward the end of the day, when workers are likely to be restless.

From the point of view of management, then, Muzak is a useful tool in the effort to maximize both productivity and prof-its. However, some people object to its presence, labeling it as a type of unregulated air pollution. Still others see it as an Orwellian nightmare, a manipulation of the subconscious. But Muzak's effectiveness seems to lie in the fact that most people never really listen to it. While it may be true that no one actually likes this carefully crafted aural atmosphere, many simply ignore it, allowing its forgettable sounds to soften the contours of the day.

36. According to the passage, a 15-minute segment of Muzak with an average stimulus value of 5 would most likely be broadcast at

A. 4:30 P.M.
B. 8:15 A.M.
C. 3:00 P.M.
D. 1:15 P.M.

37. Of the following, the author is most interested in discussing

A. the origins of the Muzak Corporation.
B. how Muzak modifies physical states and psychological atmospheres.
C. how Muzak increases productivity in the workplace.
D. the ways in which Muzak differs from other "easy listening" formats.

38. It can be inferred from the passage that some critics of Muzak believe that Muzak

A. is not significantly different from other "easy listening" programs.
B. subtly manipulates the subconscious mind.
C. is actually distracting to many workers.
D. caters to the whims of supermarket consumers.

39. According to the passage, Muzak differs from other "easy listening" formats in that Muzak

I. produces measurable health benefits.
II. improves workers' job performances.
III. is programmed in order to affect behavioral changes.

A. I only
B. II only
C. III only
D. II and III only

40. It can be inferred from the statements in the passage that the author regards Muzak as

A. a paradoxical phenomenon.
B. an unnecessary evil.
C. a violation of privacy.
D. a pleasurable diversion.

Verbal Reasoning Practice Test 4 Answers and Explanations

ANSWER KEY

1.	C	9.	A	17.	C	25.	D	33.	D
2.	D	10.	D	18.	B	26.	A	34.	C
3.	B	11.	C	19.	C	27.	C	35.	D
4.	D	12.	A	20.	B	28.	C	36.	C
5.	B	13.	C	21.	B	29.	B	37.	B
6.	A	14.	A	22.	B	30.	D	38.	B
7.	C	15.	C	23.	D	31.	D	39.	C
8.	B	16.	D	24.	D	32.	D	40.	A

EXPLANATIONS

Passage I: Harriet Jacobs

Topic: Harriet Jacobs's book

Scope: Change in the text's relevance

Purpose: To support Yellin's theory that book is true

Mapping the Passage:

¶1. *Incidents* = primary source; not a novel.

¶2. Why initially received as fiction.

¶3. Additional reason why received as fiction: racial prejudice.

¶4. Why and how Yellin discovered Jacobs was author.

¶5. How Jacobs learned to write; why she remained anonymous; why she wrote the novel.

1. C

This question asks you to explain the function of the reference to *Uncle Tom's Cabin*, which the author describes as a "thinly veiled political tract in the Abolitionist cause."

Readers of *Incidents* initially considered it the same type of book. Thus, *Uncle Tom's Cabin* showed that a precedent existed for this type of fiction, which is answer (C).

Wrong Answers:

(A) Out of Scope. The author doesn't discuss racial stereotyping in either book.

(B) Out of Scope. It sets up a comparison that does not exist in the text—nothing is mentioned about the quality of *Uncle Tom's Cabin*.

(D) Opposite. *Uncle Tom's Cabin* was not confused with nonfiction, nor is *Incidents* a novel.

2. D

This is an inference (deduction) question requiring an answer choice that logically follows from the passage. The first paragraph discusses the book's value as a powerful argument against slavery, an American historical issue, even when people thought it was a novel. Thus (D)—novels can give us insights into history—restates the book's value.

Wrong Answers:

(A) Faulty Use of Detail. The author states that readers in 1861 might have considered public discussion of sexuality inappropriate, but we don't know that the author agrees with that assessment.

(B) Out of Scope. The passage doesn't discuss men achieving these standards, just women.

(C) Faulty Use of Detail. It's true that *Incidents* was written in a literary tradition popular among female readers, but we don't know anything about the readers of this book.

3. B

Three of these statements are in the passage and are used to support Yellin's argument that Harriet Jacobs was the author. The one statement that doesn't support this conclusion is (B). Although Yellin did study "the papers of Lydia Maria Child and others in her circle," she never used the fact that Child was listed as the book's editor as evidence.

Wrong Answers:

(A) Opposite. This is in the last paragraph and is cited by Yellin as part of the evidence that Jacobs wrote the book.

(C) Opposite. This is also in the last paragraph and supports the idea that Jacobs would have preferred to remain anonymous and not be listed as the author.

(D) Opposite. This is the entire second half of paragraph 4.

4. D

This application question asks us to apply the ideas from the passage to a new situation. The "situation described in the passage" is that *Incidents* was once thought to be fiction but was later proven to be nonfiction. (D) fits this scenario best; it's another situation of something at first thought to be false (as fiction would be), then proved true (as an autobiography would be).

Wrong Answers:

(A) Opposite. It's on the same general topic as the passage, substituting a well-known author for an unknown one, but is missing the key part: a new revelation that allows something to be reclassified.

(B) Out of Scope. There's no way to reconcile technology with anything analogous to Jacobs's situation. The mention of the plantation house, which is relevant to slavery, should alert us that this is a trap answer.

(C) Out of Scope. Even if the situation in question were the recognition of Jacobs as the writer of *Incidents*, she was not poorly regarded during her lifetime as far as we know from the passage, though she may have been unknown.

5. B

If former slaves often dictated their memoirs to whites, who then became the editors of the work, two of the objections to Jacobs writing *Incidents* would be refuted: A former slave could not have written such a dramatic book, nor could she have been familiar with the book's literary tradition. Jacobs could have dictated her real-life story to Child, a novelist who could have written a dramatic book in the style of other slave narratives. This would support Yellin's theory that the book was nonfiction.

Wrong Answers:

(A) Opposite. Jacobs, not Child, was the author of the book.

(C) Out of Scope. Yellin never asserts that Jacobs wrote the book by herself.

(D) Faulty Use of Detail. According to the passage, Jacobs chose to remain anonymous because of "inappropriate" matters in *Incidents*. This decision would not depend on who edited the book.

6. A

This is an application question that refers to paragraph 4. There we see that Yellin "document[ed] the existence of people and events in the book," thereby establishing the true nature of the book as nonfiction and identifying Jacobs as the author. Choice (A) is on the mark here.

Wrong Answers:

(B) Out of Scope. This might have been true when the book was published, but no such criticism after 1947 is mentioned.

(C) Out of Scope. The question asks why nothing happened between 1947 and the 1980s, not what happened "after slavery was abolished."

(D) Opposite. The passage doesn't give any information about when these libraries were "discovered." Additionally, these libraries, mentioned in the last paragraph, are only cited as evidence that Jacobs is the writer; they were not used to discover her identity.

Passage II: Kohlberg

Topic: Kohlberg's theory of moral reasoning
Scope: Theory's stages
Purpose: To explain

Mapping the Passage:

¶1. Kohlberg's theory of moral reasoning: 3 stages.

¶2. Preconventional reasoning: Children and preteens.

¶3. Conventional stage: Young adults.

¶4. Postconventional stage: Most adults.

¶5. Similarities and differences between Piaget and Kohlberg.

7.   C

This question asks about the primary purpose of the passage. The author's tone is merely descriptive, and her topic is the stages of Kohlberg's theory of the stages of moral reasoning. (C) accurately describes the main purpose of the passage and answers this question.

Wrong Answers:

(A) Out of Scope. The author mentions behavior only to illustrate that Kohlberg's theory is concerned with thought processes, not behavior.

(B) Out of Scope. The author doesn't criticize Kohlberg's theory. In this passage, the author is neutral.

D) Out of Scope. The author doesn't consider particular behaviors and never assigns values to them, such as "moral" or "immoral."

8.   B

In paragraph 3, "interpersonal concordance" is the first of the two substages characterized by comprehension of "good" and "bad" motives, so (B) is correct.

Wrong Answers:

(A) Faulty Use of Detail. This is mentioned in the third paragraph but occurs in the second substage, which follows the "interpersonal concordance" orientation.

(C) Faulty Use of Detail. This is discussed in the fourth paragraph and is part of the "postconventional" stage.

(D) Faulty Use of Detail. This is in paragraph 4 and is the last part of the postconventional stage.

9.   A

This question asks about the overall pattern of the development of moral reasoning—the stages through which reasoning passes. As you look over your map and the passage, it becomes clear that reasoning goes from the stage of avoiding tangible consequences ("trouble or punishment") all the way to reasoning on the basis of abstract, ethical ideas. With that as your prediction, the answer that jumps out is (A).

Wrong Answers:

(B) Out of Scope. The passage is about cognitive reasoning, not behavior. The last paragraph even says that "Kohlberg's stages are not directly correlative to behavior." Additionally, Kohlberg does not discuss the morality of the stages.

(C) Faulty Use of Detail. Personal needs and desires are considered in the "preconventional" stage, common to young children and preteens.

(D) Out of Scope. Kohlberg's theory doesn't define any stage as being more or less "conservative" than another.

10.   D

The fifth paragraph compares Kohlberg's views to those of Piaget. What's the difference? Piaget considers "age and external stimuli" as the factors leading to cognitive development, while Kohlberg claims that "social development" is responsible for the development of thought processes. That's (D).

Wrong Answers:

(A) **Out of Scope.** Kohlberg's theory has to do with reasoning, not behavior.

(B) **Out of Scope.** This suggests that Piaget's theory regards actual behavior, which the passage neither states nor implies.

(C) **Out of Scope.** The passage implies that both theorists are concerned with cognitive development throughout life.

11. C

This incorporation question asks you to consider statements that might weaken Kohlberg's theory. (C) states that individuals use all three stages throughout their lives; this contradicts Kohlberg's theory, which says that people successively move from one stage to the next.

Wrong Answers:

(A) **Opposite.** This study would support Kohlberg's theory, which says that people in the "postconventional" stage "take social standards into account but not as absolutes."

(B) **Opposite.** Kohlberg doesn't claim that infants and toddlers can grasp altruism, so this study would also support his theory.

(D) **Faulty Use of Detail.** This would support the author's views about Kohlberg and Piaget, but it would have no effect on Kohlberg's theory.

12. A

The author mentions "longitudinal movement" in the last paragraph. The sentence containing this phrase suggests that longitudinal movement refers to the advancement through progressively higher levels of reasoning, from childish to mature reasoning. (A) restates that idea.

Wrong Answers:

(B) **Opposite.** The question isn't referring to movements across and between substages but from one stage to the next.

(C) **Out of Scope.** The test maker keeps coming back to "behavior" as an out-of-scope answer. The trap is the possible confusion of behavior with thought, but behavior just isn't at issue in this passage.

(D) **Opposite.** The last paragraph talks about moral and cognitive development. Kohlberg's theory considers moral reasoning, while Piaget's looks at cognitive development. The passage says the two are correlated but doesn't state or imply an alternation between the two.

13. C

The "conventional" stage is marked by a consideration of good and bad motives and, later, by a respect for law and order with a view that "the law must be respected at all times." (C) correctly describes a person in this stage who would conceivably support any police action because of an unwavering belief in the need for lawful order.

Wrong Answers:

(A) **Faulty Use of Detail.** A driver who runs a red light is likely considering his or her own needs, which is part of preconventional reasoning.

(B) **Faulty Use of Detail.** This is consistent with the postconventional stage—the highest level—not the conventional stage.

(D) **Faulty Use of Detail.** This counterfeiter isn't considering the distinction between good and bad motives or respecting the law, the two tenants of the "conventional" stage.

Passage III: Asteroid Impact

Topic: Alvarez theory
Scope: Evidence for and against Alvarez theory
Purpose: To discuss

Mapping the Passage:

¶1. Mass extinction: Cause unknown; few consider extraterrestrial impact.

¶2. Alvarez's theory: Extraterrestrial asteroid impact caused extinction.

¶3. Support for Alvarez: Iridium at K-T.

¶4. More support: Lunar surface.

¶5. Critique of the Alvarez theory.

14. A

To tackle a strengthen/weaken question that cites a particular theory in the passage, make sure you understand both the question and the arguments for and against the theory before reading the answer choices. This question asks for evidence that would support those who critique Alvarez. The argument of these critics is given in the last paragraph: no crater, iridium comes from the earth's core, and the Alvarezes are only physicists. Look at statement I first, since it occurs three times in the choices. This would clearly bolster the opponents' view—if sufficient iridium deposits come from the earth's core, Alvarez supporters cannot rely on them as evidence of impact.

Wrong Answers:

II. Out of Scope. Statement II refers to "several episodes," while the Alvarez theory is concerned with only one.

III. Out of Scope. Paragraph 3 states that iridium is "very common in asteroids and comets" but not necessarily present in all of them. So finding several meteorites without iridium wouldn't change anything.

15. C

This isn't easy, but (C) is the only possible correct choice. Remember that the author is neutral (we used the neutral word "discuss" for purpose), so any answer that favors one theory over the other is incorrect. The author wouldn't want the Alvarezes' opponents to give up their view until the new theory had been fully tested against all their criticisms.

Wrong Answers:

(A) Distortion. The traditionalists' view isn't dismissed as "detrimental," just different.

(B) Distortion. Because the author of this passage is neutral, he wouldn't consider either side to be "unrivaled," which would indicate his total support.

(D) Distortion. The critics are not unreceptive to new evidence. The last paragraph gives their rebuttal to the Alvarezes' evidence, proving they do consider new evidence. In this case, they simply don't think it proves the Alvarez theory.

16. D

This evaluation question asks why the author includes a detailed description of the environmental conditions proposed by the Alvarezes for the end of the Cretaceous period. Look back at the second paragraph. These details clarify the mechanism by which an asteroid impact could have led to extinctions. The meteorite didn't simply smash all species into extinction; it led to an environment that couldn't sustain them, as (D) says.

Wrong Answers:

(A) Distortion. On the MCAT, *demonstrate* means "prove." According to the passage, the Alvarez theory is still being debated.

(B) Faulty Use of Detail. The lack of a known crater site is mentioned at the end of paragraph 4, but it is not relevant to environmental conditions.

(C) Faulty Use of Detail. The fourth paragraph argues that the earth is vulnerable to meteorite collisions. This statement is based on the number of lunar impacts but is irrelevant to the Alvarezes' description of environmental conditions in paragraph 2.

17. C

The number of asteroids and comets suggested by the author's word *teeming* is an essential part of the argument made by Alvarez supporters about how frequently collisions must have occurred in earth's history. If the earth and moon "lie within the same swarm of asteroids and comets," it's more than likely that many of them struck the earth, supporting (C).

Wrong Answers:

(A) Faulty Use of Detail. These details about the effects of an asteroid impact are completely unrelated to the number of asteroids and comets around the earth.

(B) Faulty Use of Detail. Like (A), this answer choice also incorrectly looks at the results of an asteroid impact.

(D) Opposite. The fact that the earth is in an area "teeming with asteroids" supports the theory that it experiences numerous asteroid impacts, contradicting the traditionalists'

theory that the earth's geography can be explained by gradual processes.

18. B

The details in the question stem relate to the statements in the passage about the size of the impact craters on the moon and the Alvarezes' theory that a six-mile-wide meteorite caused the Cretaceous extinctions. According to the passage, the craters on the moon are only "31–58 miles in diameter," significantly smaller than the 500-mile crater a six-mile asteroid would have caused, according to this new information. Therefore, something much smaller than a six-mile-wide asteroid must have caused the craters on the moon, making it less likely that an asteroid with a six-mile diameter struck the earth.

Wrong Answers:

(A) **Opposite.** The new information weakens, not strengthens, the theory.

(C) **Faulty Use of Detail.** The passage doesn't explicitly say that there is any relationship between the amount of devastation caused by an asteroid and the size of its crater.

(D) **Opposite.** The author wouldn't have cited such evidence if it were irrelevant.

Passage IV: Gender Work

Topic: Gender-based trends in U.S. labor
Scope: Evolution from Colonial era to Industrial Revolution
Purpose: To discuss

Mapping the Passage:

¶1. Gender-based work trends; change from Colonial era to Industrial Revolution.

¶2. Colonial era: Family = self-sufficient; work = civic duty for women.

¶3. Industrial Revolution: Gender gap widened.

¶4. Women's role in Industrial Revolution.

¶5. Men's role in Industrial Revolution.

19. C

The fourth paragraph discusses the difficulties women faced in the Industrial Revolution, and the fifth paragraph talks about the struggles men faced. Therefore, the passage supports (C).

Wrong Answers:

(A) **Out of Scope.** The passage doesn't mention an "economic downturn" after the Colonial era.

(B) **Out of Scope.** This passage does not discuss social classes in the Colonial era.

(D) **Out of Scope.** The women's movement in the 20th century is not discussed in the passage.

20. B

The author looks at the status of the working class during the Industrial Revolution (paragraph 4) in contrast to that of the middle- and upper-class families of the same era. Lower-class women, due to financial limitations, could not achieve the socially ideal gender role, which is exactly what (B) says.

Wrong Answers:

(A) **Out of Scope.** The author never mentions the status of the working class during the Colonial era.

(C) **Out of Scope.** The passage does not talk about attitudes of one class toward another.

(D) **Opposite.** Paragraph 4 discusses the working class's struggle to conform to the "Cult of True Womanhood," so these people must have viewed it as their ideal.

21. B

Almost the entire passage discusses gender differences between these two periods. While Colonial women were integral to their families' survival and thus were encouraged to work by their husbands (paragraph 2), women in the Industrial Revolution were relegated to "domestic responsibility." Thus, men were less accepting of women's labor after the Industrial Revolution than before, and that's (B).

Wrong Answers:

(A) **Out of Scope.** The passage doesn't discuss the relative prosperity of these two eras.

(C) **Out of Scope.** We don't know how hard it was for men during the Colonial era, only during the Industrial Revolution.

(D) **Out of Scope.** While this may be historically true, the treatment of children during the Colonial era and the Industrial Revolution is never mentioned in the passage. Never bring your own knowledge or opinion to a passage. Every correct answer is supported by what the author wrote, not what the reader thinks.

22. B

The "Cult of True Womanhood" held women to strict rules of "piety, purity, domesticity, and submissiveness." Under this ideal, a woman was not allowed to work to help support her family; this was solely the responsibility of her husband. (B) is the only example of a woman not breaking any of the tenets of "True Womanhood."

Wrong Answers:

(A) **Opposite.** This looks like a working-class woman's life in the Industrial Revolution.

(C) **Opposite.** A woman with her own tailoring business (which would provide her with financial independence) was frowned upon by the strictures of the Cult. Don't be misled by the reference to "in her home." She's still a worker, which the Cult doesn't support.

(D) **Out of Scope.** Men's problems are not part of the "Cult of True Womanhood."

23. D

Of the statements provided, the author would be least likely to agree with (D). While women played different roles during the Colonial era and Industrial Revolution, women during both time periods were held to certain social expectations. Colonial women were expected to be active participants in the labor force; during the Industrial Revolution, women were expected to be the moral authorities in their homes. Though the roles were different, the author doesn't make any reference to which is more important.

Wrong Answers:

(A) **Opposite.** The author of the passage would agree that the Industrial Revolution was a time of great advancement but also of harmful socioeconomic restrictions.

(B) **Opposite.** The author would also agree with this. The financial contributions of working-class women during the Industrial Revolution were key to economic survival, but these women were not encouraged to join the labor force as Colonial women were.

(C) **Opposite.** In paragraphs 1 and 2, the author makes it clear that neither the Colonial era nor the Industrial Revolution were periods of total equality between men and women.

Passage V: Augustan Age

Topic: Augustan Age satires

Scope: Swift's satires

Purpose: To compare and contrast two

Mapping the Passage:

¶1. Augustan Age: Major writers produced satires and argued about the genre (Pope, Addison, Johnson).

¶2. Swift: Mixed opinion on satire.

¶3. Swift wrote satires using unreliable narrators ("ironic personae").

¶4. Differences between the narrators in *Argument* and *Proposal*.

¶5. Similarities between these narrators.

24. D

This is a short—but for many readers, difficult—passage. Stick to Kaplan's strategic approach, and you'll be fine. Statement I occurs in three choices, so consider it first. In the second paragraph, Swift refers to satirizing individuals' foibles, and Swift's two works deal with larger, societal ills. So this statement is true. Statement II is supported by the example of *The Rape of the Lock* in paragraph 1. Statement III can also be found in paragraph 1. Addison doesn't like satire because it can be a tool for "irreparable harm."

Wrong Answers:

None. I, II, and III are all true.

25. D

The correct answer to this application question will fit into one of the categories of satire mentioned in the passage. Swift's two most famous works are indirectly and ironically "instructional" on the subjects of religion and politics. (D) matches this type of writing. The "pedantic academic" mentioned may have confused you, but Swift's works are definitely "disguised attack(s)."

Wrong Answers:

(A) Opposite. A polemic uses an earnest, direct approach, while a satire uses an indirect one.

(B) Opposite. An exposé is also direct.

(C) Out of Scope. This could be a *setting* for satire, but it's not an actual satire.

26. A

The first paragraph describes Johnson's criticism of the subject matter in Pope's mock epic. In the next sentence, the author claims that Pope's piece was "ideal to lambaste" conventions. (A) correctly states that Johnson's criticism, which is directed at the subject of a satire, too narrowly defines this genre.

Wrong Answers:

(B) Opposite. According to the author, the subject matter is "ideal," not flawed.

(C) Out of Scope. While Johnson found the choice of topic questionable, the passage gives no indication that he failed to find it humorous.

(D) Faulty Use of Detail. Pope's writing criticizes the "traditional epic," which is a literary form, not "everyday life."

27. C

The first sentence says that the "Augustan Age has been called 'The Great Age of Satire,'" which means that satire did not previously have a dominant position; (C) correctly matches this prediction.

Wrong Answers:

(A) Out of Scope. The author mentions several themes of satire used during the Augustan Age, but not before it. Also, be wary of an extreme word such as *only*.

(B) Out of Scope. The passage doesn't discuss "heroic poetry" before the Augustan Age.

(D) Out of Scope. There's no support for this in the passage.

28. C

The first paragraph gives a brief synopsis of the plot in Pope's *The Rape of the Lock*. This summary is followed by Johnson's criticism of the work's subject matter—the purpose for which the plot is included—and then Johnson's contention that it's not an appropriate subject for satire, (C).

Wrong Answers:

(A) Out of Scope. In the last sentence of the first paragraph, the author states that this story line was ideal for its specific purpose—not that it was ideal for all Augustan satire.

(B) Faulty Use of Detail. The passage contrasts Pope's position to Addison's by referencing *Epilogue to Satires*.

(D) Opposite. The author says that Pope's piece was "ideal," not "frivolous."

29. B

Addison thought that satire should not be used because of the "irreparable harm" it did to the persons who were its subject. He assumed the injury to the individual was more important than any value the work could have for the reader or society as a whole. This matches (B).

Wrong Answers:

(A) Opposite. Addison's view was that satire hurt its target, meaning he believed it was effective.

(C) Out of Scope. We don't know anything about Addison's opinion on how well readers understood satire.

(D) Faulty Use of Detail. This is Johnson's criticism, not Addison's.

30. D

This issue is discussed in the second half of the third paragraph. Swift felt satire "conveyed strong opinions" well because the "juxtaposition of the literal and the veiled" meanings of the narrator resulted in "complicated, subtle operations" in the mind of the reader. Though (D) is densely worded, it reflects Swift's view.

Wrong Answers:

(A) Opposite. According to the last two sentences of paragraph 2, the one thing Swift questioned about satire was whether it could reach those with "hardened hearts."

(B) Distortion. The passage doesn't state that satire was the "only genre" Swift could have used, and we have no idea whether the unreliable narrator was Swift's favorite.

(C) Faulty Use of Detail. The first two sentences of the last paragraph say that Swift's narrators show his "concern for reason gone awry" but not why he chose serious subjects.

Passage VI: Smokers

Topic: Smoking by U.S. women
Scope: Effect of relationships on their smoking behavior
Purpose: To analyze the results of a study

Mapping the Passage:

¶1. Increase in smoking among young women despite overall decrease.

¶2. Study looked at women's habits related to parental and peer smoking behavior.

¶3. Smoking behavior of mother (but not father) correlates with probability that a woman starts.

¶4. Continued smoking habits correlate with those of close female friends (not male).

¶5. Stopping smoking also correlates with behavior of female peers.

31. D

This question concerns the effect of a young woman's closest female friends on her smoking behavior. The third sentence of the fourth paragraph states that a young woman's closest female friends play a major role in the maintenance of her smoking habit—that is, the frequency and duration of her habit, so (D) is our answer.

Wrong Answers:

(A) Opposite. It contradicts the fourth paragraph.

(B). Faulty Use of Detail. Although a woman's friends have a strong influence on her smoking habits, the passage does not say they "encourage her to smoke heavily."

(C) Faulty Use of Detail. The passage only looks at the parents' influence on whether a woman starts smoking.

32. D

This is a detail question about the consequences of male smoking behavior. Both the third and fourth paragraphs, as well as the last two sentences of the fifth paragraph, indicate that male smoking behavior doesn't seem to affect female smoking habits, which is (D).

Wrong Answers:

(A) Opposite. The passage states, on two occasions, that female smoking behavior is unrelated to that of their male friends.

(B) Out of Scope. Males' influence on the smoking of other males isn't discussed in the passage.

(C) Opposite. The last paragraph states that "only the smoking behavior of female friends" affected a woman's decision to stop smoking.

33. D

This question asks for a *weakener* of Smith's argument. Smith argues that a young woman's smoking habits are initially influenced by her mother and later by the smoking habits of her female friends. According to Smith, the smoking habits of males play no role in explaining young women's smoking behavior. If it were discovered that the smoking habits of both parents significantly influence a daughter's initial decision to smoke (D), this would mean that the father's smoking habit does indeed influence a female's smoking behavior. This discovery would contradict and therefore weaken Smith's argument.

Wrong Answers:

(A) Opposite. This is exactly what the study showed. It would strengthen Smith's argument.

(B) Opposite. This would also strengthen Smith's argument.

(C) Out of Scope. Smith's argument only looks at how personal relationships, not financial status, affect women's smoking habits.

34. C

Your map says that the passage is about a study which uses extensive statistics and research on women's smoking. This prediction closely matches answer (C).

Wrong Answers:

(A) Out of Scope. This study doesn't refute anything, and no earlier hypothesis is offered.

(B) Out of Scope. We have no idea if the theory is popular.

(D) Out of Scope. We don't know if Smith's theory is controversial.

35. D

The second sentence of the first paragraph states that in the early 1970s, the percentage of males smoking leveled off at 19 percent. Therefore, (D) is correct.

Wrong Answers:

(A) Faulty Use of Detail. The number of teenage females currently smoking is 26 percent.

(B) Opposite. The passage states that the number of young males smoking reached a "plateau" in the 1970s, meaning it leveled off rather than decreased.

(C) Faulty Use of Detail. Again, the passage states that 26 percent of teenage women currently smoke.

Passage VII: Muzak

Topic: Muzak
Scope: The uses and effects of Muzak
Purpose: To describe

Mapping the Passage:

¶1. Muzak: Widely played to modify an environment.

¶2. Origins of Muzak and how it increases productivity.

¶3. Possible reason for Muzak's effectiveness; cites research.

¶4. Muzak is carefully planned to get desired effect.

¶5. Objections to Muzak, but author supports it.

36. C

This is a detail question whose topic is discussed in paragraph 4. The higher the mood rating, the more invigorating a song, so a segment with an average stimulus value of 5 would be rather lively. The passage then says that more stimulating segments "air at 11 A.M. and 3 P.M." so (C) is the correct answer.

Wrong Answers:

(A) Opposite. The passage says that "more soothing segments," which would have a lower rating, play toward the end of the day, which would be 4:30 P.M.

(B) Out of Scope. The passage does not discuss music played at the beginning of the day.

(D) Opposite. Music played right after lunch, such as at 1:15 P.M., is more soothing.

37. B

For this main idea question, check and match your Purpose, Scope, and Topic. That turns out to be (B).

Wrong Answers:

(A) Faulty Use of Detail. Only the second paragraph discusses the origins of Muzak. Never choose a detail for the answer to a main idea question. One detail can't characterize the entire passage.

(C) Faulty Use of Detail. This is only in paragraph 3.

(D) Faulty Use of Detail. This is from paragraph 4.

38. B

This is an inference question about critics of Muzak, who are discussed in the last paragraph. The two main objections mentioned are that it is "unregulated air pollution" and "a manipulation of the subconscious." Among the answer choices, (B) uses almost the same words as the passage.

Wrong Answers:

(A) Out of Scope. The fourth paragraph says that Muzak is different from other "easy listening" music, but the criticism doesn't mention this relationship.

(C) Opposite. Both the first and fifth paragraphs state that most workers don't actively listen to the music, but it seems to benefit rather than distract them.

(D) Faulty Use of Detail. Muzak seems to encourage buying, but that's not the same as catering to the whims of the consumer.

39.　C

This asks how Muzak differs from other easy listening formats. Paragraph 4 tells us that the difference is in the way that Muzak is programmed based on the time of day, so choice III is correct. The programming is the only difference mentioned, so (C) is the correct answer.

Wrong Answers:

I. Opposite. According to the third paragraph, any calming music lowers heart rate and blood pressure.

II. Opposite. The second and third paragraphs each give an example of productivity increasing from listening to music other than Muzak.

40.　A

This is a question regarding the author's view of Muzak. In the first sentence of the passage, the author writes that Muzak represents the "paradoxical success story of a product designed to be ignored." The author reiterates this idea when he finishes the passage by restating this apparent contradiction. Thus, we can easily infer that the author finds Muzak to be a paradoxical phenomenon, (A). Don't be surprised when the correct answer to an inference question seems to be almost exactly what the author already stated. Correct inference answers really *are* the author's stated conclusions, just in slightly different words.

Wrong Answers:

(B) Opposite. According to the passage, the author views Muzak favorably, or at worst neutrally, but definitely not as an "evil."

(C) Out of Scope. Although the last paragraph says "some people" call Muzak "Orwellian nightmare", this is clearly not the author's viewpoint.

(D) Opposite. In the last sentence, the author states that no one likes Muzak. That certainly doesn't suggest that it's a pleasurable diversion.

Verbal Reasoning
Practice Test 5

Time—60 minutes

Directions: There are seven passages in this Verbal Reasoning test. Each passage is followed by a set of questions. After reading a passage, select the one best answer to each question. If you are not certain of an answer, eliminate the alternatives that you know to be incorrect and then select an answer from the remaining alternatives.

PASSAGE I (QUESTIONS 1–5)

In 1855, excavations at the site of the ancient city of Larsa, in present-day Iraq, unearthed a large number of tablets traceable to Sumero-Babylonian times, approximately 1900–1500 B.C.E. The materials appeared to be receipts, accounts, and tables. Interpretation revealed that the number system of this ancient civilization was sexagesimal (counting was by 10s and 60s). The symbols used were quasipositional; the symbol for "1" could also signify the powers of 60 and even 10 times the powers of 60, depending upon the specific nature of the transaction.

It is now known that not only the number system but also the system of linear measure used by the Sumero-Babylonian society was based on 60. A clay tablet recovered at Larsa some time after the initial findings, believed to be a standard text copied as part of the school curriculum, shows a systematic and progressive sequence of linear measure utilizing units that represented specific quantities of barley, the society's food staple and currency. Six she (grains) were equal to 1 shu-si (finger), 30 shu-si equaled 1 kush (cubit), 12 kush equaled 1 nindan, 60 nindan equaled 1 USH, and 30 USH added up to 1 beru. The factors used to convert from one unit to another—6, 30, 12, 60, and 30—are multiples of six, and each is a factor of 60, the base in the sexagesimal number system.

Later excavations revealed that the Sumero-Babylonian mathematical system was a successor of sexagesimal systems that had appeared both in earlier eras and in other geographical locations. Tablet fragments discovered in the 1920s at Jemdet Nasr in Iraq disclosed that the numerical and linear systems first noted in 1855 probably had been in use as early as 2900–2800 B.C.E. The pictographic inscriptions appeared to be a precursor of a Sumerian form of writing known as cuneiform, while the numerical symbols—circles, cuplike shapes, and slashes—were similar to those on the tablets found at Larsa. In both, the notations reflected computation in multiples of 10 and 60 while the basic unit of measure was the she or grain. The Jemdet Nasr findings are thus considered proto-Sumerian.

Research at Susa, the ancient Elamite city located in present-day Iran, has revealed that even this separate culture probably used the mathematical system noted at the various Sumerian sites. Initial excavations at Susa uncovered tablets inscribed with both the cuneiform writings and numerals of Sumero-Babylonia. Later excavations there revealed evidence of a society in existence at least a millennium before that of the Elamites. This proto-Elamite culture, which was roughly contemporary with that of the proto-Sumerians, used numbers and linear measures virtually identical to theirs, despite a completely different style of writing.

1. This passage was most likely taken from

A. a newspaper feature about ancient market transactions.

B. a journal article regarding ancient numerical systems.

C. a lecture on archeological discoveries in the Near East.

D. an encyclopedia entry on Sumero-Babylonian forms of writing.

2. Based on the information in the passage, which of the following archeological findings is LEAST likely?

A. A tablet or pictographic writing dating from 2700 B.C.E. using the units she and shu-si

B. A tablet containing sexagesimal numbers and cuneiform writing dating from 3200 B.C.E.

C. A tablet inscribed with cups and slashes describing a transaction involving measurement in terms of fingers and cubits

D. A tablet dating from 1300 B.C.E. showing a table of measurements with conversion factors of 6, 30, 12, 60, and 30

3. Which of the following characteristics could be common to both a Sumerian and a proto-Sumerian tablet?

A. Slashes and circles

B. Cuneiform inscriptions

C. Positional notation using the number 0

D. A system of measure based on the finger as the smallest unit

4. Which of the following most probably is the sequence in which the societies mentioned in the passage flourished?

A. Proto-Elamite, Elamite, proto-Sumerian, Sumero-Babylonian

B. Proto-Elamite, Elamite, Sumero-Babylonian, proto-Sumerian

C. Elamite, proto-Sumerian, Sumero-Babylonian, proto-Elamite

D. Proto-Sumerian, proto-Elamite, Elamite, Sumero-Babylonian

5. The author mentions excavations at Susa in order to

A. prove that the proto-Sumerian culture was dominant in the ancient Middle East.

B. explain the ways in which an aspect of proto-Sumerian culture spread to other areas of the ancient Middle East.

C. support the notion that sexagesimal mathematical systems were used by several ancient Middle Eastern societies.

D. indicate that the mathematical system used in Sumero-Babylonian times was heavily influenced by proto-Elamite culture.

PASSAGE II (QUESTIONS 6–11)

"Big bang"—the spontaneous explosion that created the universe some 12 billion years ago—initiated processes that led to an uneven distribution of luminous matter throughout the universe. The study of the genesis and evolution of the universe is a relatively young discipline. Before the 20th century, astronomers knew little about space beyond our own galaxy, the Milky Way, and could only speculate about the existence of "external" galaxies. In the 20th century, the development of sophisticated observation technology, including the radio telescope, particle accelerators, and satellites, made it possible for astronomers to study the components and properties of the universe and to formulate theories about its development.

One popular theory of the universe's development, introduced in 1972 by Soviet astronomers Zel'dovich and Sunyaev, proposes that gases present in the early universe became quite dense and unevenly distributed in response to gravitational forces. Over time, dense pockets of gas formed vast sheets of luminous material, which astronomers refer to as "pancakes." Because these gaseous pancakes were located in regions of the universe where multiple clusters of galaxies now exist, Zel'dovich and Sunyaev reasoned that early in the universe's development, the pancakes must have fragmented into galactic clusters and individual galaxies; in other regions of the universe, limited quantities of gas prevented the development of luminous matter, leaving much of space "empty."

Zel'dovich and Sunyaev's attempt to explain the development of the universe had its origin in their observations of the distribution of galaxies. Galaxies are grouped in structures called "clusters" that vary in size; small clusters may contain only a few galaxies while the largest clusters may contain many thousands of them. Clusters, in turn, form structures known as "superclusters" that are so large that any individual member galaxy, in motion for billions of years, will have traversed only a fraction of its supercluster's diameter. Astronomers have identified four superclusters thus far, but disagree about their precise boundaries.

Whatever the exact boundaries of superclusters, scientists believe that even these huge structures occupy only a small part of the total area of the universe. Most of space consists of empty regions known as "voids" devoid of luminous matter. Astronomers are still unsure of the exact composition of voids, but speculate that they are made up of nonluminous "dark matter" that cannot be seen and appears, in observation from Earth, as nothing more than vast areas of nothingness.

However, while the Zel'dovich-Sunyaev theory describes and explains the uneven distribution of luminous matter, it only partially accounts for the conditions of the universe today. Zel'dovich and Sunyaev failed to address the continued expansion of the universe. To understand this aspect of the universe's development, astronomers had to refer back to the work of Edwin Hubble, a prominent astronomer of the 1920s and 1930s. Using a technique known as "red shift analysis," Hubble developed the concept of diverging galaxies. In astronomical observation, the more distant a celestial body is from the Milky Way, the more its light shifts to the red end of the spectrum, and Hubble observed that the light emitted from galaxies moved further to the red end of the spectrum over time. He concluded that other galaxies must be moving away from our own. The divergence of galaxies was later codified as Hubble's Law, from which astronomers have been able to infer that, in a continuing response to the huge initial release of energy in the "big bang" explosion, celestial bodies—including galactic clusters, superclusters, voids, and the universe itself—are expanding.

6. Based in the information in the passage, we can infer that the galaxies are moving

    A. in a random fashion.
    B. toward the Milky Way.
    C. out of their original clusters.
    D. because of a massive energy discharge.

7. According to the passage, which of the following is true of the composition and properties of the universe?

    A. There are no more than four superclusters in our universe.
    B. Gravitational forces have no effect on concentrations of gas.
    C. Galaxies will eventually assume fixed positions in the universe.
    D. The distribution of galaxies today reflects the effects of gravity on gaseous formations.

8. We would be justified in concluding that the author considers the Zel'dovich-Sunyaev theory to be

    A. illuminating but incomplete.
    B. enlightening and comprehensive.
    C. uninformed but original.
    D. insightful but lacking evidence.

9. While observing the movement of galaxies, an astronomer on earth notices that light emitted from galaxy A is further to the red end of the spectrum than light coming from galaxy B. Based on this astronomer's observations, it can be inferred from the passage that

    A. galaxy B is further from the Milky Way than galaxy A.
    B. galaxy B is moving away from the Milky Way faster than galaxy A.
    C. galaxy B is diverging at a faster rate than galaxy A.
    D. galaxy B is closer to the Milky Way than galaxy A.

10. The author introduces "Hubble's Law" principally in order to

    A. contradict the theory of diverging galaxies.
    B. explain the technique of "red shift analysis."
    C. prove the existence of "dark matter."
    D. supplement the Zel'dovich-Sunyaev theory.

11. It can be inferred from the passage that at some time in the future,

    I. the huge amount of energy released by the "big bang" explosion will be exhausted.

    II. the Milky Way will be larger than its present size.

    III. the configuration of the universe will remain constant.

    A. I only
    B. II only
    C. I and II only
    D. I, II, and III

PASSAGE III (QUESTIONS 12–17)

Located on the western borderlands of the Russian Empire and later the Soviet Union, the regions that would one day become Belarus and Moldova had long been part of a buffer zone used to protect Russia from Western influences and military forces. The imperial and Soviet governments attempted to fully integrate the two regions' economies into their own and to Russify their people in order to bind them seamlessly into the their respective empires. For a long time, these efforts seemed to work, but in 1991, Belarus and Moldova declared their independence from the Soviet Union.

In both Belarus and Moldova, many conservatives wish to return to the days of the Soviet Union for a variety of reasons, some economic, some nostalgic, and some fearful. Both Belarus and Moldova stated their intention of having democratic political systems, but making the change from a communist government to a real democracy proved difficult, not the least because of officials who viewed democracy as too chaotic and unstable, unlike the predictability that had characterized their previous political lives.

The two countries are a study in contrasts. Belarus is mostly ethnic Belarusian (and overwhelmingly Slavic) in population. The tsars and commissars who sought to meld Belorussia with Russia succeeded to a remarkable extent: independent Belarus still identifies closely with Russia, and Belarusian nationalists are in the minority. But Moldova has a majority population of ethnic Romanians, who are not Slavs. Regardless of Russian and Soviet efforts to Slavicize them, most ethnic Romanians were able to maintain their identity and looked to Romania as the source of their culture. When the Soviet Union began to crumble, Moldova sought to distance itself from Russia, despite the wishes of the Transnistrians, who in 1990 proclaimed the "Dnestr Moldavian Republic," with a pro-Soviet extralegal government, on the east bank of the Nistru River. The Transnistrians want no part of a possible reunification with Romania, where they would be a small minority instead of a powerful political force.

Despite the differences between the two countries, the focal point for those who wish to maintain each country's independence is the same—the national language, the same rallying point as in the revolutions of 1848. Those revolts all failed in their immediate goals, but they eventually led to greater representation of ethnic groups in legislatures and to greater cultural autonomy, including the use of languages that, until then, had been dismissed by the authorities as peasant vernaculars. However, while nationalists in the last century sought to codify (and sometimes even form) a literary language, the task of the nationalists in 1991 was to revive that language and divest it of its Russian and Soviet accretions.

To those who have never undergone forced cultural assimilation, the issue may seem trivial. To those who have had their use of language restricted, however, the matter goes beyond mere defiance. Language is the medium of the culture on which their daily lives and identities are based. To define what language can be spoken is to define the identity not only of the individual but also of the country. Moldovans kept Russian as a language of interethnic communication but subsequently entered a debate as to what their own language was to be called: Was it Moldovan or Romanian? President Lukashyenka explained that the term *Moldovan* was used in the constitution for political reasons—to assuage fears of imminent reunification with Romania. Again, politics, language, and emotions were thoroughly entangled. Belarusians, the majority of whom prefer to use Russian in their daily lives, have dealt with the language issue differently. They returned Russian to its status of official language, alongside Belarusian.

12. Based on the passage, we can reasonably expect the author to argue that the reason the Transnistrians want to realign with Russia, and not to reunite with Romania, is because

   I. they fear the political instability and unpredictability of democratic political systems.

  II. they consider the Nistru River the correct and natural Moldavan boundary.

 III. they would be a small and powerless minority if Moldova unifies with Romania.

  A. I only
  B. II and III only
  C. I, II and III
  D. III only

13. Which of the following, if true, would most WEAKEN the author's claims about the goals of the Transnistrians?

  A. The Russian government also wishes to establish closer relations with Moldova.

  B. Transnistrians seek to protect economic interests that include illegal sales of arms and drugs.

  C. The majority of Moldovans agree that the Transnistrians should secede from Moldova.

  D. There were no Transnistrians in Moldova during the revolutions of 1848.

14. The author probably mentions the revolutions of 1848 (paragraph 4) in order to

  A. establish that language has been a point of contention in Soviet states for over a century.

  B. argue that, as those revolutions failed, so too the present nationalist cause is doomed.

  C. point out that language was an artificial issue, since the national language had to be invented.

  D. explain why the Transnistrians have historically felt themselves to be outsiders in Moldova.

15. Based on the passage, the author believes that the major cause of controversy in Moldova today is the issue of

  A. use of Russian as an official language.
  B. possible reunification with Romania.
  C. the legal status of the Slavic minority.
  D. use of Romanian as an official language.

16. If the president of Belarus were to propose expanding its economic and political union with Russia, we can assume that the majority of the Belarusian population would

  A. accept any cooperative relations that didn't threaten Belarus independence.

  B. threaten to revolt if Russian influence over Belarus were increased.

  C. support him only if equal unity could be simultaneously established with Europe.

  D. We can't predict any response based on the information in the passage.

17. If we were to learn that much of the leadership in Belarus has traditionally considered their country evenly divided between its pro-Western and pro-Russian provinces, this would be LEAST consistent with

  A. the author's claim that Belarus was a buffer zone protecting Russia from the West.

  B. the author's assertions about the success of Russification in Belarus.

  C. the explanation for why the Transnistrians wish to unite with Russia rather than with Romania.

  D. the conservatives' wish to return to the days of the Soviet Union.

PASSAGE IV (QUESTIONS 18–23)

As formal organizations, business corporations are distinguished by their particular goals, which include maximization of profits, growth, and survival. Providing goods and services is a means to this end. The following statement from the board of directors of the 3M Company is exemplary in this regard: "The objective of the 3M Company is to produce quality goods and services that are useful and needed by the public, acceptable to the public, and in the best interests of the global economy—and thereby to earn a profit which is essential to the perpetuation of the useful role of the company."

These goals provide the raison d'être and ultimate ethical values of the 3M Company. If, for example, a number of individuals (outsiders or even insiders) believe that a company's aggressive marketing of infant formula in third-world countries is morally wrong, the company is unlikely to be moved by arguments based on ethos alone as long as what it is doing remains profitable. But if those opposed to the company's practice organize a highly effective boycott of the company's products, their moral views will soon enter into the company's deliberations indirectly as limiting operating conditions. The dissenters can, at this point, no more be ignored than a prohibitive increase in the costs of certain raw materials.

Although the concepts and categories of ethics may be applied to the conduct of corporations, there are important differences between the values and principles underlying corporate behavior and those underlying most individuals' actions. As individuals, we are often concerned with integrity, autonomy, and responsibility even when they cannot be shown to further a basic goal such as overall happiness; we regard them as important and valuable in themselves and not simply as a means to some other more basic end.

If corporations are by their nature end or goal directed, how can they acknowledge acts as wrong in and of themselves? Is it possible to hold a corporation criminally responsible for acts that if performed by a human person would result in criminal liability?

The first case of this type to achieve widespread public attention was the attempt to prosecute the Ford Motor Company for manslaughter as the result of alleged negligent or reckless decision making concerning the safety engineering of the Pinto vehicle. Although the defendant corporation and its officers were found innocent after trial, the case can serve as an exemplar for our purposes.

In essence, the prosecution in this case attempted to show that the corporation had produced and distributed a vehicle that was known to be defective at the time of production and sale, and that even after a great deal of additional information accumulated regarding the nature of the problems, the corporation took no action to correct them. The obvious noncorporate analogy would be the prosecution of a person who was driving a car with brakes known to be faulty, who did not have them repaired because it would cost too much, and who killed someone when the brakes eventually fail and the car did not stop in time. Such cases involving individuals are prosecuted and won regularly.

If corporations have no concept of right or wrong because they are exclusively goal directed, can they be convicted in cases of this type, and what purpose would be served by such a conviction? Perhaps we can make a utilitarian argument for convicting corporations of such crimes. The argument would be that of deterrence; conviction and punishment would deter other corporations from taking similar actions under similar circumstances. However, there appears to be considerable evidence that deterrence does not work on corporations, even if, arguably, it works on individuals. The possibility of being discovered and the potential magnitude of the fine merely become more data to be included in the analysis of limiting conditions.

18. A claim that things have ethical value to corporations only insofar as they are instrumental in furthering the ultimate goals of the corporation is

A. necessarily true, given the information presented in the passage.

B. perhaps true, and supported by the information presented in the passage.

C. perhaps true, but not supported by any information in the passage.

D. necessarily false, given the information presented in the passage.

19. In the context of the author's reference to an organized body of people united in a belief and their subsequent action, the phrase "limiting operating conditions" (paragraph 2) refers primarily to

A. the factors that will adversely impact a company's profit-making capacity.

B. the prevailing moral opinions of the public concerning a company's products.

C. the availability of raw materials necessary for producing a particular good.

D. the difficulty a company's officers have in trying to ignore ethical issues.

20. Implicit in the author's discussion of whether or not a corporation can be convicted in cases like the one involving the Pinto vehicle is the assumption that

A. most corporations have committed both moral and legal transgressions.

B. a corporation has an identity above and beyond its individual members.

C. few corporate persons will question their corporation's actions.

D. corporations do not always believe that the end justifies the means.

21. If a company that produced shampoo products opted to stop the routine testing of its products on animals because it decided that it is wrong to cause the animals pain, what effect would this have on the argument made in the passage?

A. It would strongly support the argument.

B. It would support the argument somewhat, but not conclusively.

C. It would neither support nor substantially weaken the argument.

D. It would substantially weaken the argument.

22. The author's analogy of the alleged actions of the Ford Motor Company to those of a person who knowingly drives with faulty brakes suggests that

A. Ford should have been convicted of the crime of manslaughter in the trial.

B. the Ford corporation was capable of understanding the moral concepts of right and wrong.

C. the problem with the safety engineering of the Pinto had to do specifically with its brakes.

D. Ford may have ignored the Pinto's defects because they would be too costly to correct.

23. Which of the following assertions would most strengthen the author's claim that deterrence will not work on corporations?

A. The possibility of punishment does not deter many individuals from committing crimes.

B. The penalties imposed on companies have amounted to a small fraction of their profits.

C. Strict antipollution laws have cut down on the waste dumped by companies into rivers.

D. The trial of a corporation often extends over a period of several years.

PASSAGE V (QUESTIONS 24–30)

For more than a century, there has been a dispute among scholars over the authorship of the heroic poem *Beowulf*. Was *Beowulf* the work of one author or of several? Can the author or authors be identified as pagan or Christian? Of the theories that have attempted to come to grips with these questions, three have been especially prominent.

The earliest of the three, the "tribal-lay" theory, stresses that *Beowulf* is an amalgam of older Germanic and Nordic tribal myths. Proponents of this theory argue that the poem in its final form is the work of several authors whose earlier works were joined together by a number of later editors. This conclusion is based on the poem's numerous digressions from the main theme. These digressions, including Sigemund's battle with the dragon, are only tenuously linked to the hero Beowulf's struggles with monsters and men. Interestingly, while many critics see the poem as a Christian allegory with Beowulf as the champion of goodness battling the forces of evil, "tribal-lay" theorists seem to ignore the poem's obvious Christian overtones and consider its ethical tone to be a reflection of lay Germanic and Nordic codes of loyalty to tribe and vengeance to enemies.

Like the "tribal-lay" theory, the "growth by accretion" theory supports the notion of multiple authorship. But according to the "accretion" view, *Beowulf* began as a short, simple work of mythology by a single author and was gradually transformed into a long, intricate poem as later authors added to it over a period of several centuries. As evidence in support of this view, scholars point to the mixture of pagan rituals and themes with Christian values. This strange combination of conflicting motifs, some believe, could only have been the result of multiple authorship.

A third theory originates from a paper by J. R. R. Tolkien entitled "*Beowulf*: The Monsters and the Critics." In his paper, Tolkien argued that *Beowulf* was the work of a single Christian author, probably a member of a royal court, who used pagan material as the basis of his poem. Scholars who believe this "Christian authorship" theory argue that it is not at all surprising that a Christian would have written such a poem. At the time of *Beowulf*'s writing, sometime between the years 650 and 850, the bulk of the population of England—including much of the literate strata—was only nominally Christian and still clung to pagan beliefs and practices. Although Christianity had gained a foothold in England, it had yet to displace pagan culture. "Christian authorship" theorists reason that a nominal Christian would have been perfectly comfortable incorporating both pagan and Christian elements into the same work. These scholars further argue that since the Anglo-Saxons were engaged in constant warfare with the Vikings, Scots, and Picts at the time of *Beowulf*'s writing, its author may have deliberately emphasized certain pagan motifs, particularly the cult of the warrior, for the political purpose of bolstering morale among both the aristocracy and the masses at a time when they were under constant military pressure.

Although it is not possible to conclusively prove that one theory is correct and the other two wrong, most scholars favor the Tolkien view. The "tribal-lay" and the "growth by accretion" theories are generally dismissed because of the epic's essential unity despite disparate references and seemingly conflicting motifs. Most scholars find historical analyses of the context of the author's writing provide the best resolutions to the poem's apparent contradictions.

24. The author mentions Sigemund's battle with the dragon (paragraph 2) in order to

    A. show that the Christian theme of good versus evil is central to *Beowulf*.

    B. provide support for the notion that *Beowulf* is an incorporation of more ancient tribal myths.

    C. prove that *Beowulf* is the work of a single pagan author.

    D. provide an allegorical representation of the Anglo-Saxon struggle with Vikings, Scots, and Picts.

25. According to the "Christian authorship" theory, the emphasis on the pagan cult of the warrior in *Beowulf* is a reflection of

A. major themes in Germanic and Norse culture.
B. the author's position as a military official in a royal court.
C. political upheavals in England at the time of the epic's writing.
D. an eighth-century decline in Christian faith among Anglo-Saxons.

26. Which of the following statements is/are compatible with the ideas of the "growth by accretion" theorists?

I. *Beowulf* represents the result of contributions made by multiple authors.

II. Conflicting motifs in *Beowulf* indicate that the poem is not the work of a single author.

III. The essential unity of *Beowulf* defies the constant turmoil and warfare of the period in which its author wrote.

A. I and II only
B. I and III only
C. II and III only
D. I, II, and III

27. According to the passage, a major distinction between the "tribal-lay" and "growth by accretion" theorists is

A. the degree of emphasis each group places on the epic's historical context.
B. the different ways in which the theorists interpret the poem's allegorical references.
C. their varied conceptions of the multiple authorship of *Beowulf*.
D. the way in which each group accounts for *Beowulf*'s Christian elements.

28. Which of the following would most seriously weaken the "Christian authorship" theory?

A. During an excavation of an 11th-century Norwegian church, archeologists find a partially translated manuscript of *Beowulf*.
B. Historians now believe that Anglo-Saxon conflicts with the Vikings, Scots, and Picts were much more intense and long lasting than previously thought.
C. Recently discovered documents indicate that *Beowulf* is an English translation of a Germanic myth of earlier origin.
D. Some linguists have concluded that *Beowulf* was written by a literate peasant, because the poem contains phrases and terms used by peasants but not found in the language of aristocrats.

29. The passage suggests that most scholars favor the "Christian authorship" theory because

A. it is able to locate many of the obscure references made in *Beowulf* in Germanic and Norse mythology.
B. other theories fail to appreciate the significance of Christian elements in *Beowulf*.
C. it is able to resolve inconsistencies in *Beowulf* by referring to the context in which it was written.
D. no other theory attempts to explain the epic's disparate references and varied motifs.

30. The author mentions a paper written by J. R. R. Tolkien (paragraph 4) in order to

A. lend authoritative support to multiple authorship theories.
B. discredit the notion that *Beowulf* was written by a Christian.
C. disprove previous theories regarding *Beowulf*'s authorship.
D. introduce a contextual analysis of the writing of *Beowulf*.

PASSAGE VI (QUESTIONS 31–35)

The earliest telescopes were refractors, in that they used lenses to bend incoming light. By using refractive lenses, early astronomers were able to gather light and view images with greater resolution and magnification than possible with the naked eye. But because pioneer telescope makers knew relatively little about optics, their lenses exhibited two serious defects. The first problem, spherical aberration, is a distortion that occurs when a lens with round surfaces fails to focus light from a point object to a point image. The second problem, chromatic aberration, stems from the fact that an ordinary lens refracts different wavelengths of light to slightly different degrees, resulting in a different focal length for each color and, therefore, an out-of-focus image with a colorful halo.

A number of scientists, among them Johannes Kepler, realized that spherical aberration could be corrected simply by using a differently shaped lens. A solution to chromatic aberration, however, proved more difficult. When Sir Isaac Newton announced that it seemed impossible to correct chromatic aberration, scientists turned their attention to reflecting telescopes. Like refractors, these telescopes also increased light, resolution, and magnification of an image, but reflectors use curved mirrors in lieu of clear lenses in order to avoid the chromatic distortion of refraction. However, early reflecting telescopes had their problems too: the mirrors they utilized were made of metal alloys, which absorbed light and thus obscured images. One solution to this problem was to build larger telescopes, since bigger mirrors mean greater light reception and brighter images. Unfortunately, the opticians and foundries of the day were not yet up to the challenge. Mirror technology progressed slowly, as did the development of better reflector telescopes.

Chromatic aberration remained a problem in refractors, until Englishman Peter Hall discovered that a compound lens (i.e., one that combined different surfaces) could compensate for the dispersion of different colors by focusing them back together. Unfortunately, his findings were little known. Later, mathematician Leonhard Euler hit upon a similar solution using two lenses with water between them. Soon after, noted optician John Dolland followed Euler's lead and sandwiched a piece of flint glass between two pieces of crown glass, an arrangement that corrected both chromatic and spherical aberration. As a result of this advancement and subsequent modifications, the refractor once again became the telescopic instrument of choice and remained so for about 100 years.

But the refractor continued to have one inescapable limitation—a constraint on the maximum effective lens diameter, which limits the light-gathering property of the telescope. For this reason, as well as because of technical advances in mirror making, the reflector would once again assume prominence. At the Great Exposition of 1851, Varnish and Mellish presented the first chemical technique for layering silver onto glass. The mirrors that ultimately resulted from this breakthrough were silvered on the front and represented a double advantage. First, the silver surface (financially feasible because of the small amount of silver required) increased reflectivity of mirrors some 50 percent. Second, using glass in place of metal eliminated problems of shrinkage and cracking.

The refractor never again surpassed the reflector. With further advances in the development of heat-resistant glass and casting techniques, larger and larger mirrors became possible, and astronomers saw farther and farther into the universe.

31. Of the following, the author is most interested in discussing

A. how different shapes of lenses influence resolution and magnification in telescopes.

B. why refractors have become more popular than reflectors.

C. how two basic telescope designs alternately succeeded each other in importance and popularity.

D. the ways in which technological constraints have shaped the course of science.

32. The author mentions the views of Sir Isaac Newton (paragraph 2) in order to

A. explain why scientists initially turned toward reflecting telescopes.

B. emphasize the severity of the problem of spherical aberration.

C. show that early scientists often reached erroneous conclusions.

D. tacitly challenge the view that Sir Isaac Newton was a brilliant scientist.

33. According to the passage, chromatic aberration can be corrected by

A. a lens with rounded surfaces.

B. using glass in place of metal alloys.

C. building larger telescopes for greater light reception.

D. an arrangement of two lenses separated by water.

34. The passage implies that the development of better telescopes was primarily hindered by

A. technological constraints.

B. imprecise methodologies.

C. disinterest among scientists.

D. unavailability of materials.

35. According to the passage, which of the following characteristics is/are common to both reflector and refractor telescopes?

I. Increased resolution

II. Compound lenses

III. Light-gathering capacities

A. I only

B. I and II only

C. I and III only

D. II and III only

PASSAGE VII (QUESTIONS 36–40)

The following passage was written in 1994.

The population of the United States is growing older and will continue to do so until well into the next century. For the first time in American history, elders outnumber teenagers. The U.S. Census Bureau projects that 39 million Americans will be 65 or older by the year 2010, 51 million by 2020, and 65 million by 2030. This demographic trend is due mainly to two factors: increased life expectancy and the occurrence of a "baby boom" in the generation born immediately after World War II. People are living well beyond the average life expectancy in greater numbers than ever before. In fact, the number of U.S. citizens 85 years old and older is growing six times as fast as the rest of the population.

The "graying" of the United States is due in large measure to the aging of the generation born after World War II, the "baby boomers." The baby boom peaked in 1957, with over 4.3 million births that year. More than 75 million Americans were born between 1946 and 1964, the largest generation in U.S. history. Today, millions of "boomers" are already moving into middle age; in less than two decades, they will join the ranks of America's elderly.

What will be the social, economic, and political consequences of the aging of America? One likely development will involve a gradual restructuring of the family unit, moving away from the traditional nuclear family and toward an extended, multigenerational family dominated by elders, not by their adult children.

The aging of the U.S. population is also likely to have far-reaching effects on the nation's workforce. In 1989, there were approximately 3.5 workers for every person 65 and older; by the year 2030, there'll be only 2 workers for every person 65 and older. As the number of available younger workers shrinks, elderly people will become more attractive as prospective employees. Many will simply retain their existing jobs beyond the now-mandatory retirement age. In fact, the phenomenon of early retirement, which has transformed the U.S. workforce over the past four decades, will probably become a thing of the past. In 1950, about 50 percent of all 65-year-old men still worked; today, only 15 percent of them do. The median retirement age is currently 61. Yet recent surveys show that almost half of today's retirees would prefer to be working, and in decades to come, their counterparts will be doing just that.

Finally, the great proportional increase in the number of older Americans will have significant effects on the nation's economy in the areas of Social Security and health care. A recent government survey showed that 77 percent of elderly Americans have annual incomes of less than $20,000; only 3 percent earn more than $50,000. As their earning power declines and their need for health care increases, most elderly Americans come to depend heavily on federal and state subsidies. With the advent of Social Security in 1935, and Medicaid/Medicare in 1965, the size of those subsidies has grown steadily until by 1990, spending on the elderly accounted for 30 percent of the annual federal budget.

Considering these figures, and the fact that the elderly population will double within the next 40 years, it's clear that major government policy decisions lie ahead. In the first 50 years of its existence, for example, the Social Security fund has received $55 billion more in employee/employer contributions than it has paid out in benefits to the elderly. Yet time and again the federal government has "borrowed" this surplus without repaying it in order to pay interest on the national debt.

Similarly, the Medicaid/Medicare system is threatened by the continuous upward spiral of medical costs. The cost of caring for disabled elderly Americans is expected to double in the next decade alone. And millions of Americans of all ages are currently unable to afford private health insurance. In fact, the United States is practically unique among developed nations in lacking a national health care system. Its advocates say such a system would be far less expensive than the present state of affairs, but the medical establishment and various special interest groups have so far blocked legislation aimed at creating it. Nonetheless, within the next few decades, an aging U.S. population may well demand that such a program be implemented.

36. The author concludes that the majority of elderly people living in the United States at the time the passage was written

   A. were earning less than $20,000 per year.
   B. will suffer some sort of disability between the ages of 65 and 75.
   C. were unable to purchase their own homes.
   D. continued to work at least 20 hours per week.

37. The fact that health care costs for disabled elderly Americans were expected to double in the next ten years indicates that

   A. the federal government will be unable to finance a national health care system.
   B. the Medicaid/Medicare system will probably become even more expensive to maintain in the future.
   C. money will have to be borrowed from the Social Security fund in order to finance the Medicaid/Medicare system.
   D. "baby boomers" will be unable to receive federal health benefits as they grow older.

38. According to the U.S. Census Bureau, the elderly population at the time the author wrote was

   A. larger than the population of teenagers.
   B. larger than the population of "boomers."
   C. smaller than the number of elderly people in 1950.
   D. smaller than the number of elderly people in 1970.

39. The passage suggests that, at the time the author wrote, many elderly people had over the prior three decades

   A. supplemented their incomes by working past the age of retirement.
   B. lost their Social Security benefits.
   C. experienced a doubling in their cost of living.
   D. come to depend heavily on government subsidies.

40. According to the author, the federal government had not yet instituted a program mandating health care for all U.S. citizens because

   A. the federal deficit must first be eliminated.
   B. such a program would be too expensive.
   C. legislative lobbies had prevented it.
   D. Medicaid and Medicare had made it unnecessary.

Verbal Reasoning Practice Test 5 Answers and Explanations

ANSWER KEY

1. B	9. D	17. B	25. C	33. D
2. B	10. D	18. B	26. A	34. A
3. A	11. B	19. A	27. C	35. C
4. D	12. D	20. B	28. C	36. A
5. C	13. B	21. D	29. C	37. B
6. D	14. A	22. D	30. D	38. A
7. D	15. B	23. B	31. C	39. D
8. A	16. A	24. B	32. A	40. C

EXPLANATIONS

Passage I: Number Systems

Topic: Sexagesimal mathematical system
Scope: Widespread use in ancient Babylonia
Purpose: To discuss

Mapping the Passage:

¶1. Sumero-Babylonian number system.

¶2. Linear measure system also based on 60.

¶3. Sumero-Babylonian system successor of earlier sexagesimal systems.

¶4. Elamites also used same system, as did their predecessors.

1. B

Consider the tone of the passage and the detail used in it. The author must have a good grasp on her subject, so she's probably an expert. What's her main topic? Numbers. OK, she's an expert in ancient number systems. That's (B). Journals tend to be read by those who are experts or interested in the field, and (B) is also the only answer that refers to numbers.

Wrong Answers:

(A) Opposite. A newspaper article would never be written in this kind of specific depth—it would have more general appeal, and the purpose of the passage is not to write about market transactions.

(C) Out of Scope. We're dealing not with archeology in general but with findings about numerical systems.

(D) Faulty Use of Detail. The passage only briefly mentions Sumero-Babylonian writing (cuneiform) in the course of its discussion of ancient numerical systems.

2. B

For this one, we're going to have to research each detail carefully. Forget the numbers and focus on the easier clue: cuneiform writing. This appears in paragraph 3, where we read that cuneiform came after the pictographic inscriptions on the tablets from Jemdet Nasr. Those were dated from 2900–2800 B.C.E., so cuneiform must have developed after that. (B) dates cuneiform at 3200 B.C.E.—too early, so this answer is the least likely.

Wrong Answers:

(A) Opposite. According to the third paragraph, the Jemdet Nasr tablets used pictographic writing at least from 2900–2800 B.C.E., and the symbols were "similar to those on the tablets found at Larsa." In both tablets, the "basic unit of measure was the she," so it's quite possible the Jemdet ones also used the shu-si.

(C) Opposite. The tablet described in paragraph 2 used fingers and cubits and had similar numerical symbols to the tablet described in the next paragraph—circles and slashes.

(D) Opposite. A tablet from 1300 B.C.E. using factors of 60 falls right in line with when that system seems to have been used: 1900–1500 B.C.E.

3. A

This question takes us right to paragraph 3, where we're told that the proto-Sumerian system used cups and slashes as symbols, similar to those on the Larsa tablets. We already read that the Larsa site is dated from Sumerian (okay, Sumerian-Babylonian, but why quibble?) times, so both seem to have used cups and circles—thus, answer (A).

Wrong Answers:

(B) Opposite. Proto-Sumerian writing was pictographic; the later Sumerian writing was cuneiform.

(C) Out of Scope. The use of 0 is never mentioned.

(D) Out of Scope. The she (grain), not the shu-si or finger, is the smallest unit mentioned.

4. D

Here's another question requiring methodical research. Just take a deep breath and attack it. On the other hand, if it seems to be taking forever to get the answer, you might just want to guess. You can easily eliminate (B) and (C) because of the "proto" placement problem (see explanations below). You now have a 50-50 chance of guessing the right answer and moving on. Of the four societies described in the passage, only two are assigned specific historical dates: the Sumero-Babylonians are said to have flourished in the years 1900–1500 B.C.E., while the proto-Sumerians existed in the years 2900–2800 B.C.E. Paragraph 4 places the proto-Elamites contemporary with the proto-Sumerians; the Elamites were at least 1,000 years later, although there is not enough detail to determine their actual date. Thus, in the final sequence, the proto-Elamites and proto-Sumerians should be placed in immediate proximity to one another, followed by the Elamites and the Sumero-Babylonians (or vice versa). Only (D) fulfills this requirement.

Wrong Answers:

(A) Faulty Use of Detail. This has the position of the Elamite eras wrong.

(B) Faulty Use of Detail. Proto-Sumerian can't come after its successor, Sumerian-Babylonian.

(C) Faulty Use of Detail. This time, proto-Elamite is in the wrong position.

5. C

Finally, an easier question. Why does the author mention the excavations at Susa? To support the idea that sexagesimal mathematical systems were used by several ancient Middle Eastern societies, leading directly to answer (C).

Wrong Answers:

(A) Distortion. The author doesn't prove (i.e., assert beyond any doubt) that proto-Sumerian culture was dominant in the ancient Middle East; neither does she suggest proto-Sumerian dominance.

(B) Out of Scope. There's nothing in the passage about how cultures spread.

(D) Opposite. It's the other way around; Sumerian and proto-Sumerian cultures exerted influence upon neighboring cultures, including the Elamites. That's probably why the mathematical system is referred to as "Sumero-Babylonian," not "Elamite."

Passage II: The Universe

Topic: The development of the universe
Scope: Zel'dovich and Sunyaev theory
Purpose: To explain

Mapping the Passage:

¶1. Study of the origins and evolution of universe is a young discipline.

¶2. Zel'dovich and Sunyaev theory explains uneven distribution of luminous matter.

¶3. Galaxies are grouped into clusters, superclusters.

¶4. Most of space = dark matter.

¶5. Failure of theory: Does not account for expansion of universe (Hubble's Law).

6. D

The first sentence of paragraph 1 says that the "big bang" resulted in matter spreading across the universe. The last sentence of the passage adds that galaxies are diverging as a result of the "release of energy in the 'big bang' explosion," causing the continued expansion of the universe. So galaxies are moving as a result of a massive energy discharge, (D).

Wrong Answers:

(A) Opposite. The final paragraph tells us that galaxies diverge, moving away from each other. That's in one specific direction, not in random ways.

(B) Opposite. Based on his observations, Hubble "concluded that other galaxies must be moving away from our own."

(C) Out of Scope. We're told in the final paragraph that celestial bodies, including galactic clusters, are expanding but not necessarily moving out of their original clusters.

7. D

The first few sentences of the second paragraph state that gravitational forces in the early universe determined the current distribution of galaxies by concentrating gas in certain regions of the universe, so (D) correctly describes an aspect of the universe.

Wrong Answers:

(A) Distortion. The third paragraph states that "astronomers have identified four superclusters thus far," but that doesn't mean these are the only four.

(B) Opposite. The second paragraph tells us that gravitational forces had an effect on gaseous "pancakes." (How's *that* for a scientific term?) And did you jump at the phrase "no effect"? You should, since you know that most extreme answers are wrong.

(C) Out of Scope. Nowhere in the passage is there any indication that galaxies will eventually stop moving.

8. A

This question asks you about the author's view of the Zel'dovich-Sunyaev theory. At the beginning of the final paragraph, the author notes that the Zel'dovich-Sunyaev theory has contributed greatly to our understanding of the universe. But he goes on to say that this theory can't explain the universe's continual expansion. (A) captures the author's attitude.

Wrong Answers:

(B) Opposite. If the theory were comprehensive, there would be no need for an additional theory to explain things more thoroughly.

(C) Opposite. The author finds the theory interesting and illuminating. That can't go along with uninformed.

(D) Opposite. Almost the entire passage is taken up with evidence.

9. D

Red-shift analysis is discussed in the middle of the last paragraph; the more distant a celestial body from the point of observation, the more its light shifts to the red end of the spectrum. If light emitted from galaxy A is further to the red end of the spectrum than light emitted from galaxy B, we can infer that galaxy B is closer to earth and the Milky Way than galaxy A is. (D) does the trick.

Wrong Answers:

(A) Opposite. As your research showed you.

(B) Out of Scope. In order to determine the speed of a galaxy, we need to see how the red shift changes over time, which is more information than this question gives us.

(C) Out of Scope. Here's the speed issue again.

10. D

"Hubble's Law" is in the last paragraph—the one in which the author refers to another theory to supplement the Zel'dovich-Sunyaev theory. Just look to match that idea, and you'll come up with (D).

Wrong Answers:

(A) Opposite. Hubble's Law *is* the theory of diverging galaxies.

(B) Opposite. Red-shift analysis is included only to help explain Hubble's Law, not the other way around.

(C) Faulty Use of Detail. Hubble's Law doesn't deal with dark matter, which is discussed in the previous paragraph.

11. B

Since statement I appears in three answers, start there. There's no suggestion in the passage that the energy will be exhausted, so this has to be wrong. Right away, you know the answer is (B). You don't even have to check out II and III, though II is a correct inference based on data that show the universe is expanding.

Wrong Answers:

I. Out of Scope. Although we may assume that the energy will be exhausted, based on our own knowledge of physics, the passage doesn't discuss this possibility.

III. Opposite. Since the last paragraph says that everything in the universe is expanding, we can conclude that its configuration won't stay the same.

Passage III: Belarus and Moldova

Topic: Belarus, Moldova, and Russia
Scope: Differences between Belarus's and Moldova's independence from the Soviet Union
Purpose: To explain how language is a focal point in the ethnic disputes.

Mapping the Passage:

¶1. Russia attempted to "Russify" Belarus and Moldova to buffer itself from the West.

¶2. Both countries converting to unpredictable democracy.

¶3. Ethnic differences.

¶4. National language = primary issue for those aspiring for independence.

¶5. Importance of language.

12. D

Stay flexible when answering Roman numeral questions. You could start with statement III, which appears in three choices, or you could scan for the lovely clue word *Transnistrians* and go directly to paragraph 3. There it's made clear that the Transnistrians fear becoming a small minority and losing their political power. Scan the answer choices, and you'll see that III says the same thing. So III is in. Since it's the only reason given, nothing else could fit, leaving us (D) only.

Wrong Answers:

I. Faulty Use of Detail. According to the second paragraph, it wasn't the Transnistrians but the "officials who viewed democracy as too chaotic and unstable."

II. Out of Scope. Transnistrians were based on the east side of the river, but we're never told that they consider that the natural boundary.

13. B

The third paragraph contains the author's claims about the Transnistrians; they didn't want to reunify with Romania so they could maintain their political power. Anything that indicates another reason would weaken that idea. (B) is definitely another reason.

Wrong Answers:

(A) Out of Scope. This has nothing to do with the Transnistrians.

(C) Out of Scope. This doesn't relate to the Transnistrians' reasons but to other Moldavans'.

(D) Faulty Use of Detail. Those revolutions are relevant to the importance of language to a culture, not to the political differences among Moldavans.

14. A

The revolutions are mentioned in the same paragraph as the importance of language, so they obviously have some connection, as (A) indicates.

Wrong Answers:

(B) Faulty Use of Detail. There's no connection made between the failures of those revolutions and the present situation.

(C) Opposite. Language was not an artificial issue—it was the *central* issue.

(D) Faulty Use of Detail. The Transnistrians are discussed in the previous paragraph, so their situation couldn't have anything to do with the revolutions.

15. B

The major cause of controversy in Moldova is in the third paragraph: the majority of Moldovans are ethnic Romanians, who are expected to consider "a possible reunification with Romania"—one the Transnistrians "want no part of." Even calling their language "Romanian" instead of "Moldovan" would spark "fears of imminent reunification with Romania." That's answer (B).

Wrong Answers:

(A) Faulty Use of Detail. The issue of the use of Russian is handled lightly; it's simply kept "as a language of interethnic communication," apparently without debate or strife. That's not "major."

(C) Out of Scope. The legal status of the Slavic minority is not relevant to the language issue.

(D) Faulty Use of Detail. The debate is not about whether a Romanian language is to be used, only what to call it.

16. A

We're told in the third paragraph that in Belarus, the population is mostly Slavic, that the tsars and commissars "succeeded to a remarkable extent" in Russifying the people; that is, Belarusians identify closely with Russia, and nationalists are in the minority. In the fourth and fifth paragraphs, we find that Belarusians "prefer to use

Russian in their daily lives." Overall, Belarus seems fairly closely allied to Russia—although it, like Moldova, doesn't want to give up its democracy, despite its difficulty (paragraph 2). So it's likely the people in Belarus wouldn't mind working with Russia as long as they can stay separate. Match that with answer (A).

Wrong Answers:

(B) Opposite. Threatening to revolt doesn't reflect the Belarusians' friendly feelings toward Russia.

(C) Out of Scope. The rest of Europe has nothing to do with this.

(D) Opposite. The passage gives us plenty of information to make a prediction, as we did.

17. B

A new assertion that the country was equally Western and Russian is inconsistent with the statement that in Belarus, the "tsars and commissars who sought to meld Belorussia with Russia succeeded to a remarkable extent." So Belarus was brought into the Russian fold. The question, however, contradicts this, so the answer is (B).

Wrong Answers:

(A) Faulty Use of Detail. This is a tempting answer but not necessarily true. Belarus could still be a buffer zone, if not a completely neutral one.

(C) Out of Scope. Transnistrians are in Moldova, not Belarus.

(D) Faulty Use of Detail. This is true for both Belarus and Moldova and is consistent with what the author says in paragraph 2.

Passage IV: Business Ethics

Topic: Ethics

Scope: Corporate vs. individual

Purpose: To argue the difference and why prosecuting corporations for ethical crimes doesn't work

Mapping the Passage:

¶1. Goals of corporations (3M example).

¶2. Methods for making corporations respond to moral concerns.

¶3. Contrast corporations with individual ethics.

¶4. Asks if corporations can be held responsible for ethical crimes.

¶5. Failed attempt to prosecute a corporation for such crimes (Ford).

¶6. Details of ¶5.

¶7. Argument in favor of prosecution: Deterrence, but doesn't work with corporations.

18. B

The author argues that this is true, and gives an example in paragraphs 1 and 2. (C) and (D) can be eliminated. But this argument *necessarily* true? There's nothing in the argument to indicate that there could never be an exception. (B) is the only choice left standing.

Wrong Answers:

(A) Distortion. This is a very tempting wrong answer choice, but we have only a few examples here, not a definite rule.

(C) Opposite. There's plenty of support for the author's argument in the passage.

(D) Opposite. The information in the passage doesn't prove the claim, but it does support it.

19. A

Again, make sure you research the relevant text in the passage, checking your map for the structural context. What are the limiting operating conditions? A boycott is compared to an increase in the price of materials. Even if you're having trouble deciphering the phrase, you can figure that it must have something to do with a hit to the company's profit. (A) rewards you immediately for drawing the connection.

Wrong Answers:

(B) Faulty Use of Detail. While public opinions might cause the boycott, the company isn't concerned with them. Note the part of the passage that says "moral views will . . . enter into the company's deliberations *indirectly*."

(C) Faulty Use of Detail. Just like (B), this choice takes an example of limiting operating conditions and makes it the main condition. Beware of confusing examples with the principle they're exemplifying.

(D) Out of Scope. There's nothing in the passage, let alone this section of it, that discusses the moral struggles of a company's officers.

20. B

Paragraphs 5–6 discuss the Pinto case, in which the Ford Motor Company and its officers were prosecuted for manslaughter. So (B) is assumed: The corporation is more than the sum of its parts. If that were false, why would Ford *and* its officers have been prosecuted? Remember to use the denial test if you're in doubt about an assumption.

Wrong Answers:

(A) Distortion. This is a classic trap. Just because *some* corporations have done so doesn't mean that *most* have. Watch out for extreme words.

(C) Out of Scope. Whether or not individuals question the actions of their company has no effect on the author's argument.

(D) Out of Scope. Even if corporations don't *always* assume this, the Ford case, which is the type of situation with which the author is concerned, shows that they sometimes do.

21. D

A new situation: Evaluate it in the context of the passage's broad themes. Where does a company that voluntarily gives up profit to spare animals from pain fit in the author's idea of corporations? It doesn't. It's an example of ethical concerns trumping economics, which the author claims doesn't happen. We're looking for an answer choice that somehow indicates weakening, and (D) alone fits this.

Wrong Answers:

(A) Opposite. The author argues that companies "are exclusively goal directed" and don't make decisions based solely on morals.

(B) Opposite. For the same reason (A) is incorrect.

(C) Distortion. Essentially, this choice says the new case wouldn't have an effect, when it would.

22. D

This question tests your understanding of a specific analogy, so review the details. What other information is there about the hypothetical person who didn't repair her bum brakes? It would cost too much to do so. The right answer probably ties Ford and cost together. A quick scan yields (D).

Wrong Answers:

(A) Out of Scope. The analogy only has to do with causes of the crime, not with shoulds and should-nots. The author also mentions later that convicting corporations probably wouldn't be effective anyway.

(B) Out of Scope. This is another choice that digresses from the analogy we're concerned with. Also, the author says corporations have no sense of right or wrong.

(C) Faulty Use of Detail. This answer choice is trying to confuse the analogy of the brakes with the real situation we're considering. A clear grasp of the real and the hypothetical eliminates this choice quickly.

23. B

For this "strengthen" question, quickly paraphrase the author's reasons for claiming (in the last paragraph) that deterrence won't work: Companies will just treat it as an economic consideration like any other. Search for a choice that reflects this. Only (B) has to do with economics. Further, it reinforces the idea that companies will shrug off potential penalties that have little economic consequence.

Wrong Answers:

(A) Out of Scope. We're concerned with corporations rather than individuals.

(C) Out of Scope. No economic factors are in play in this choice.

(D) Out of Scope. There are no clear economic factors in this choice either. Knowing the scope of questions as well as passages and paragraphs helps to eliminate many answers quickly.

Passage V: *Beowulf*

Topic: *Beowulf*

Scope: Authorship

Purpose: To compare and contrast three theories

Mapping the Passage:

¶1. Authorship of *Beowulf* disputed: One author or several? Pagan or Christian?

¶2. Tribal lay theory

¶3. Accretion theory

¶4. Tolkien theory

¶5. Critics favor Tolkien theory

24. B

The author mentions Sigemund's battle with the dragon in his discussion of the "tribal-lay" theory in paragraph 2. This theory considers *Beowulf* a mix of older myths and the work of many authors or editors. Sigemund's battle is considered a digression, a characteristic of the "tribal-lay" theory. Only (B) says that.

Wrong Answers:

(A) Faulty Use of Detail. This would be closer to the Tolkien theory.

(C) Out of Scope. There's no theory about a single pagan author.

(D) Faulty Use of Detail. The battles between the Anglo-Saxons and the Vikings, Scots, and Picts are discussed in regard to the "Christian authorship" theory.

25. C

The "Christian authorship" theory holds that *Beowulf*'s author might have emphasized pagan motifs—like the cult of the warrior—to boost morale for political purposes during a time of military upheavals. Therefore, the cult of the warrior is a reflection of political upheavals in England at the time of its writing, and that's (C).

Wrong Answers:

(A) Faulty Use of Detail. Themes in Germanic and Norse culture are stressed in the "tribal-lay" theory, not the "Christian authorship" theory.

(B) Out of Scope. Although Tolkien argues that the Christian author of *Beowulf* was probably a member of a royal court, he doesn't say that the writer was a military official.
(D) Opposite. Christianity wasn't declining; it had "gained a foothold."

26. A

The "growth by accretion" theory (paragraph 3) states that *Beowulf* is the product of a number of authors over a period of centuries. Considering that, statement I is true and is part of our answer. Proponents of this theory point to conflicting pagan and Christian themes as evidence of *Beowulf's* multiple authorship, so statement II is also true and is also part of the answer to this question. However, statement III plays on the "Christian authorship" theory's emphasis on unity, which has nothing to do with the "growth by accretion" theory.

Wrong Answers:

III. Opposite. The "growth by accretion" theory cites a "strange combination of conflicting motifs," which is the opposite of unity. Additionally, this theory holds that several authors wrote *Beowulf*, and this choice refers to the singular "its author."

27. C

Both the "tribal-lay" and "growth by accretion" theories hold that *Beowulf* was written by multiple authors. Notice the contrast word "But" in the second sentence of paragraph 3. Here's where the difference lies, and it has to do with a short, simple work getting longer and more intricate because different authors added their own writing to it. That difference is reflected in (C).

Wrong Answers:

(A) Out of Scope. The distinction between these theories has nothing to do with historical emphasis.
(B) Out of Scope. These theories are not concerned with interpretation of allegory.
(D) Opposite. The author stresses that "tribal-lay" theorists tend to ignore the poem's "obvious Christian overtones"

entirely, so they wouldn't account for references they don't recognize in the first place.

28. C
The "Christian authorship" theory rests on the belief that *Beowulf* had a single Christian author who wrote the poem, based on pagan material, sometime between the years 650 and 850 C.E. That author must have been English, since there are all sorts of references to England in the paragraph. Anything that runs contrary to this idea would weaken the theory. If it were discovered that *Beowulf* is an English translation of an earlier Germanic myth, the theory that *Beowulf* originated in England would be severely weakened.

Wrong Answers:

(A) Opposite. It's perfectly consistent to think that a partially translated (presumably into Norwegian) manuscript of *Beowulf* may have existed in an 11th-century Norwegian church.
(B) Out of Scope. The length and intensity of these conflicts wouldn't affect *Beowulf's* authorship in the least.
(D) Faulty Use of Detail. Just because Tolkien points to a member of a royal court doesn't mean the poem couldn't have been written by a literate peasant—who would still be one (presumably Christian) author.

29. C
Right there in paragraph 5, the author states that most scholars prefer the "Christian authorship" theory—one person wrote the poem—because of the "essential unity" of the work. Match that with (C). When you resolve inconsistencies, you come up with unity.

Wrong Answers:

(A) Faulty Use of Detail. Germanic and Norse mythology are part of the "tribal-lay" theory.

(B) Out of Scope. The Christian elements are not part of the answer as given in the last paragraph.

(D) Opposite. All three theories attempt to explain the varied references and motifs.

30. D

The paper referred to was written by Tolkien and introduces a theory about the authorship of *Beowulf*. That's about all we can say about why the paper was included in this passage, and (D) comes closest to it, especially if we interpret *analysis* as a part of theorizing, which we should.

Wrong Answers:

(A) Opposite. Tolkien's theory requires one author, not several.

(B) Opposite. A Christian author is a central idea of Tolkien's theory.

(C) Distortion. *Disprove* is an extreme word that leaves absolutely no doubt that something is incorrect. As three different theories show, there's lots of doubt. Besides, the author himself says no theory can be proved conclusively (last paragraph).

Passage VI: Telescopes

Topic: Telescopes
Scope: Reflector and refractor
Purpose: To discuss their history

Mapping the Passage:

¶1. Early telescopes = refractors but had problems.

¶2. Mirrors discovered as solution, but technology not yet up to speed.

¶3. Compound lens fixed refractor problem.

¶4. Mirror technology improved.

¶5. Reflectors surpass refractors.

31. C

This is a main idea question, and the main idea is all about telescopes: two kinds, several problems, changes in popularity. That's a good match for (C).

Wrong Answers:

(A) Faulty Use of Detail. As mentioned before, never choose a detail as the answer to a global question.

(B) Opposite. The main idea is not which telescope is more popular, and the author says that reflectors, not refractors, are currently more popular, so this can't be right.

(D) Out of Scope. The passage is about telescopes, not all of science. Out-of-scope is another classic wrong answer for a global question. Avoid it.

32. A

Let's go back to the second paragraph and put the author's reference to Sir Isaac Newton into context. After Newton said that chromatic aberration, the main problem with refractors, couldn't be corrected, "scientists turned their attention to reflecting telescopes." This matches (A) almost perfectly.

Wrong Answers:

(B) Opposite. Not only does the passage say that spherical aberration is simply corrected, this answer is also wrong because Newton is mentioned in reference to *chromatic* aberrations.

(C) Distortion. Newton is only one example of an early scientist reaching a wrong conclusion. The passage doesn't suggest that they "often" did so.

(D) Out of Scope. The author is absolutely not critical of Newton. This is too judgmental.

33. D

A straightforward detail question. Scan for "chromatic aberration," and you'll soon find that that Leonhard Euler provided a solution to chromatic aberration: two lenses with water between them. That's a quick match with (D).

Wrong Answers:

(A) **Faulty Use of Detail.** According to the passage, a lens with rounded surfaces may cause spherical aberration but solves nothing.

(B) **Faulty Use of Detail.** This is an issue with reflectors. Chromatic aberration occurs with refractors.

(C) **Faulty Use of Detail.** Building bigger telescopes was a solution to a problem with reflecting telescopes.

34. A

You might figure this out from the frequent mention of problems with materials and construction; or from the mention that "technology progressed slowly" (paragraph 2); or from the last paragraph, where the author says that new technology (she cites "heat-resistant glass and casting techniques") has made all the difference to modern astronomers. So (A) it is.

Wrong Answers:

(B) **Out of Scope.** Methodology isn't an issue in the passage.

(C) **Opposite.** The passage mentions numerous scientists who were quite interested in developing better telescopes.

(D) **Out of Scope.** Although the passage says telescopes were limited by the lens size, it does not imply that this constraint occurred because materials were unavailable.

35. C

Start with statement I; it's in three answers. It must be true because paragraph 2 states that "like refractors [reflectors] also increased . . . resolution." (D) is out, so what about statement II? Nope, that only refers to refractors. (B) is out. And III—light-gathering? Yes, all telescopes do that. So the answer is (C).

Wrong Answers:

II. **Faulty Use of Detail.** Though refractors "used lenses to bend incoming light," reflectors "use curved mirrors in lieu of clear lenses." Therefore, this property doesn't apply to both types of telescope.

Passage VII: Elderly Americans
Topic: The aging American population
Scope: Effects on the country
Purpose: To explain

Mapping the Passage:

¶1. Trend toward elderly population in America.

¶2. Reason: Aging of the Baby Boomers.

¶3. One likely consequence: Multigenerational families.

¶4. Effects on the nation's workforce.

¶5. Problems will arise with Social Security and health care.

¶6. Problems with the Social Security fund.

¶7. Problems with the American health care system.

36. A

Paragraph 5 states says that 77 percent of elderly Americans earn less than $20,000 per year. That's an easy choice—it's (A).

Wrong Answers:

(B) **Out of Scope.** The passage doesn't discuss the possibility of suffering a disability.

(C) **Out of Scope.** The author doesn't say the elderly can't buy homes. Don't confuse this with the idea of a "multigenerational family."

(D) **Out of Scope.** We know many older people still work, but we don't know how many hours.

37. B

Let's see—if health care costs double, it must make paying for it harder. Match that simple prediction with (B).

Wrong Answers:

(A) **Distortion.** Stay away from an answer with *unable* in it and note that the reference to national health care is not about affording it but about its not being available in the United States. Finally, a national health care system might be less expensive than the current system.

(C) **Faulty Use of Detail.** The passage says that money is borrowed to pay interest on the national debt. It's not associated with medical costs.

(D) **Distortion.** This statement is too pessimistic.

38. A

Take a brief look at the answers. We're dealing with something larger or smaller, and the answer is right in the second sentence. The elderly outnumber teens, so answer (A) it is.

Wrong Answers:

(B) Faulty Use of Detail. Since the "boomers" are the largest generation in U.S. history, numbering 75 million, (B) is highly unlikely.

(C) Opposite. The author never actually states how many elderly people there are in the current U.S. population, but the current number must surely be greater than the number in 1970 since this group is "growing six times as fast as the rest of the population."

(D) Opposite. There are more elderly people now than ever before.

39. D

Since you don't know where the answer will come from in the passage, you have to go through the choices one by one. At the end of paragraph 6, we see that elderly Americans have come to depend on government subsidies, as reflected in (D).

Wrong Answers:

(A) Opposite. Only 15 percent of 65-year-old men still work.

(B) Out of Scope. There is no evidence that any elderly people have lost their Social Security benefits.

(C) Out of Scope. Health care costs are expected to double, but the passage doesn't tell us about the cost of living.

40. C

Health care is in the last paragraph, so quickly go there. We find that the "medical establishment and various special interest groups" have blocked a move to a national health care system. This easily matches (C).

Wrong Answers:

(A) Out of Scope. The passage never ties a national health care system to the elimination of the federal deficit.

(B) Opposite. It might be less expensive than what we have now.

(D) Opposite. It's the problems with Medicare/Medicaid that may make a national health care program necessary.

Verbal Reasoning
Practice Test 6

Time—60 minutes

Directions: There are seven passages in this Verbal Reasoning test. Each passage is followed by a set of questions. After reading a passage, select the one best answer to each question. If you are not certain of an answer, eliminate the alternatives that you know to be incorrect and then select an answer from the remaining alternatives.

Passage I (Questions 1–5)

In the famous Harrisburg case of 1971–1972, the defendants—Father Phillip Berrigan and seven other Catholic radicals—were charged with conspiring to raid draft boards, destroy records, and kidnap presidential adviser Henry Kissinger. A team of liberal social scientists, realizing that the highly politicized nature of the case made jury composition an especially crucial factor, volunteered to assist the defense by developing a strategy to effect the selection of a sympathetic jury.

The first stage in the project consisted of a telephone survey in which calls were made to 840 randomly selected Harrisburg households to determine the general demographic characteristics of the population. In the project's second stage, the research team interviewed two-fifths of the initial group of 840 in order to pinpoint more exactly their attitudes and prejudices. Respondents were asked about their media contact, faith in the government, prior knowledge of the defendants and their case, and other factors that might bear on their responses as jurors. With the information thus compiled, the sociologists developed a rating system that could be applied to each prospective juror and that, it was hoped, would indicate the attitude he or she would possess going into trial. Certain types—for example, Presbyterians and Episcopalians, the college-educated, and those who had broad contact with the metropolitan news media—were considered potentially hostile to the radical, antiwar defendants; other types, such as African Americans, women, and those with no religious affiliation, were judged more likely to be sympathetic. The defense lawyers were guided by the ratings in their challenges to supposed potentially hostile jurors.

Though the defense was pleased with the initial results, the third and fourth stages of the project—courtroom observation and post-trial follow-up—revealed unforeseen weaknesses. Most significantly, two jurors rated "likely sympathetic" were the only two who finally held out for the defendants' conviction. In addition, the follow-up study indicated that the jury's deliberations had been influenced as much by the relative weakness of the government's case and the unpersuasiveness of its witnesses as by the predispositions reflected in the initial surveys.

After reviewing the above material, one scholar concluded that it is impossible for researchers to link attributes such as education or religion to social attitudes in a way that yields reliable predictions about actual behavior.

1. The primary purpose of this passage is to

   A. examine the results of an attempt to apply social science research.
   B. prove the problem-solving relevance of social science methodology.
   C. describe the various methodological procedures of social scientists.
   D. argue that social science research is being exploited for political purposes.

2. The passage suggests that the attempt to profile "sympathetic" jurors failed because of

   A. the random nature of the telephone survey.
   B. inconsistencies in attitudes and behavior.
   C. the inadequacy of current statistical methods.
   D. haphazard collection of irrelevant demographic information.

3. Which of the following accurately reflects the sequence of steps followed in constructing the profile of a "sympathetic" juror?

   A. Personal interviews, telephone survey, development of a rating system, courtroom observation, post-trial analysis
   B. Development of a rating system, telephone survey, personal interviews, courtroom observation, post-trial analysis
   C. Courtroom observation, development of a rating system, personal interviews, telephone survey, post-trial analysis
   D. Telephone survey, personal interviews, development of a rating system, courtroom observation, post-trial analysis

4. The passage implies that social scientists made which of the following assumptions prior to the trial?

   A. The news media in Harrisburg supported the radicals.
   B. Individuals are not truthful on surveys of their attitudes.
   C. Religious people are likely to support radical political behavior.
   D. Social science research should be used to achieve political goals.

5. According to the profile of "sympathetic" jurors discussed in this passage, which of the following individuals would be LEAST likely to support the radicals?

   A. A poorly educated, irreligious man who ignores the local media
   B. A poorly educated, religious woman who ignores the local media
   C. A highly educated, religious man who avidly consumes local news
   D. A highly educated, irreligious woman who avidly consumes local news

Passage II (Questions 6–11)

Paleontologists distinguish three major eras in the history of multicellular life: the Paleozoic, Mesozoic, and Cenozoic. The fossil record of this 600-million-year period has traditionally been interpreted as showing continuity and progression; even the unusual extinct organisms are routinely assigned to the phyla occupied by their assumed modern relatives. However, the recent reconsideration of a large group of mainly Paleozoic marine remains, collectively known as the "*Problematica*," has sparked debate over this practice.

The bizarre, banana-shaped *Tullimonstrum* and spiked, spiny *Hallucigenia* are cited by the revisionists as examples of *Problematica* that cannot be cleanly fit into any modern phylum. These creatures have in fact been deemed morphologically unique enough to warrant phyla of their own. But members of another group of *Problematica*, the pre-Paleozoic *Ediacaran* fauna, illustrate the more usual taxonomic practice: they are assigned variously to such phyla as *Coelenterata* (because of the radial grooves some of them exhibit) or *Annelida* (because others show bilateral symmetry). Revisionists argue that these classifications reflect superficial morphological similarities while ignoring the fact that *Ediacaran* fauna utilized a fundamentally different approach to survival from those of their supposed present-day relatives. The *Ediacaran* fauna carried out gas exchange and absorption of nutrients directly through their external surfaces; this was possible only because of their extremely thin cross section. Among modern animals, only a few parasites such as tapeworms take this approach, and these creatures are otherwise unlike the *Ediacaran* fauna. *Coelenterates* and *annelids*, on the other hand, have evolved internal organs to provide surface areas for gas exchange and absorption.

The disagreement over the *Problematica* reflects a more significant breach over the nature of evolutionary selection. Conventional theorists believe that the Cambrian explosion—the yet unexplained appearance of large numbers of multicellular organisms on earth between 570 and 500 million years ago—yielded a few basic phyla: in essence, a large number of organisms that fit into a small number of essentially different "body plans." By the end of the Cambrian, almost all modern animal phyla had evolved. (The plant phyla appeared more slowly.) The remainder of the Paleozoic and the entirety of the Mesozoic and Cenozoic eras were given over to the evolution of a great variety of species using these basic body plans. Extinctions, including those of the *Problematica*, eliminated species or whole groups of species within these basically viable phyla. The extinction of an entire phylum, such as *Tullimonstrum*, is admitted grudgingly as an exception to the general pattern.

Revisionists interpret the Cambrian explosion as the virtually simultaneous appearance of a much larger number of animal phyla than exists today; each was a separate "experiment" in basic design. Hence, the *Problematica* are viewed not as unsuccessful variants of viable body plans, but as distinct body plans in their own right. While the Paleozoic seas were filled with large numbers of distinct phyla, the number of species in each phylum was low—often only one or two. In contrast, the Cenozoic seas have a much smaller number of phyla, but many more species—there are at least 20,000 species of fish alone. Hence, the number of marine phyla has fallen, while variation within the surviving phyla has been prodigious.

The revisionists agree with taxonomic traditionalists that modern marine species are products of natural selection, but contend that the selection process eliminated not only particular maladaptive traits but entire approaches to survival—not only species but also body plans and, thus, entire phyla. The unusual solution to respiration and absorption seen in the *Ediacaran* fauna, for example, was discarded as a viable alternative for the vast majority of animals at the same time as the *Ediacaran* fauna themselves were wiped out: given the improbability of duplicating an entire body plan through chance mutation, it was unlikely that this particular approach would ever be tried again. Before the Mesozoic was far advanced, these flawed approaches to survival had been permanently removed from the pool of organisms that would have the opportunity to undergo speciation and evolutionary refinement.

6. By inference from the passage, the *Problematica*

    A. differed from one another morphologically and in their approach to basic life functions.

    B. had begun to decrease in number significantly by the close of the Mesozoic era.

    C. existed exclusively as marine creatures of the Paleozoic era.

    D. recently have been assigned to their own phylum.

7. According to the passage, a central difference between the conventional and revisionist interpretations of the fossil record is that

    A. conventional theorists do not account for the disappearance of *Problematica* from the late Paleozoic–middle Mesozoic fossil record.

    B. revisionist theorists emphasize the effects of selection for overall design in addition to selection for specific characteristics.

    C. revisionist theorists draw their conclusions from a quantification of the number of species existing in each of the three major eras.

    D. revisionist theorists believe ancient life forms were subject to random and unpredictable evolutionary pressures.

8. Researchers who question conventional paleontologists' conclusions would agree with which of the following statements?

    A. Modern organisms have undergone little change since their initial appearance in the early Paleozoic era.

    B. The depiction of all morphologically unusual life forms as unsuccessful variations upon workable body plans distorts critical patterns of evolution.

    C. Imperfections in the fossil record due to natural phenomena preclude the drawing of any definite conclusions about evolutionary processes.

    D. The Cambrian explosion permanently disrupted the orderly patterns of evolution that had previously existed.

9. According to revisionist paleontologists, no modern species are evolutionary descendents of the *Hallucigenia* because

    A. the body plan of the *Hallucigenia* was just one of many distinct approaches to survival that arose in the aftermath of the Cambrian explosion.

    B. the organisms arising from the Cambrian explosion became extinct before they could undergo evolution.

    C. the *Hallucigenia* ultimately proved to be unfit in comparison with other species of that phylum and were therefore edged out of their particular niche.

    D. the elimination of the *Hallucigenia* phylum as a result of overall flaws in design implied the extinction of all future variants on that design.

10. It may be inferred that revisionist paleontologists would believe which of the following is true of traditional taxonomic classification?

    A. It reflects the outdated and inaccurate belief that evolution is guided by natural selection.

    B. It imposes constraints upon those who would contest conventional evolutionary theory.

    C. It enables researchers to concentrate on the theoretical rather than the practical aspects of the fossil record.

    D. It is skewed toward phyla containing living representatives.

11. Conventional theorists comparing multicellular life at the beginning of the Cambrian era with that at the beginning of the Cenozoic era would assert that

    A. the number of phyla increased and the number of species increased.

    B. the number of phyla remained the same and the number of species increased.

    C. the number of phyla decreased and the number of species increased.

    D. the number of phyla decreased and the number of species remained the same.

Passage III (Questions 12–16)

The use of human subjects in medical experiments has been a troublesome issue for the scientific community, one complicated by the fact that there are really two separate situations in which such research might be appropriate. Therapeutic experimentation involves the use of new drugs and/or procedures on patients in clinical settings as possible treatments for actual ailments. Nontherapeutic experimentation is conducted upon healthy individuals to determine whether a new treatment or substance has undesirable side effects.

Therapeutic experimentation dates back to the eighteenth century, when the healing effects of bloodletting and castor oil were put to the test against diseases ranging from cholera to pneumonia. The purpose of therapeutic experimentation is quite clear: to ameliorate an individual's illness. The greatest fear aroused by therapeutic experimentation is that physicians may try new therapies recklessly; many members of the medical community therefore insist that it be undertaken solely with the full consent of the patient, and only after conventional treatments have failed.

Since nontherapeutic experimentation confers no benefit on the subject (at best, participants maintain their current state of health; at worst, their health may seriously deteriorate), it has been more controversial. While the need for nontherapeutic experimentation is now generally accepted, there is still controversy over how best to select or encourage volunteers, given the risk of injury. Money and other enticements have been offered to potential participants, although such inducements generally have been considered unethical. As early as 1721, British critics protested King George's offer of a pardon to condemned prisoners who agreed to submit to variolation (inoculation with infectious smallpox matter) to determine whether subjects would subsequently develop the disease or would instead become immune. It was argued that the prisoners were deprived of a truly free choice, since they faced death sentences if they refused. Commentators have also questioned the propriety of experimenting on medical students, soldiers, and pharmaceutical industry employees, all of whom may be vulnerable to pressure by superiors who may have a vested interest in the project.

The medical community and concerned observers have yet to agree upon the type of individual whose participation in a nontherapeutic experiment could be deemed truly voluntary.

Although those conducting both therapeutic and nontherapeutic experiments have attempted to take precautions by pretesting their research on animals and by imposing limits on their field of potential subjects, there remains an inevitable risk for human volunteers. To minimize possible hazards, certain traditional safeguards have been utilized. The so-called "golden rule" of human biomedical research has traditionally mandated that no investigator undertake a project unless he or she would willingly participate in that experiment. In 1929, for example, Dr. Werner Forssman passed a catheter into the right ventricle of his own heart to demonstrate that the procedure was both safe and comfortable. The principal ethical question evoked by the "golden rule" is that a physician's right to experiment on his or her own body does not necessarily entitle the doctor to subject others to the same risk.

A second important safeguard has been the securing of an "informed consent" from the volunteer. However, the British Medical Association, among other groups, has questioned whether subjects without a minimal level of scientific or medical knowledge can give a truly informed consent, rather than simply accepting the recommendations of their physicians. The difficult task, faced by all scientists who use human subjects in medical research project, is the dispassionate dissemination of accurate and comprehensible information to potential volunteers.

12. In which of the following ways is therapeutic experimentation different from nontherapeutic experimentation?

    A. It offers volunteers improved health as an incentive.

    B. It cannot be initiated without the consent of the patient's physician.

    C. It is only performed on healthy volunteers.

    D. It has been fully accepted by the medical community, while nontherapeutic experimentation is generally rejected.

13. The variolation of prisoners cited in the passage (paragraph 3) is most similar in principle to which of the following procedures?

    A. Drawing a certain amount of blood from a volunteer with a suspected case of malaria

    B. Inserting a catheter into the heart of a subject experiencing an undetermined cardiac event

    C. Assessing the pain-reducing capacities of a new aspirin

    D. Administering a new sedative and monitoring subjects for allergic reactions

14. On the subject of biomedical experimentation, the scientific community has been

    A. divided over the necessity of obtaining an informed consent from potential subjects.

    B. more supportive of therapeutic research than of nontherapeutic experiments.

    C. largely opposed to the sentiments expressed by other members of society on this issue.

    D. disillusioned by the government's delayed acceptance of nontherapeutic testing.

15. It may be inferred that the selection of subjects for nontherapeutic research projects is complicated by all of the following EXCEPT that

    A. potential volunteers usually are unwilling to take part in an experiment that does not offer financial compensation.

    B. potential subjects may be unduly influenced by the opinions of those in relative positions of authority.

    C. researchers and nonscientists who intend to take part in an experiment may have different views as to what constitutes an acceptable level of risk.

    D. potential volunteers often do not have an adequate understanding of a proposed project.

16. The author believes that all scientists who conduct medical experiments involving human volunteers must

    A. make certain that only people with a background in science or medicine are used as test subjects.

    B. ensure that subjects receive an impartial and intelligible explanation of the project.

    C. refrain from initiating experimental therapy unless conventional treatments have proven ineffectual.

    D. allow research on human subjects only after tests on animals have proved a drug safe.

Passage IV (Questions 17–21)

The giant panda's isolated existence in a few alpine regions on the periphery of the Tibetan plateau and distinctive black and white markings have made it the object of great fascination. While the general public tends to view the panda as a kind of living teddy bear, biologists are not sure how to view this enigmatic species. It defies easy classification. Ever since its discovery in the middle of the 19th century, a controversy has been raging among biologists over the question of the panda's relation to other species.

The discoverer of the giant panda, Armand David, considered the panda a species of bear distinct from any other. Later, biologist Alphonse Milne-Edwards argued that the panda should not be classified as a bear, but should be placed in a distinct family of its own. Over the course of the next 120 years, biologists have alternately placed the giant panda with bears in the Ursidae family, with raccoons in the Procyonidae family, or in its own Ailuropodidae family.

Systematists, who classify animal species on the basis of traits, consider the classification of the panda according to whether its traits are "homologous" or merely "analogous" to similar traits in other species. Homologous traits are those which have developed as a result of common ancestry; every species possessing a particular trait is descended from the same ancestor. Every member of the cat family, for instance, has only four toes on its hind feet. The extent to which various species are related is determined by the number of homologous traits they share. The greater the number of homologous traits species share, the closer the relationship among them. Analogous traits, on the other hand, result from convergence, a process whereby species descended from different ancestors develop similar traits due to environmental stimulus. The wings of an eagle and those of a butterfly, for example, perform the same function, but these two species do not share a common ancestry.

Unfortunately, the genetic basis of homologous traits is poorly understood, and problems in distinguishing the effects of environment and genes make it difficult to identify analogous relationships. Consequently, such analyses of observed traits have raised more questions regarding the panda's lineage than they have solved. While the giant panda may look like a bear, it also has many traits that bears do not possess. The giant panda, like the red panda (a relation of the raccoon and a member of the Procyonidae family), is mainly an herbivore, its diet consisting primarily of bamboo. This type of diet has contributed to the development of a more massive head and jaw structure in the giant panda than in the typical bear. Giant pandas also have thumbs, which are used to strip leaves from bamboo stalks, while bears do not have a similar digit. Many bears hibernate at certain times of the year, but giant pandas do not. Furthermore, most bears growl or roar, but giant pandas bleat. In terms of chromosome structure, bears have thirty-seven pairs, red pandas have twenty-two pairs, and giant pandas only twenty-one. It is not surprising, then, that emphasis of certain traits to the exclusion of others has made it possible for biologists to argue in support of a variety of different panda classifications.

Tests recently developed to supplement methods of classification based on the observation of traits may help to resolve the issue of the panda's proper classification. These tests are based on the "molecular clock" hypothesis, which contends that the genetic material of populations which are reproductively isolated diverges steadily over time. By examining the genetic material of various species, biologists can determine when they diverged from a common ancestor. Employing a technique known as DNA hybridization, biologists have been able to demonstrate that the giant panda is more closely related to bears than to raccoons. Other methods, including gel electrophoresis, two-dimensional electrophoresis, and immunological surveys, have supported the conclusion that while the giant panda belongs to the Ursidae family, its ancestors split from the main Ursid line more than 15 million years ago.

17. According to the passage, which of the following is NOT true of homologous traits?

  A. Homologous traits stem from the sharing of a common ancestry.
  B. The degree of relationship among various species can be determined by the number of homologous traits they share.
  C. Homologous traits develop as a result of the process of convergence.
  D. Systematists refer to homologous traits in classifying animals.

18. By inference from the passage, which of the following most probably represents an analogous trait?

  A. Body hair of humans and body hair of apes
  B. Scales of snakes and skin of humans
  C. Wings of falcons and wings of mosquitos
  D. Thumbs of pandas and digits of raccoons

19. According to the information in the passage, which of the following animals are most closely related?

  A. Four animals that share five homologous traits
  B. Three animals that share five analogous traits
  C. Two animals that share ten homologous traits
  D. Two animals that share ten analogous traits

20. Which of the following best sums up the main idea of the last paragraph?

  A. The giant panda is properly classified as a bear, even though its ancestors split off from the bear family long ago.
  B. Because the giant panda is primarily a plant eater, it deserves to be placed with raccoons and red pandas in the Procyonidae family.
  C. Various techniques based on the "molecular clock" hypothesis have not shed any light on the issue of the panda's proper classification.
  D. Biologists are now able to approximate when various species diverged from a common ancestor by examining the genetic material of those species.

21. This passage was most likely written by a

  A. geologist.
  B. geneticist.
  C. biologist.
  D. chemist.

Passage V (Questions 22–28)

The term *groupthink* was coined by Irving Janis in 1972 to describe breakdowns in group decision making. Janis claimed that groupthink has led to several disastrous decisions in U.S. foreign policy, such as the Kennedy administration's support for the Bay of Pigs invasion in 1961. According to Janis's hypothesis, groupthink may occur when a highly cohesive group led by a strong leader with a predilection for a specific solution faces a crisis situation. Because individual members fear rejection by the group and desire that the morale of the group remain high, the group excludes outside information, ignores alternative solutions, and may make a decision that, in retrospect, is obviously wrong.

To test groupthink under laboratory conditions, Matie Flowers separated 160 undergraduate students into forty groups of 4. Two factors were independently considered in the experiment: style of leadership (open or closed) and group cohesiveness. An open leader was instructed to encourage discussion of all possible solutions and to refrain from offering a solution until each member of the group had expressed his or her opinion. A closed leader was told to state a preferred solution at the beginning of the session and to make clear that the main objective of the group was to arrive at a consensus. In groups defined as having low cohesiveness, the members were strangers, while in groups with high cohesiveness, the individuals were acquainted. Each team was presented with the same crisis situation; each member of a team was assigned a role and given a different fact sheet (facts listed depended on the specific role played by the individual).

Individuals led by an open leader offered significantly more solutions than did members of teams with closed leaders. However, cohesiveness had no apparent effect on the number of solutions proposed. Groups with open leaders dealt with significantly more facts in making a decision. Teams with a closed leader mentioned more facts after a decision had been reached than did groups led by an open leader. Cohesiveness had no significant effect on the introduction of facts.

Although some effects of groupthink apparently occurred in the experiment, group cohesiveness was not critical in producing the effects. One likely explanation for this inconsistency suggests that the problem stems from two different conceptions of "high group cohesiveness." Janis had based his concept of group cohesiveness on the behavior of individuals who had worked and socialized together over a long period of time; Flowers, however, grouped individuals who were less intimately acquainted. Thus, the experiment may have failed to simulate the type of high cohesiveness that occurs in real social groups faced by actual crisis situations.

22. It can be inferred from the passage that group decision making

   A. is most successful under a strong leader.
   B. is only successful in highly cohesive groups.
   C. can sometimes lead to disastrous results.
   D. limits the number of possible solutions.

23. According to the passage, the goal of Flowers's experiment was to

   A. demonstrate that group cohesiveness does not influence groupthink.
   B. contest the theory that groupthink is restricted to crisis situations.
   C. test Janis's hypothesis under laboratory conditions.
   D. prove that groupthink stems from strong leadership styles.

24. The author most likely mentions the 1961 Bay of Pigs invasion (paragraph 1) in order to

   A. discredit the reputation of the Kennedy administration.

   B. illustrate the long-term effects of policy decisions.

   C. provide an example of the effects of groupthink in a crisis situation.

   D. show that poor decisions are made in crisis situations.

25. Which of the following factors did Flowers attempt to vary in her groupthink experiment?

   I. Style of group leadership

   II. Severity of crises encountered by groups

   III. Degree of cohesion among group members

   A. I only

   B. I and III only

   C. II and III only

   D. I, II, and III

26. Which of the following would most WEAKEN Janis's groupthink hypothesis?

   A. A study that concludes individuals fear being rejected by the group more than making a wrong decision

   B. An experiment that suggests an open leadership style rarely results in faulty decision making

   C. A theory that implies groupthink is common to government and military organizations

   D. A study that concludes leaders rarely approach a crisis with a solution in mind

27. Which of the following best expresses the author's conclusions regarding the Flowers experiment?

   A. Because group cohesiveness did not influence groupthink, Janis's theory is clearly false.

   B. Because leadership style seems to affect group decision-making processes, Janis's theory is obviously true.

   C. Since group cohesiveness did not seem to affect group decision-making processes, Janis's theory may be true only under certain conditions.

   D. Since group cohesiveness had no significant effect on groupthink, it should not be considered a factor in Janis's schema.

28. According to the passage, the "inconsistency" in research findings, referred to in paragraph 4, probably stems from the fact that

   A. groups led by closed leaders in Janis's study dealt with facts after, not before, decisions were made.

   B. Flowers believed that strong leadership style was the prime cause of groupthink, while Janis emphasized the role of group cohesiveness.

   C. despite Flowers's expectations, groups with open leaders offered fewer solutions than did those with closed leaders.

   D. Flowers and Janis based their studies on varying concepts of group cohesiveness.

Passage VI (Questions 29–35)

Two important concepts of social philosophy are utilitarianism, which aims to calculate and institute the greatest good for the greatest number, not necessarily excepting the possibility of sacrifice and suffering on the part of a minority; and the notion of the social contract, which states that a society exists by the implicit agreement of all its citizens, and on that basis owes certain obligations to them. These two concepts are contrasting but not necessarily contradictory; nonetheless one or another has often enjoyed ascendancy since their initial formulations by Bentham and Locke, respectively. In this century utilitarianism has long been a de facto orthodoxy among political philosophers. The 1971 publication of John Rawls's *A Theory of Justice*, however, gave the contractarian view a needed and welcome restatement.

Since they will determine the "clauses" of the social contract, the nature and needs of the parties must be carefully considered. Rather than adopt an implausible Rousseauean vision of uncorrupted, harmonious "natural man," the new contractarians postulate a group of rational men and women gathered for the purpose of defining a concept of justice that will guide their affairs. They further assume that these people make their decisions behind a veil of ignorance, that is, they are temporarily totally unaware of their position in society—their race, their gender, their place in the social order. Yet the principles at which they arrive will bind them once the veil is lifted.

Starting from this original position, it can be logically demonstrated that rational beings would arrive at a decision ensuring the maximum possible justice and liberty for even the least privileged member of society. For who would propose a utilitarian view of justice and risk slavery when the veil was lifted? Would the knowledge that society as a whole derived a greater benefit console him or her in servitude?

Two basic principles would most likely emerge from this hypothetical conclave. First, all would have access to the greatest degree of liberty compatible with a similar liberty for all other members of society. For example, freedom of speech thus would be inviolable, whereas the utilitarian could easily justify its abridgment for a greater social good. Second, social and economic inequality, insofar as they are inevitable, would be arranged such that they inhered in offices and stations available to all and such that whatever benefits accrue from a necessary evil would be distributed to everyone's advantage. Injustice, then, is defined as an unequal distribution of good things, with liberty first among them.

While it can be and has been argued that the blind choosers envisioned by the new contractarians might well decide to gamble on the outcome of the social order, such arguments are ultimately lacking in interest. The point of the contractarian view does not lie in what real people "would" do in an admittedly impossible situation. Rather, it is to provide an abstract model that is intuitively satisfactory and a machinery for making ethical decisions.

29. The primary purpose of the passage is to

    A. outline and defend a contractarian view of justice.

    B. propose a radical solution to social problems.

    C. compare the utilitarian and contractarian theories of justice.

    D. explore the political theory of John Rawls.

30. According to the passage, people considering justice behind a "veil of ignorance" (paragraph 2) would

    A. select a principle favoring the group they would belong to when the veil was lifted.

    B. select a principle that would be fair to everyone regardless of birth and status.

    C. be unable to agree on a single principle.

    D. demand an end to social and political inequality.

31. By inference from the passage, utilitarianism and contractarianism necessarily

A. conflict with each other.
B. agree on major points.
C. start from similar ideas of human nature.
D. involve differing notions of the desirable society.

32. Assume that an aged parent is being artificially kept alive, causing the family financial and emotional hardships. The passage implies that a utilitarian would most likely respond to this situation by

A. balancing the potential burdens on the family against the burdens to society.
B. arguing that the parent, as a member of the "contracting" unit, had a right to an equal voice in the decision.
C. keeping the parent alive only if doing so was beneficial to society as a whole.
D. upholding the parent's right to life against any potential lessening of the family's hardship.

33. Which of the following is an assumption of the contractarian model?

A. The decision makers act without any knowledge of the consequences.
B. All members of the contracting group will place a high value on personal liberty.
C. Justice can only be secured by ensuring that all positions have equal power and status.
D. The contracting parties will seek to safeguard their liberties at the expense of the rights of others.

34. By inference from the passage, a party to the social contract who decided "to gamble on the outcome of the social order" (paragraph 5) would select a principle of justice

A. allowing unequal access to liberty and other social goods.
B. based on a Rousseauistic vision of humanity.
C. based on the greatest possible equalization of both personal freedom and material circumstances.
D. benefiting the gambler in his or her future life.

35. Which of the following would a "new contractarian" regard as an absolute right that must not be abridged?

A. Personal liberty
B. Social equality
C. Economic equality
D. Racial equality

Passage VII (Questions 36–40)

Suppose you are about to make a speech attempting to persuade your audience that more spending on education is necessary or that the budget deficit should be reduced through cuts in domestic spending. There are a few different ways you might approach your argument. When it comes down to it, though, you must find a way of presenting your material to your audience that is most effective. What factors make a one-sided argument so effective that they seem to be the tactic of choice for most modern propagandists?

If a communicator mentions the opposition's arguments, it might indicate that he or she is an objective, fair-minded person; this could enhance the speaker's trustworthiness and thus increase his or her effectiveness. On the other hand, if a communicator so much as mentions the arguments of the other side of the issue, it might suggest to the audience that the issue is a controversial one; this could make members of the audience vacillate.

With these possibilities in mind, it should not come as a surprise that there is no simple relation between one-sided arguments and the effectiveness of the communication. It depends to some extent upon how well informed the audience is and on the audience's initial opinions on the issue. Citing research contrary to one's thesis must be a measured risk. If the audience is not already aware of this research, they might be unduly swayed in the wrong direction. Research generally finds that the more well informed the members of the audience are, the less likely they are to be persuaded by a one-sided argument and the more likely they are to be persuaded by an argument that brings out the important opposing arguments and then attempts to refute them. We should underscore that the research does not favor the effectiveness of a simple two-sided argument: It favors the effectiveness of presenting both sides and pointing out the weaknesses in your opponent's position.

This makes sense: A well-informed person is more likely to know some of the counterarguments; when the communicator avoids mentioning these, the knowledgeable members of the audience are likely to conclude that the communicator is either unfair or unable to refute such arguments. On the other hand, an uninformed person is less apt to know of the existence of opposing arguments. If the counterargument is ignored, the less well-informed members of the audience are persuaded; if the counterargument is presented, they might get confused.

The message-dense nature of the mass media often makes it difficult to respond intelligently to what we receive. It takes considerable mental effort to process effectively the stream of one short message after another. Advertisers have observed that consumers frequently find comparative advertising confusing; they mistake one brand for another, leading to a situation in which the advertiser is publicizing the competition. For this reason, comparative advertising is rarely used by the leading brand (why give an upstart free publicity?); it is used mostly by a challenger that might gain from being confused with the leader.

Another factor influencing the effectiveness of one- versus two-sided persuasion is the partisanship of the audience. As we might expect, if a member of the audience is already predisposed to believe the communicator's argument, a one-sided presentation has a greater impact on his or her opinion than a two-sided presentation.

36. Suppose that the president of the United States wants to persuade foreign policy experts in Congress to support the deployment of American troops overseas. The president should do which of the following to convince these experts to support troop deployment?

A. Make a one-sided argument that addresses only the potential benefits of such a policy

B. Make a one-sided argument that addresses only the potential costs of such a policy

C. Make a two-sided argument that addresses both the potential benefits and potential costs of such a policy

D. Make an argument that appeals to emotions rather than one that addresses the facts

37. Implicit in the authors' discussion of audience receptivity to messages is the assumption that

A. advertisements are an ineffective means to get people to buy consumer products.

B. the mass media attempt to shape public opinion to suit their own interests.

C. most people do not generally think carefully about what they are told by others.

D. the less people know about an issue, the more likely they are to accept the opinion of others.

38. Based on the arguments and information put forth by the author in the passage, which of the following statements is true?

A. One-sided arguments are generally less effective than two-sided arguments when the message is being delivered to a knowledgeable audience.

B. Comparative advertising is always an effective way for a company to sell more of its products.

C. Highly educated people are more receptive to two-sided arguments than less highly educated people.

D. Communicators who employ one-sided arguments are usually not fair-minded people.

39. The existence of which of the following phenomena would challenge the information in the passage?

I. A well-informed, unbiased person who reacts unfavorably to a one-sided message, but favorably to a two-sided message

II. A poorly informed, unbiased person who reacts unfavorably to a one-sided message, but favorably to a two-sided message

III. A well-informed, unbiased person who reacts favorably to a one-sided message

A. I only

B. III only

C. I and II only

D. II and III only

40. If the claims made in the passage are correct, how would a communicator who is aware of these claims be expected to react to a knowledgeable, open-minded audience?

A. The communicator would not try to make an argument.

B. The communicator would present a one-sided argument.

C. The communicator would present a two-sided argument.

D. The communicator would appeal to the audience's emotions.

Verbal Reasoning Practice Test 6
Answers and Explanations

ANSWER KEY

1.	A	9.	D	17.	C	25.	B	33.	B
2.	B	10.	D	18.	C	26.	D	34.	A
3.	D	11.	A	19.	C	27.	C	35.	D
4.	D	12.	A	20.	A	28.	D	36.	C
5.	C	13.	D	21.	C	29.	A	37.	D
6.	A	14.	B	22.	C	30.	B	38.	A
7.	B	15.	A	23.	C	31.	D	39.	D
8.	B	16.	B	24.	C	32.	C	40.	C

Passage I: Harrisburg Jury

Topic: Harrisburg case

Scope: Jury selection and social science

Purpose: To discuss the limitations

Mapping the Passage:

¶1. Harrisburg case: Social scientists try to select sympathetic jury.

¶2. Procedural steps.

¶3. Problems with jury selection system.

¶4. One scholar: Can't predict jury behavior based on the survey attributes.

1. A

For this global question, refer back to your Purpose, Scope, and Topic—all of which match (A).

Wrong Answers:

(B) Opposite. As indicated in the last paragraph, the real thrust of the passage is that social science methods didn't work.

(C) Faulty Use of Detail. Methodology is part of the passage, but the text does not consider "various" procedures.

(D) Out of Scope. The author states that social science is being used, but definitely not "exploited," for political purposes.

2. B

The last paragraph says that based on the results of this trial, it is not possible to link the survey's attributes to the way people actually make decisions. In other words, people seem to be inconsistent in their behavior, which matches (B).

Wrong Answers:

(A) Faulty Use of Detail. The survey chose respondents at random, but that wasn't why the predictions failed.

(C) Out of Scope. The passage doesn't say anything about the inadequacy of current statistical methods.

(D) Out of Scope. There's no suggestion that the demographic data collected was irrelevant or collected haphazardly.

3. D

The sequence starts in paragraph 2, so you start there too. According to the text, the "first stage in the project consisted of a telephone survey." Only (D) lists this as the first step.

Wrong Answers:

(A), (B), and (C) all have the steps in the wrong sequence.

4. D

Logic tells you that the social scientists must have thought they could successfully predict a sympathetic jury. If not, why would they even have tried? Match that prediction with (D) and don't quibble with the word *should* when you'd rather use *could*. After all, you can prove that all other answers are wrong, so the right one must be (D).

Wrong Answers:

(A) **Out of Scope.** The news media has nothing to do with social science and jury selection.
(B) **Opposite.** If social scientists thought people weren't truthful on surveys, they wouldn't have used people's answers to try to develop a sympathetic jury.
(C) **Opposite.** Presbyterians and Episcopalians were supposed to be hostile to the radicals, while those with no religious affiliation were considered "sympathetic."

5. C

Paragraph 2 provides a list of people who wouldn't support radicals: people who are college educated, religious, and attentive to the local media. (C) is the obvious match.

Wrong Answers:

(A), (B) and (D) all have the wrong mix of attributes.

Passage II: *Problematica* Species

Topic: *Problematica*
Scope: Taxonomy
Purpose: To discuss and debate

Mapping the Passage:

¶1. Recent reconsideration of Paleozoic marine → debate about phyla.
¶2. Examples of *Problematica*: Can't fit into any modern phylum.
¶3. Conventionalists: Initially few basic phyla.
¶4. Revisionists: Initially many "experimental" phyla.
¶5. Revisionists believe entire phyla were eliminated.

6. A

Paragraph 2 tells us that *Tullimonstrum* and *Hallucigenia* are assigned their own distinct phyla, while the *Ediacaran* fauna belong either in a new phylum or phyla (revisionist view) or in one of two modern phyla (conventional view). Thus, the three examples of *Problematica* all belong in different phyla and are morphologically distinct. In addition, the *Ediacaran* fauna had an approach to basic life functions distinct from that of nearly all modern animals; by inference, it was also distinct from that of *Tullimonstrum* and the *Hallucigenia*. All this adds up to what is stated in (A).

Wrong Answers:

(B) **Faulty Use of Detail.** The *Problematica*, creatures with body forms that didn't work, were extinct early in the Mesozoic era, according to the last paragraph.
(C) **Distortion.** Although the *Problematica* discussed in the passage were all marine, it does not state that others (if there were any) couldn't have been terrestrial.
(D) **Opposite.** The whole problem is phylum assignment, and it hasn't been resolved.

7. B

Revisionists and conventionalists differ about where to place the *Problematica*. Revisionists say *Problematica* don't belong to any modern phylum because their overall different and unsatisfactory body plans led to extinction. Conventionalists say different: that natural selection acted upon each phylum to eliminate some of its "branches" (species) but not the phylum itself. (B) comes closest, noting the difference between considering an entire body plan versus specific characteristics.

Wrong Answers:

(A) Out of Scope. We know what revisionists think about why *Problematica* disappeared. We don't specifically know what the conventionalists would say, but this doesn't mean they don't account for it in some other way

(C) Faulty Use of Detail. The comparison of numbers of species is evidence for the revisionists' conclusions, not the basis of the conclusions.

(D) Out of Scope. Both the conventionalists and revisionists believe that evolution occurred, but they differ in their beliefs about how it occurred.

8. B

Be careful about the wording of this question. It's actually asking what the revisionists would agree with. We've already reviewed their theory about distinct, but unworkable body plans and extinction. From that, we can assume (B); people who think only about *workable* body plans have missed something in the fossil record.

Wrong Answers:

(A) Opposite. Both sides agree that evolution took place, so change was a given.

(C) Opposite. Even though the fossil record may be imperfect, both sides draw conclusions.

(D) Out of Scope. Nothing is suggested in the passage about evolution before the Cambrian explosion.

9. D

Hallucigenia are examples of *Problematica*, and by now we know what revisionists think happened to them: They became extinct because their body plans were unworkable. The body design didn't work; the creatures became extinct: no *Problematica*, no descendents, no variations. (D) comes closest to this.

Wrong Answers:

(A) Faulty Use of Detail. Although the revisionists believed that the *Hallucigenia* were "just one of many distinct" body plans, this doesn't explain why *Hallucigenia* have no descendents today but many other phyla do.

(B) Opposite. Revisionists believe many organisms arising from the Cambrian explosion did evolve and were the ancestors of modern species, as noted in the first sentence of paragraph 5.

(C) Opposite There *were* no other species in the same phylum. As the revisionists keep saying, *Hallucigenia* was in a phylum all by itself.

10. D

Revisionists believe the traditional system of taxonomic classification reflects the idea that all fossils may be grouped within existing taxonomic categories. If scientists deal only with existing phyla, (D) must be correct.

Wrong Answers:

(A) Opposite. The last paragraph states that revisionists agree with traditionalists on natural selection.

(B) Out of Scope. Not only is this not in the passage, but since the revisionists have developed their own theory, they've obviously not been stopped by constraints.

(C) Out of Scope. The passage doesn't discuss the theoretical versus practical parts of fossils.

11. A

This is going to take some research, but paragraph 3 states: "By the end of the Cambrian, *almost* all modern animal phyla had evolved." Since the conventional theory holds that few—if any—ancient phyla have become extinct, the implication is that more phyla and species were living at the beginning of recent (Cenozoic) times than at the beginning of the Cambrian (A).

Wrong Answers:

(B) Opposite. According to the conventionalists, the Cambrian explosion initially produced "a few basic phyla" that evolved into numerous other phyla.

(C) Faulty Use of Detail. This is the revisionist, not the conventionalist, conclusion.

(D) Opposite. Both revisionists and conventional theorists agree that the number of *species* has increased since the beginning of the Cambrian.

Passage III: Medical Studies on Humans

Topic: Biomedical research

Scope: Use of human subjects

Purpose: To explain the difficulties

Mapping the Passage:

¶1. Therapeutic vs. nontherapeutic experimentation.

¶2. Therapeutic experimentation history.

¶3. Problems with nontherapeutic.

¶4. No agreement on definition of truly voluntary.

¶5. Golden Rule of research.

¶6. Informed consent.

12. A

Paragraph 2 notes that the purpose of therapeutic experimentation is to "ameliorate an individual's illness"; that is, to treat and hopefully relieve disease. But according to paragraph 3, nontherapeutic experimentation doesn't have this goal, which matches (A).

Wrong Answers:

(B) Out of Scope. The role of the patient's physician isn't discussed in either type of research.

(C) Opposite. Nontherapeutic research is done on healthy people.

(D) Opposite. The third paragraph states that "the need for nontherapeutic experimentation is now generally accepted."

13. D

Paragraph 3 tells us that the variolation experiment involved inoculating healthy volunteers with infectious smallpox to determine whether they acquired immunity. It was thus a *nontherapeutic* experiment (its goal was not to treat an existing illness); participants would either maintain their health or contract smallpox. The only choice that discusses another nontherapeutic experiment, similar in principle to variolation, is (D).

Wrong Answers:

(A) Opposite. This would be therapeutic—performed with an eye to diagnosing, and presumably treating, an illness.

(B) Opposite. Therapeutic again—designed to treat a real illness.

(C) Opposite. You guessed it: therapeutic. You would assess pain-reducing ability by testing it on someone with pain in order to lessen the pain (if you tested it on a person at all, which is not inherent in the answer).

14. B

According to paragraph 2, therapeutic research dates back to the 18th century, its "purpose … is quite clear," and the only serious reservation concerns the behavior of the researchers. Nontherapeutic research, however, "has been more controversial" because of limited or unethical incentives, uncertainty over volunteers, and similar questions (paragraph 3). Obviously then, therapeutic experimentation is less controversial and matches (B).

Wrong Answers:

(A) Out of Scope. While the last paragraph deals with problems of informed consent, there's nothing about divided opinions.

(C) Out of Scope. The passage doesn't make a comparison between the opinions of the scientific community and society at large.

(D) Out of Scope. There's nothing in the passage about the government's acceptance of testing.

15. A

This scattered detail question requires some slow and careful research. Take a look at the answer choices and, one by one, check them out in the passage. You're looking for one that isn't supported there. Scattered throughout the passage you'll find everything but (A). Although the passage states that "money and other enticements have been offered," it doesn't imply that volunteers are "usually" unwilling to take part unless they're paid. Be careful of answer choices that distort what the passage says, often making an extreme statement that is not supported.

Wrong Answers:

(B) Opposite. This is mentioned in the last sentence of paragraph 3.

(C) Opposite. This is what paragraph 5 is all about.

(D) Opposite. This is one of the problems of informed consent in the last paragraph.

16.   B

The author states a personal belief only in the last sentence: "The difficult task, faced by all scientists who use human subjects in medical research projects, is the dispassionate dissemination of accurate and comprehensible information to potential volunteers." In other words, as much as possible, researchers need to make sure volunteers know what they're getting into. This opinion is paraphrased in (B).

Wrong Answers:

(A) Out of Scope. No one recommends that experimentation be limited to volunteers who have a scientific or medical background.

(C) Faulty Use of Detail. Although the second paragraph states that therapeutic experiments are usually conducted "only after conventional treatments have failed," this question asks about "all scientists," which would also include those performing nontherapeutic experiments.

(D) Distortion. The fifth paragraph begins with the statement that scientists "have attempted to take precautions by pretesting their research on animals," but the passage doesn't imply that the author believes it must always happen.

Passage IV: Panda Bear
Topic: Giant panda
Scope: Classification
Purpose: To discuss problems and progress

Mapping the Passage:

¶1. Panda's relationship to other species debated.

¶2. Panda's classification has varied.

¶3. Homologous, analogous traits.

¶4. Differences between pandas and other bears.

¶5. Molecular biology → panda is a bear.

17.   C

Homologous traits are discussed in the third and fourth paragraphs, so look there for the answer to this scattered detail question. As always with these kinds of questions, let the answers guide your research. When you do so, you'll find everything but (C), which is wrong because it refers to analogous traits. So (C) is the odd man out and the right answer.

Wrong Answers:

(A) Opposite. According to the third paragraph, homologous traits "have developed as a result of common ancestry."

(B) Opposite. The third paragraph also states that the relationship between two species "is determined by the number of homologous traits they share."

(D) Opposite. Systemists are in paragraph 3, the one that describes homologous traits.

18.   C

This is an application question, asking you to apply your understanding of analogous traits and relationships among animals. Analogous traits develop as a result of environmental stimuli, rather than stemming from common ancestry. The correct answer must present two animals that are not related but possess traits that serve similar functions. Falcons and mosquitoes, in (C), are not descended from the same ancestor, yet both have developed a similar trait—wings used for flight—so (C) is the answer.

Wrong Answers:

(A) Opposite. Humans and apes are descended from a common ancestor, so their shared trait of body hair is probably homologous, not analogous.

(B) Opposite. Scales and skin are not shared traits.

(D) Opposite. Pandas have thumbs and raccoons don't, so the digits can't perform the same function and thus aren't shared traits.

19.   C

Notice that all the answers involve either homologous or analogous traits, so you'll be looking at what makes both these traits indicative of a close relationship between species. You'll get all the information you need in paragraph 3, but it boils down to this: The more homologous traits two species share, the closer they are related. Which answer has most homologous traits? (C).

Wrong Answers:

(A) Faulty Use of Detail. Five homologous traits look good, but they can't beat ten, as in (C). Don't get sidetracked by the number of animals in this answer. We're not dealing with how many animals there are but how many homologous traits there are.

(B) Faulty Use of Detail. Analogous traits show convergence, not common ancestry.

(D) Faulty Use of Detail. Same problem as (B), but worse because now there are even more analogous traits.

20. A

As your map shows, the last paragraph is all about new technology that shows that the panda is a bear. That's all you need to match with (A).

Wrong Answers:

(B) Faulty Use of Detail. The fourth paragraph talks about the giant panda's eating habits, but this question asks about the main idea of the fifth paragraph.

(C) Opposite. The molecular clock method helped classify the panda.

(D) Faulty Use of Detail. This is one use of molecular biology, but the answer isn't focused on the panda, which is, after all, the subject of the passage.

21. C

Now who would write about classifying an animal, particularly in light of traits? "Biologist" should be your first thought, and that's (C).

Wrong Answers:

(A) Opposite. Geologists study the earth, as you know.

(B) Opposite. Although the last paragraph discusses genetics and DNA, a geneticist would be more specialized than the scientist who wrote this general passage.

(D) Opposite. Chemists study chemistry, which is not the focus of the passage.

Passage V: Groupthink

Topic: Groupthink
Scope: Flowers's study
Purpose: To report and discuss findings

Mapping the Passage:

¶1. Irving Janis's theory of groupthink.
¶2. Methods and details of study.
¶3. Results.
¶4. Failures of the study design.

22. C

In this inference question, look for an answer that closely mirrors something in the passage and must be true based on what you read. Sometimes this is easier done by eliminating wrong answers. As you research the possibilities, you'll see that (C) is right in line with the example given in paragraph 1—a "disastrous decision" resulting from groupthink.

Wrong Answers:

(A) Opposite. The Bay of Pigs decision was made by a group with a strong leader, and it wasn't particularly successful. Don't confuse an open leader with a strong one.

(B) Distortion. Watch out for words such as *only*. They usually indicate a wrong answer, except when the passage author herself is extreme. Then an extreme answer simply mirrors the author. But that's not the case here.

(D) Opposite. The passage suggests that the more people involved in an interactive decision-making process, the more possible solutions result.

23. C

Your map says it all: Flowers's goal was to test groupthink, (C). Predict and match—that's the way to save time on the MCAT.

Wrong Answers:

(A) Distortion. A test is not a proof; it's a research tool. Besides, Flowers didn't have a biased agenda, as this answer suggests.

(B) Out of Scope. She wasn't contesting (i.e., trying to disprove) anything. Again, Flowers conducted a neutral experiment.

(D) Out of Scope. This is wrong for the same reasons that (A) and (B) are wrong.

24. C

The Bay of Pigs crisis is given as an example of how groupthink has led to disastrous decisions in foreign policy. That prediction quickly takes you to (C).

Wrong Answers:

(A) Out of Scope. Janis didn't set out to discredit the Kennedy administration. An example supports a thesis, and his thesis has nothing to do with the administration.

(B) Out of Scope. The author discusses the decision-making process in the Bay of Pigs invasion, not the results of those decisions.

(D) Out of Scope. The Bay of Pigs decision *was* a poor one, but this answer is too broad and is not the reason it is mentioned in a passage about groupthink.

25. B

You'll find all of Flowers's criteria in the second paragraph. There are only two: style of leadership and cohesiveness. That fits statements I and III, so match those with the right answer, (B). You could, of course, have started with I since it appears in three of the four answers. Either way you'd get (B).

Wrong Answers:

II. Opposite. The second paragraph states that "each team was presented with the same crisis situation."

26. D

To weaken (or strengthen) a hypothesis, first review the hypothesis quickly. Janis's theory is that there are factors that contribute to groupthink results. How was this test-ed? Flowers set up groups with different membership and leader types, mirroring real situations, then gave each of them the same crisis situation. Some groups were led by a strong, closed leader with a solution in mind. Obviously, Flowers must theorize that such groups exist. But (D) says that this situation rarely happens. That would weaken the hypothesis and would thus be the right answer.

Wrong Answers:

(A) Opposite. This would strengthen the hypothesis. The author mentions this issue in the last sentence of the first paragraph.

(B) Opposite. Again, this supports Janis. He states that it's the strong leader with a bias toward a specific solution, not the open leader, who is likely to lead a group to a faulty decision.

(C) Opposite. The passage starts out with an example from government foreign policy, so groupthink must apply there, and there's no reason to believe it wouldn't also apply to the military, a group set up much like the government.

27. C

All paragraphs except the last one deal with the groupthink hypothesis and experiment, so the only place the author could make himself known would be that last paragraph. When you reread it, you find that the author doesn't comment on whether or not Janis is correct but on Flowers's and Janis's different interpretations of "high group cohesiveness." Considering that, he could conclude that you'd get different results under different interpretations, and that points to (C).

Wrong Answers:

(A) Distortion. The author doesn't make this very extreme comment.

(B) Distortion. The first part of the answer seems possible, but the exaggerated conclusion isn't in the passage. A correct answer is completely, not partially, right.

(D) Out of Scope. Though group cohesiveness had no effect in the experiments, the author ends the passage by saying "the experiment may have failed" to test Janis's hypothesis accurately. This statement implies that the effect of group cohesiveness should be re-examined, not removed from the theory.

28. D

The question takes us directly to the last paragraph again, where the "inconsistency" is mentioned as a possible result of the two interpretations of "high group cohesiveness." That research quickly leads to you answer (D). As this question shows, it's good to use research from a previous question to help in answering another.

Wrong Answers:

(A) **Faulty Use of Detail.** Closed-leader groups did deal with more facts after the decision was made, but that's not what the author thinks led to the inconsistency.

(B) **Out of Scope.** The author doesn't identify which factor Janis or Flowers considered more important in groupthink.

(C) **Faulty Use of Detail.** In reality, closed leaders offered fewer solutions, and again, this is not the reason for the inconsistency.

Passage VI: Utilitarianism and Contractarian View
Topic: Social philosophy
Scope: Contractarian
Purpose: To outline and defend a contractarian view of justice

Mapping the Passage:
¶1. Utilitarianism vs. social contract.
¶2. The contractarian philosophy.
¶3. Principles of it.
¶4. More principles.
¶5. Criticism and rebuttal of principles.

29. A

Although the author initially seems to be contrasting utilitarianism and contractarianism, she never really follows this up. And note the contrast word "however" in the last sentence of the first paragraph. Contrast words clue you in to author purpose, and since this one is followed by reference to the contractarian view, that's probably what the au-

thor is concerned with. Other than the first paragraph and a bit of the second, the passage is all about the new contractarianism. Thus, (A) is correct.

Wrong Answers:

(B) **Out of Scope.** There's no reference to or even inference of either view being radical.

(C) **Faulty Use of Detail.** As the explanation above notes, this may look like a compare/contrast passage at first, but it quickly focuses on the contractarian view only.

(D) **Faulty Use of Detail.** Rawls is in paragraph 1 only, and we know that a detail can't answer a main idea question.

30. B

Though the "veil of interest" appears in paragraph 2, the principles derived from it are in paragraphs 3 and 4. Since this is a tough question about a tough passage, let the answers help you. Check them out one by one and see which is compatible with a contractarian principle. (B), a restatement of "maximum possible justice and liberty for even the least privileged member of society," does the job.

Wrong Answers:

(A) **Opposite.** The whole point of the "veil of ignorance" is to exclude special group interests that lead to inequality. While behind this veil, the decision makers would be "totally unaware of their position in society."

(C) **Opposite.** The fact that there are principles must indicate that certain ideas are agreed upon.

(D) **Opposite.** This sounds like a worthy goal, but in paragraph 4, we find that social and economic inequality are, to a point, "inevitable." The reference to "political" can be inferred from the general idea of inequality.

31. D

Although utilitarians call for "the greatest good for the greatest number," it's clear from paragraph 1 that this may involve sacrificing the interests of a minority. Contractarians, on the other hand, believe society "owes certain obligations" to all its members—which implies that at least some interests of all the members of society must be satisfied, even if this requires reducing the absolute amount of "good" in the world as defined by the utilitarians. Thus, the two ideas start from differing notions of the desirable society, as in (D).

Wrong Answers:

(A) Opposite. The author says that the "two concepts are contrasting but not necessarily contradictory."

(B) Out of Scope. We really don't know many of the major points of utilitarianism, so it's impossible to say whether the two social philosophies agree on them. We do know, however, that they don't agree on one major point: the concept of society.

(C) Out of Scope. Paragraph 2 says that new contractarians don't subscribe to Rousseau's view of the "natural man," but that's *new* contractarians. The question is about contractarians in general, and we don't know much about them.

32. C

Utilitarianism accepts "sacrifice and suffering on the part of a minority" for the "greatest good for the greatest number" (society). In this case, the aging parent is the minority, and the family—representative of society—is burdened by the parent. According to utilitarian theory, the only reason to continue the burden is if keeping the parent alive somehow benefits society, as (C) says.

Wrong Answers:

(A) Opposite. Balance would be more the contractarian view.

(B) Opposite. This is the contractarian view again.

(D) Opposite. Utilitarians are willing to sacrifice the minority to lessen a burden on society, thus increasing the greater good.

33. B

Paragraph 2 makes plain that the members of the contracting group will select what they consider the most beneficial and fair social structure. Paragraph 3 goes on to say that one of these rules would be maximum possible liberty, jus-

tifying this conclusion by asking the rhetorical question of who would risk slavery when the veil was lifted. But what if someone *would* risk a loss of liberty? What if someone valued personal comfort above liberty? He might agree to being really well paid, clothed and sheltered, living a life of luxury, but not free. Thus, the contractarians' assertion that their system leads to a free society is true only if no one wants to risk loss of liberty, which is what they must assume. (B) is correct.

Wrong Answers:

(A) Opposite. The decision makers actually know the general consequences of their decision (equality); they simply are unaware of the specific personal consequences.

(C) Opposite. Remember, contractarians believe a certain amount of injustice is "inevitable."

(D) Opposite. Utilitarians might do this—though it seems a bit extreme—but contractarians wouldn't. Since everyone is entitled to equal access (paragraph 4), it wouldn't be possible for the contracting parties to safeguard their own liberties at the expense of others.

34. A

Didn't you just know you'd get a question on this strange reference? Don't worry about it; do the best you can and move on. But let's think. We're dealing with someone who would gamble on the outcome and look for something that would be a potential reward to her. (forget the "justice" stuff—think "reward" instead). Look back at paragraph 4; access to equality, not actual equality (which doesn't seem possible given the "inevitable" social and economic inequality), is the goal. If the gambler had access to something others didn't, that could be to her good, though it would mean unequal access for someone else. You can stop right there and choose (A).

Wrong Answers:

(B) Opposite. As paragraph 2 describes it, Rousseau views man as "uncorrupted" and "harmonious." There are no social inequities to gamble on in this view, so a gambler wouldn't likely choose it.

(C) Opposite. Having opportunities others don't have wouldn't provide equal freedom and circumstances.

(D) Distortion. The best he or she could do would be to select a principle of justice *more likely*, but not definitely, to be of personal benefit.

35. D

Let's use elimination. As you check the answers, you see that all but racial equality can, if necessary, be abridged. Social and economic equality can be abridged—in fact, they inevitably are—but that inequality must inhere in offices and not in accidents of birth, and since a person's race is just such an accident, (D) is the answer.

Wrong Answers:

(A) Opposite. As the second sentence of paragraph 4 makes clear, personal liberty can be abridged if it interferes with the personal liberty of another.

(B) Opposite. The fourth paragraph says that "social and economic inequality . . . are inevitable."

(C) Opposite. This is also inevitable.

Passage VII: One-Sided Arguments

Topic: Arguments

Scope: One-sided vs. two-sided

Purpose: Discuss the effectiveness of both

Mapping the Passage:

¶1. Asks why one-sided arguments are effective.

¶2. Problems and benefits with two-sided.

¶3. One-sided better with uninformed audience; two-sided with informed one.

¶4. Explanation for previous evidence.

¶5. Why advertisers use one-sided messages.

¶6. Biased audiences respond to a one-sided argument; unbiased audiences to two-sided.

36. C

An application question. What does the effectiveness of an argument depend on, according to an author? The knowledge and preconceptions of the audience. Foreign policy experts are by definition knowledgeable about the subject, so a two-sided argument that points out the weaknesses in the opposing position will be most effective. (C) is right on target.

Wrong Answers:

(A) Opposite. This sort of argument would be better suited to an uninformed or partisan audience.

(B) Opposite. Arguing against his own policy wouldn't help the president.

(D) Out of Scope. The author never argues the merits of an argument that appeals to emotions.

37. D

This is an inference question: Review the relevant arguments the author makes. The author argues that audiences are receptive to one-sided arguments if they're not knowledgeable about the subject, two-sided ones if they are. What assumption is implicit in this and necessary to make the argument work? Answer: That audiences without knowledge can be convinced one way or the other. (D) matches well with this. If in doubt, use the denial test. If people who don't know much about an issue are unlikely to accept the opinions of others, a one-sided argument wouldn't be at all effective. The author's argument falls apart, and the answer as it is written must therefore be a necessary assumption.

Wrong Answers:

(A) Distortion. The author mentions one ineffective method of advertising in paragraph 5, but that doesn't mean that all advertising is ineffective.

(B) Out of Scope. The author never mentions the concerns of mass media.

(C) Out of Scope. While *some* people may be inattentive and careless thinkers, that doesn't mean that *most* people don't listen carefully.

38. A

Another inference question: We need to find something in line with the author's points. A good grasp of these will immediately lead to (A), which is explicitly stated in the third paragraph: "the more well informed the members of the audience are, the less likely they are to be persuaded by a one-sided argument and the more likely they are to be persuaded by" a two-sided one.

Wrong Answers:

(B) Distortion. The author argues that comparative advertising is effective only in certain situations—when a challenger is trying to gain on the leading brand.

(C) Out of Scope. A tricky answer choice. The author is talking about knowledgeable audiences, not highly educated ones. Don't confuse the two.

(D) Faulty Use of Detail. This author suggests in paragraph 4 that the *audience* may consider the communicator unfair but doesn't suggest anywhere that this is actually the case.

39. D

Look for answer choices that counter the author's one-sided/two-sided argument breakdown. All answer choices appear equally often, so start with Roman numeral I, which essentially restates the author's characterization of a well-informed listener. Get rid of (A) and (C). Statement II, however, counters the author's argument that uninformed audiences will prefer one-sided messages. Eliminate (B). While you have the correct answer at this point, checking statement III shows the flip side of statement II, another instance of an audience member who doesn't fit into the author's profiles.

Wrong Answers:

I. Opposite. According to the passage, a well-informed, unbiased person *should* respond more favorably to a two-sided message.

40. C

An application question. Simply apply the author's general arguments to the specific situation. If a communicator knows the author's arguments are true and is speaking to a knowledgeable and unbiased audience, which argument will she choose? The two-sided one. (C) gives you the quick points.

Wrong Answers:

(A) Opposite. Why not? The situation fits the author's two-sided scenario perfectly.

(B) Opposite. This would fit the profile of a communicator speaking to the opposite type of audience.

(D) Out of Scope. The author never argues that arguments should appeal to emotions.